BLACK EPHEMERA

Black Ephemera

*The Crisis and Challenge
of the Musical Archive*

Mark Anthony Neal

NEW YORK UNIVERSITY PRESS

New York

NEW YORK UNIVERSITY PRESS
New York
www.nyupress.org

References to Internet websites (URLs) were accurate at the time of writing. Neither the author nor New York University Press is responsible for URLs that may have expired or changed since the manuscript was prepared.

Library of Congress Cataloging-in-Publication Data
Names: Neal, Mark Anthony, author.
Title: Black ephemera : the crisis and challenge of the musical archive / Mark Anthony Neal
Description: New York : New York University Press, 2022. | Includes bibliographical references and index.
Identifiers: LCCN 2021027741 | ISBN 9781479806881 (hardback) | ISBN 9781479806904 (paperback) | ISBN 9781479806911 (ebook) | ISBN 9781479806935 (ebook other)
Subjects: LCSH: African Americans—Music—History and criticism. | Popular music—United States—History and criticism. | Sound recording industry—United States. | African Americans—Archival resources.
Classification: LCC ML3556 .N38 2022 | DDC 780.8996/073—dc23
LC record available at https://lccn.loc.gov/2021027741

New York University Press books are printed on acid-free paper, and their binding materials are chosen for strength and durability. We strive to use environmentally responsible suppliers and materials to the greatest extent possible in publishing our books.

Manufactured in the United States of America

10 9 8 7 6 5 4 3 2 1

Also available as an ebook

CONTENTS

Introduction

The Crisis and the Challenge of the Archive

I was thirteen years old when my mother gave me my first boom box, as a Christmas gift. It was relatively small in comparison to the one Radio Raheem carried around in Spike Lee's film *Do the Right Thing*. As with Radio Raheem, though, the boom box—as well as the Walkman that would replace it a few years later—offered me the opportunity to carry my music with me. Indeed, one of the stories I heard frequently about my father was that, as a teenager, he went nowhere without his transistor radio. I am my father's son. The boom box's best feature by far was that it allowed me to record programs from my favorite New York City radio stations, WABC-AM and WCBS-FM. In the years before I had the money to start collecting music, or the confidence to begin siphoning from my father's rather formidable collection, those over-the-air radio recordings constituted an archive of my musical tastes—even with the voices of Harry Harrison, Dan Ingram, or Chuck Leonard tagged on to the intros of so many of the songs.

When I had my first part-time job as a teen, I devoted more than half of my earnings to buying vinyl recordings from places like the Tower Records on 4th and Broadway and J&R Music World, and Bondy's Record Store both down on Park Row. My ultimate aim, however, was not collecting vinyl but crafting and curating pause-button mixtapes. For me, mixtapes not only reflected my love of music, but also the thought that went into constructing these sonic representations of my passions, desires, and moods. Like deejays who worked for months on the mixes that folks would hear on the dancefloor at the club, I always understood that these mixtapes were my intellectual property; not simply a compilation of songs thrown together randomly or sequenced by some record company executive, they represented attempts at meaning-making that surpassed the intent of the artists or their producers and distributors. What I didn't understand as well at the time is that, in making those mixtapes, I was also functioning as an archivist, as much of my own taste as of the transition from analog to digital.

I still have many of those tapes, though I rarely listen to any of them anymore, if only because car manufacturers no longer equip new vehicles with cassette players. The emergence of both handheld digital devices that can store thousands of sound recordings—my iPod Classic once held more than sixteen thousand songs—and, more recently, of music streaming platforms, has radically transformed my relationship to my sonic archive. Instead of dutifully "crate-digging," as early hip-hop producers and deejays referred to the act of locating obscure vinyl source material, or rifling the cut-out rack at a record store to find that one track to complete my mixtape, I can retrieve material almost instantly. I can still remember the look on my late father's face when I showed him my first iPod and explained that there was music on it. For a man who could remember listening to 78s, and who ignored the 8-track and cassette revolutions, maintaining his commitment to his beloved 33 1/3s, it became a challenge maintaining a connection to the sonic world.

For the multibillion-dollar music industry, the question is simply how to build a better delivery system to consumers. For example, hip-hop artist and entrepreneur Shawn Carter (Jay-Z) and his Roc-Nation label signed a five-million-dollar deal with smartphone provider Samsung, who made the first one million copies of his 2013 album *Magna Carta Holy Grail* available via download exclusively to Samsung Galaxy owners days before its official release. Indeed, the innovative nature of the deal forced the Recording Industry Association of America (RIAA) to reevaluate its monitoring of gold and platinum sales, since those one million Galaxy owners didn't actually choose to purchase *Magna Carta Holy Grail*.[1]

In this era of big data and algorithms, the accessibility of the archive of contemporary and historical Blackness—what I'll call "big Black data"—is unprecedented. The fact that we can, with relative ease, access earlier iterations of Black visual forms like Bert Williams's 1916 silent film short *A Natural Born Gambler*, or any number of Josephine Baker performances from the 1920s (an archive that Beyonce Knowles Carter is quite familiar with) via YouTube, for example, has transformed what it means for scholars to teach and research Blackness in the digital age. While I celebrate the new availability of these archives of Blackness and have contributed to them myself, I am ambivalent when it comes to the question of who holds the responsibility for curating them. The footprints of those who left archival vestiges of their fugitivity, like Maroons fleeing plantations, serve as vital lifelines of freedom and survival for those whom the archives have been obscured and distorted. In addition to logical and theoretical concerns around intellectual property— can there be ownership of a historical commons of Blackness, for example?— old-fashioned citation practices apply less in the more amorphous digital realm, particularly with regard to Blackness.

Before I settled on the working title for this project, *Black Ephemera*, I consistently worded the subtitle as the "crisis" or "challenge" of the archive. In many ways both are accurate: what I might call the *crisis* of the archive responds to the general state of Black cultural criticism today. In becoming more available to the general public—as opposed to resources such as *Negro Digest*, its successor *Black World*, *Liberator Magazine*, or the first decade of *Essence*, which are more difficult to locate—Black cultural criticism has become defined, in part, by the increased global commodification of Black culture and the so-called democratization of opinion, if not expertise, via the Internet. The resulting demystification of the labor that produces Black culture and cultural criticism renders the archive disposable, truncated, and in many ways irrelevant to commercial enterprise. Under these circumstances, anyone can access Black culture without bearing responsibility for its care and sustenance. This proves a challenge to the Black cultural critic invested in the continued work of mystification: a theorizing of Black culture that remains grounded in the archive and its capacity to generate expansive and liberatory notions of Blackness not intended for mass consumption. The crisis and challenge of the Black archive not only pose questions of knowledge, but of the way knowledge moves or manifests within the Black archive that are obscure, ephemeral, fugitive, precarious, fluid, and increasingly digital—qualities that challenge the very idea of what constitutes an archive.

Though *Black Ephemera* is largely concerned with the Black archive—the catalog of an iconic Black music label, the historical and contemporary iterations of Black women's trauma in popular culture, Black mourning as rendered in digital and analog culture, the "great" American Songbook as redefined by two legendary Black musical artists, and the abstracting of the Black archive—it remains tethered to music as its primary source. While one might think of Black music as the historical lingua franca of Blackness, my concern is that Black music itself has actually been reduced to, at best, ephemera, like a stack of vinyl albums in a closet, and, at worst, the ambient background of the continued exploitation and commodification of Black culture.

In sharing these concerns, I find a precedent in the writers and artists who comprised what literary scholar Howard Rambsy II calls "the Black arts enterprise." Rambsy specifically cites the efforts of figures like Dudley Randall and Hoyt Fuller to create literary magazines and anthologies that were "collectively and largely responsible for providing widespread exposure to both the writings and the activities of black poets during the 1960s and 1970s."[2] As Rambsy notes, these curated projects aimed to convey meanings beyond the specific content of each poem or essay. Writing about an issue of *Black World* published after a series of state-sanctioned attacks directed at the Black Panther Party, including the December 1969 assassination of Fred Hampton and Mark Clark, Rambsy observes that poems by Charles Moreland and Charyn Sutton that addressed the attacks "appear next to each other, thus amplifying the documentation of violence against African Americans, as well as the willingness of the editorial staff to catalogue such injustices."[3]

Like so many works in which Black writers and artists have attempted to index the political realities and aesthetic urgencies of their historical moment, the popularity of Black Arts Movement texts, in concert with the heightened visibility of the Black liberation movement, created a mainstream commercial desire—hunger, really—to consume narratives of Black militancy and resistance. For some, like Dudley Randall, White publishing houses and journals offered the opportunity to "alert readers to the existence of a network of Black literary spaces."[4] The editors of some volumes exploited the idea that the Black literary anthologies produced by major publishing houses in the 1970s were *of* the Black community, but that also meant that the finished product had to be able to "live" in those same communities.

As Toni Morrison commented about the 1974 anthology *The Black Book* that she edited while working as an editor at Random House, its publisher, "Black people from all over helped with it, called about things to put in it."[5] Morrison's comments reflect the way *The Black Book* anticipated not only the kinds of crowd-sourcing that would appear two generations later during the digital era—as well as the utilization of mixed-media that we see in the digital realm, as Rambsy also notes—but also the predigital musical genre of hip-hop, through generations of sampling practices and various iterations of the mixtape. According to Rambsy, "The juxtaposition of words and images in *The Black Book* provides a clear example of how an editor used a mixed-media approach to amplify and sharpen ideas about African American history and culture."[6] In this regard *The Black Book's* beyond-the-text style might be thought of as an analog to the hypertext in the digital era. In his introduction to Larry Neal's *Black Boogalo*, the late Amiri Baraka hints at what he calls a "post 'literary' world," pointing out to readers the rich work that mixed poetry with music, such as Nikki Giovanni's mashing of poetry and gospel music on *Truth Is on the Way* (1970), while in part conjuring the hip-hop enterprise itself. What can't be lost in this moment was the importance of Morrison's role as an editor within a major publishing house and her attendant role as a curator of Black culture.

Though *The Black Book*, or Morrison's work in general, is not thought of as part of the Black Arts Movement, it does offer a culmination of sorts of the strategies used to address what have historically been issues related to the production, circulation, and archiving of Blackness—concerns that are exponentially heightened in the digital era. Even as previous generations of cultural workers and critics were faced with a limited archive—or, at least, limited access to archives—they were also challenged by the difficulty of securing capital to build and maintain the archive and often keenly aware that relinquishing their intellectual property to the highest bidder might be an unavoidable necessity (British media company Getty Images being one prominent commercial archival gatekeeper). Recent years have seen the emergence of alternative models such as the collaboration between the Ford Foundation, J. Paul Getty Trust, John D. and Catherine T. MacArthur Foundation, and Andrew W. Mellon Foundation to caretake the visual archives of the Johnson Publishing Company, the longtime publisher of *Ebony* and *Jet* magazines until its demise in 2019. In this instance, an equitable response to the challenges of accessing the archives was spearheaded by Darren Walker of the Ford Foundation and Elizabeth Alexander of the Mellon Foundation, both of whom are, notably, African American.

Archives frequently need benefactors, a fact that no contemporary figure may have understood better than Henry Louis Gates Jr., who is best known in scholarly circles for his groundbreaking study of African American literary theory *The Signifying Monkey* (1988) and for coediting *The Norton Anthology of African American Literature* (1996), and who has positioned himself as a singular arbiter and curator of African American arts and letters. Gates's work with the Black archive has extended beyond the traditional literary realm into the digital arena, with the creation of Encarta Africana with Microsoft and Kwame Anthony Appiah, a comprehensive multimedia encyclopedia of the "global Black experience" that used technology to realize a vision originally conceived by W. E. B. Du Bois.[7] As Gates remarked at the product's launch in early 1999, "For the first time, the story of the black world and its people will be told in a way never before possible—through images, video, music, and text brought together in a unique experience."[8] Gates and Microsoft donated thousands of copies of the product to K-12 institutions, and Gates subsequently developed the Africana website, a precursor to his online news magazine The Root. Citing Gates's work with the Human Genome Project and his development of signature public television programming aimed at exploring the significance of race, Lisa Nakamura and Peter A. Chow note that "Gates' new career as a digital media producer signals a new form of racial technology, posed as a curative to the older racist techne of enforced forgetting and information erasure or management."[9]

Black Ephemera deliberately posits the archive in opposition to such grandiose endeavors, however valuable they might be, and focuses instead on those artifacts that, broadly defined, might be thought of as literal afterthoughts—as culture not in need of curation. In the first chapter, "Love in the Stax: Death, Loss, and Resurrection in Post-King Memphis," I examine the legendary Memphis Stax recording label, which famously lost almost all of its archive to a competing interest in 1968, only months after the death of its most successful artist, Otis Redding, and the assassination of Martin Luther King Jr. in Memphis. I look at the company's strategy in rebuilding its archive, owed in large part to the vision of record company executive All Bell, by redefining the subject matter that popular Black music could address. Though well-known among fans of traditional Soul music, the legacy of the Stax label is relatively obscure compared to that of Motown Records and the Philadelphia International Records of the same period.

In chapter 2, "'I Got the Blues of a Fallen Teardrop': Erasure, Trauma, and a Sonic Archive of Black Women," I explore how Black sonic culture negotiates the invisibility and trauma of Black women. The chapter begins with an examination of the post–Hurricane Katrina documentary *Trouble the Water* (2008) and the role of rap artist

Kimberly Roberts as the film's narrator, and her deployment of the sonic and vernacular world of New Orleans to document the aftermath of Katrina's violence. The chapter's goes on to discuss Ricardo Cortez Cruz's experimental novel *Five Days of Bleeding* (1995), in which the primary female character, Zu-Zu, speaks and sings primarily through obscure song lyrics and titles, largely drawn from an archive of performances by Black women.

In the third chapter, "'Promise That You Will [Tweet] about Me': Black Death in the Digital Era," I move to examine more contemporary Black culture, looking at the ways in which collective Black mourning has been produced, curated, and archived in the digital era, via the music of Kendrick Lamar and Pharoahe Monch, and visual texts such as the music video for Flying Lotus's song "Never Catch Me" (2014) and Ryan Coogler's film *Fruitvale Station* (2013). The chapter juxtaposes these distinctly digital moments with earlier instances of Black mourning from the analog era, including the shooting death of Los Angeles teenager Latasha Harlins in 1991 and the musical memorializations of slain Black figures in the civil rights movement in the years following their deaths.

Chapter 4, "'I'll Be a Bridge': Black Interiority, Black Invention, and the American Songbook," examines the efforts of Marvin Gaye and Aretha Franklin to master the so-called "Great American Songbook": a loose term for the canon of torch songs written largely by a generation of white male songwriters and composers during the mid-twentieth century. Gaye's efforts were largely aligned with career-long efforts to record an album with the gravitas of Frank Sinatra's *In the Wee Small Hours of the Morning* (1955), an endeavor at which he failed repeatedly during his lifetime and finally achieved, ironically, after his death. Gaye's efforts, however, create an archive of music that highlights the role played by interiority in Gaye's efforts to achieve mastery. Franklin, by contrast, achieved such mastery relatively early in her career, thus creating a body of work that not only highlights the spirit of invention of a singular artist, but may well redefine the Great American Songbook. Her live recordings *Live at the Fillmore West* (1971) and *Amazing Grace* (1972),

I argue, call into question the very idea *of* an American Songbook, as historically constituted, while establishing Franklin as the singular voice of the twentieth century.

The final chapter, "Decamping Wakanda: The Archive as Maroon," imagines the Black archive as theoretical, abstract, fleeting, and fugitive, specifically examining the ways the strategies used by Maroons, who stole themselves from enslavement to establish liminal settlements of freedom and unfreedom, might be applied to criticism of the film *Black Panther* (2018), as well the films of John Akomfrah, notably *Precarity* (2018) and *The Last Angel of History* (1996). The chapter additionally explores how Black film imports analog-era musical archives as a means of establishing intimacy with lost material, notably in Charles Burnett's classic *Killer of Sheep* (1978) Barry Jenkins's *Moonlight* (2016), and Denzel Washington's 2016 film adaptation of August Wilson's 1985 play *Fences*, in which the music of Dinah Washington, Barbara Lewis, and Jimmy Scott figure prominently.

1

Love in the Stax

Death, Loss, and Resurrection in Post-King Memphis

Late in the summer of 1968, Johnnie Taylor—not to be confused with Little Johnny Taylor—walked into the Stax Recording Studios in Memphis, Tennessee, to record "Who's Making Love?" It was a breakthrough for Taylor, who was best known at the time as the vocalist who replaced Sam Cooke as lead singer of the Hi-Way Que C's, the group that Cooke fronted before achieving gospel and soul glory as the lead singer of the Soul Stirrers and, later, as the most influential Black male vocalist of his generation. By the late fall of 1968, "Who's Making Love," with its explicit references to sex, had peaked at number five on the pop charts, selling more than a million copies. The song almost single-handedly saved Stax, inaugurating a period in which the label helped redefine the subject matter and social reach of Black popular music in ways that were unimaginable just a year before Taylor's hit.

This chapter charts a transitional moment in one of the defining brands of Black cultural production in the 1960s and 1970s, which occurred in the midst of what might be described as postapocalyptic Memphis, made most manifest in the assassination of Reverend Dr. Martin Luther King Jr. on the balcony of the Lorraine Motel. Critical to its rebirth was the creative and strategic way in which Stax rebuilt a literal archive of recordings, having lost its previous catalog to a competing interest, while also reimagining the thematic archive of Black love, loss, and desire. As well as Taylor, the Temprees, Isaac Hayes, the Staple Singers, the Rance Allen Group, and the Soul Children, are some of the artists that offer the most compelling examples of Stax's strategic use of the archive.

Stax Records was founded as Satellite Records in Memphis in 1957, by Estelle Axton and her brother, Jim Stewart (the name was an acronym of the first two letters of their last names). While Detroit and Chicago emerged as centers of Black cultural production in the twentieth century, as byproducts of Black migration patterns from the South, Memphis remained a hub for Black citizens who remained in the South. Putting the Black presence in Memphis in a larger historical context, historians Aram Goudsouzian and Charles W. McKinney Jr. write, "Starting in the second half of the nineteenth century, Memphis became the most populated—and most vibrant—metropolitan area for black people in the entire Mid-South region. . . . In the crucible of segregation, African Americans in Memphis took on the task of reshaping the city—and the nation—to better conform to the principles of equality. They were creating a "light" of their own in the Bluff City."[1]

Although its founders were white, the Stax label became a totem for Black aspiration and ingenuity throughout the 1960s and early 1970s. The label itself was a critical part of the fabric of Memphis, particularly in South Memphis where it was located. As Zandria Robinson writes, "Even though Stax founders Will Stewart and Estelle Axton were white . . . by 1960, South Memphis was a definitively black neighborhood, and Stax quickly became a label driven by black artists and black music. Indeed, the label benefited from the presence of these institutions and from the residents who brought them to life."[2]

Stax and its subsidiary, Volt, hit their initial stride between 1962 and 1967, with a roster that included now-classic soul artists such as Rufus Thomas, an iconic figure who had had a previous successful career as a deejay; his daughter Carla Thomas; Booker T. & the M.G.'s; William Bell; and, most famously, Otis Redding, who was unquestionably the label's biggest star. With tracks like Albert King's "Born Under a Bad Sign," "Green Onion" by Booker T. & the M.G.'s, Rufus Thomas's "Walking the Dog," Otis Redding's "Try a Little Tenderness," "B-A-B-Y" by Carla Thomas, and "Tramp," which paired Carla Thomas with Redding, Stax/Volt positioned itself as a legitimate southern soul counterpart to Berry

Gordy's Motown enterprise in Detroit. With a sound deemed more "authentic" than Motown, and a house band led by Booker T. Jones that embodied the integrationist impulse being expressed on the streets of Memphis, the label became, on the surface, a veritable symbol of racial integration.[3]

Stax/Volt was able to rival Motown on a national scale largely due to a distribution deal cofounder Jim Stewart reached with Atlantic Records that would have lasting implications for the label. The career of Sam & Dave, whose success between 1966 and 1967 culminated in the release of the classic "Soul Man," characterized the nature of the relationship between the labels: the duo was signed as artists to Atlantic, but loaned to Stax so that their sound could be countrified by the Stax house band. Many of Sam & Dave's songs were written and produced by the duo of David Porter and Isaac Hayes, and the young Hayes's ascendency within the label structure during the postapocalyptic era in Memphis would be critical to Stax's resurrection, as would that of Stax's in-house promoter Al Bell.

After graduating from Philander Smith College, a historically Black college in Little Rock, Arkansas, Al Bell began a short organizing stint with the Southern Christian Leadership Council (SCLC), where he attended the SCLC Leadership Conference and became a student teacher. It was while working with SCLC and Martin Luther King Jr. that the themes of economic sustainability and empowerment, which undergirded the civil rights movement, began to resonate with Bell in ways that would have a lasting impact on Stax. Bell began a successful career as a deejay, first with WLOK in Memphis, later at KOKY in Little Rock, and then with WUST in Washington, DC. Bell caught Jim Stewart's attention with his ability to break Stax records in a "northern" market, and Stewart hired Bell to become Stax's national director of promotions in 1965.

One immediate change that Bell made to the company was a reevaluation of the album format. Prior to 1965, Stax had released a total of eight albums, including Otis Redding's *Otis Blue/Otis Redding Sings Soul*, which includes the original recording of "Respect," a song later

later made iconic by Atlantic artist Aretha Franklin. The year after Bell arrived, Stax/Volt released eleven albums. While Bell's motivation was to generate more income for the label, the change also reflects a particular strategy that can be deployed in the curation of sonic archives. Bell's privileging of the album format would also play a critical role at Stax in the postapocalyptic era, particularly as the album and album-oriented radio formats became more prominent among arbiters of serious pop music. By elevating the album in its business model, Stax contributed to its development into a medium that granted Black musical artists curatorial power to offer more explicit and developed ideas about the world in which they lived.

By the time Bell was made executive vice president in 1967, Stax was one of the top three independent labels in the country.[4] In early 1967, Stax artists embarked on a tour of Europe, where the reputations of Sam & Dave and Otis Redding as stellar live performers were cemented for international audiences. In late June, Redding and his Stax peers played the Monterey Pop Festival, where iconic performances of Redding and Jimi Hendrix were recorded for a documentary film, and the success of Redding's set in particular left him poised for major mainstream crossover success. After the festival, however, Stax would witness a level of tragedy that few record labels could have withstood, the most well-known of which was Redding's death, along with members of the Bar-Kays, in a plane crash outside of Madison, Wisconsin. Redding's loss to the label was made even more impactful in early 1968 when Atlantic Records was sold to Warner Brothers, necessitating that Stewart negotiate with Warner Brothers about buying Stax. While it is is hard to believe that the possible inclusion of the Stax catalog was not part of Warner Brothers' valuation of the label, or that the folks at Atlantic didn't think that Warner Brothers wouldn't offer a fair price for the outright purchase of Stax. no deal was agreed upon, effectively ending Atlantic's distribution deal with Stax. As a result, an obscure contract clause kicked in, which transferred ownership of Stax's entire catalog to Atlantic. In effect, Stax lost ownership of much of its archive.

To illustrate the value of Stax to Atlantic and its parent company, Warner Brothers, consider the example of Otis Redding's final studio album, *The Dock of the Bay*, which was released in February 1968, two months after his death. The lead single, "(Sittin' on) The Dock of the Bay," which had been released a month earlier, would be the only number-one pop song of Redding's career; it was also the first posthumous release by any artist to reach that peak position. The song remains—I would argue by far—Redding's best-known recording. As Redding biographer Mark Ribowsky told NPR on the occasion of the fiftieth anniversary of the song's release, "Let's face it: when a rock 'n' roller dies, you need a song to come out immediately to cash in on this. That's just the way the business is."[5] *The Dock of the Bay* was the last of Redding's recordings released by Stax, via their Volt subsidiary. On the basis of the single's commercial success, Atlantic mined from the archive unreleased tracks, which included now-signature Redding songs like "I Got Dreams to Remember," "Love Man," and "Hard to Handle," which was later covered by the Black Crowes and sampled by DJ Marley Marl on "The Symphony"—songs that ultimately contributed to Redding's iconic status, which matches, if not surpasses, that of Sam Cooke.

In the background of these very personal tragedies at Stax was a national tragedy: the city of Memphis had the misfortune of being the place where Martin Luther King Jr. was assassinated, contributing to a sense of collapse that might have been experienced by the Stax family in ways quite different than other Black cultural institutions at the time. King's death resonated among many of the label's Black musicians, particularly men, who compared the treatment they received in the segregated South to their experiences on the European tour. William Bell recorded "A Tribute to a King" in tribute to Redding, but it also captured the mood after King's death. The grief experienced by Black Memphis after the assassination was palpable at Stax.

Moreover, King's presence in Memphis at the time of his death was framed by a political mobilization in the city, of which the strike by Black sanitation workers that brought him there was simply the most visible.

After his murder, different political factions emerged. As Anthony C. Siracusa writes, "The fracture within Memphis's black freedom movement [was] attributed chiefly to deepening fissures between advocates of Black Power and those espousing nonviolence during the Memphis sanitation strike of 1968." At the same time, Siracusa notes, a "robust and likely illegal effort by the FBI to infiltrate and undermine both the Black Power and nonviolent wings of the black freedom movement."[6] Stax was not unaffected by these fissures in the movement and extralegal attempts to destabilize Black political mobilization. Amid calls of Black Power among young Black activists, Jim Stewart and Estelle Axton—the White faces of Stax—had to recalibrate. As the pressures mounted, executive vice president Bell—the Race Man—became a full partner with Stewart, at the expense of Axton, when Stax was sold to Gulf and Western—a shift that essentially effectively rebranded Stax as a Black-owned independent label.

"I Stand Accused": Love and Theft in the Archive

As Bell began the work of rebuilding the archive, his strategy included aggressively signing new acts that expanded the brand beyond traditional southern soul and blues, in what Bell called the "Soul Explosion." One of his largest challenges was in the valuation of the Stax label and, more broadly, of Black music itself. As Bell told the *Chicago Defender* three days before Dr. King's death, "People should consider . . . that this music is really the only music that we, as Americans, can claim as part of our heritage," adding that "it's basically the folk music of America."[7]

Among the acts that Bell developed in the postapocalyptic period were groups such as the Soul Children; the white vocalist Lynda Lyndell, who recorded the original version "What a Man" that was later covered by En Vogue and Salt & Pepa; Shirley Brown; Luther Ingram, whose single "If Loving You is Wrong," another anthem of Black infidelity, peaked at number three on the pop charts in 1972; and gospel artists the Rance Allen Group and the Staple Singers. Bringing acts like the already well-established Staple Singers and young upstarts like Rance Allen and his brothers also spoke to cultural realities in South Memphis, a point that Robinson makes, noting that "the neighborhood's gospel roots, nurtured at community churches such as Metropolitan Baptist and Second Congregational, were harnessed by Stax artists in the service of a new sound and a new historical moment in the nation and the neighborhood."[8] To support these new artists, Bell, with the assistance of Deanie Parker, Stax's director of publicity, planned to release thirty singles and twenty-eight albums recorded over an eight-month period from late 1968 to early 1969. Bell's "Soul Explosion" was referenced almost fifty years later in the "Twenty for Twenty" story line from the contemporary television series *Empire*, in which the fictional Empire label would release twenty albums to mark the label's twentieth anniversary.

Included with those twenty-eight releases were solo recordings from former partners David Porter and Isaac Hayes, whose contribution, *Hot Buttered Soul*, was a last minute add-on that not only became the most successful of those albums, but one of the most important sonic innovations in Black music in the era. Hayes's use of strings and brass to create an orchestral sound created a new sheen—upscale, urbane, aspirational—for soul music, that added polish to its "grits and gravy" image. Hayes also mined the archives of the contemporary Black artists who influenced him, such as Jerry Butler and Curtis Mayfield, but he predominantly refashioned the work of White singer-songwriters like Jimmy Webb, composer Burt Bacharach and lyricist Hal David, George Harrison, and Kris Kristofferson, whose "For the Good Times" was a hit for country star Ray Price. In each instance, Hayes and his producers so thoroughly transformed these existing compositions that they were for all intents and purposes new songs. Hayes remarked years later, "I didn't give a damn if *Hot Buttered Soul* didn't sell . . . I just wanted to do something artistic, with total freedom."[9]

Hot Buttered Soul opens with a twelve-minute version of Hal David and Burt Bacharach's "Walk on By." Originally recorded by Dionne Warwick for her third, breakthrough album, *Make Way for Dionne Warwick*

(1964), the song earned Warwick her first Grammy Award nomination and was emblematic of the pop crossover style that she, David, and Bacharach crafted. For a wide array of Black soul artists, including Jerry Butler, Lou Rawls, and Maxine Brown, Warwick's music, which included a string of top-ten pop hits like "Anyone Who Had a Heart," "Message to Michael," and "I Say a Little Prayer," provided a template for crossing over to more sophisticated, adult White audiences. Warwick's style proved so influential that even Aretha Franklin, who for all intents ended her reign as the dominant Black woman solo artist of the 1960s, recorded versions of her songs, including "Walk on By," both during Franklin's early career at Columbia Records and after her breakthrough period at Atlantic, where "I Say a Little Prayer" became a top-ten hit as the b-side of "The House That Jack Built." From this vantage point, Hayes's choices make absolute sense.

If the original "Walk on By" captured Warwick in a brisk jaunt down a busy city avenue, Hayes's version projected a deliberate soul man strut through the trials and tribulations of Soulsville, and nothing about it seemed to want to be resolved in less than the twelve minutes it took for him to make his point. As Hayes explained his strategy, "I felt what I had to say couldn't be said in two minutes and thirty seconds. So I just stretched [the songs] out and milked them for everything they were worth."[10] The recording also offers more than a passing gesture to the psychedelic revolution taking place in pop music; Hayes sounds less like he's in Memphis and more like he set up shop in Haight-Ashbury or Berkeley. In this regard, the song "Walk on By" and the album *Hot Buttered Soul* captured the aspirational theme among some Black Americans to not only leave the South, as had been the case with two streams of Black migration in the early twentieth century and in the post–World War II period, but to literally rid themselves of the shackles of the South. As a song like Gladys Knight and the Pips' "Midnight Train to Georgia" would demonstrate in the early 1970s, such an aspiration was cut with some ambivalence.

Hot Buttered Soul's closing statement is Hayes's eighteen-minute rendition of Jimmy Webb's "By the Time I Get to Phoenix," a song that earned country-pop singer Glen Campbell a Grammy Award for his 1967 version. As Hayes recalled, "I heard 'Phoenix' on the radio . . . Glen Campbell was singing it. I stopped and said 'Damn that's great.'"[11] In line with Stax's archival practices, Hayes augments Webb's stellar songwriting by providing a backstory via an eight-minute spoken-word introduction—three times the length of Campbell's recording. The introduction was part of a routine that Hayes had developed at the Tiki Club in Memphis for an audience likely not familiar with Jimmy Webb or even Glen Campbell: "I've got to create a situation these folks can relate to," he explained.[12] As Hayes relates in the actual recorded introduction, "Now I should attempt it to do it my way, my own interpretation of it. Like I said, everybody's got it's own thing, I'm gonna bring it on down to Soulsville." Hayes's invention here provides a stellar example of the way Stax artists utilized Black storytelling traditions of to augment the Stax archive.

In Hayes's retelling, the song's narrator, who was raised in the hills of Tennessee, migrated to Los Angeles, where he found his life partner. In Webb's original lyrics and Campbell's recording, Los Angeles goes unnamed as the site of departure; therefore, Hayes's naming of the city frames the song as a postwar migration tale that was reflective of the generation of Black southerners who relocated to California to work in the military-industrial complex stimulated by the Cold War. As R. J. Smith notes in *The Great Black Way: L.A. in the 1940s and the Lost African American Renaissance*, the city, which had been founded in 1781 by a group of Black and mixed-raced settlers, was the site of a cultural renaissance in the 1940s, fueled by emerging artists such as Nat King Cole, transgender performer Gladys Bentley, comedian Redd Foxx, and a young Sammy Davis Jr., among others.[13] Yet, as Hayes was coming of age, Los Angeles was also the place where Sam Cooke was killed under suspicious circumstances, and the site of days of violence in August 1965 in the aftermath of the shooting death of a Black man by police officers in the section of Watts. Since "By the Time I Get to Phoenix" is largely a song about unfaithfulness in love, the song also serves as a metaphor for the continued precarity of Black American life in a moment that also signaled possibility and hope. Hayes's narrator's travels back east, to home, through Phoenix and Albuquerque, not only because of the betrayal by his loved one, but also because of the betrayal of opportunity.

To highlight Hayes's recognition of the broader archive to which he was contributing, the singer gestures to the work of fellow soul singer Tyrone Davis ("And when he reached the driveway, you understand, he went in the bag just like my man Tyrone Davis / And he said, 'Oh, mama, mama, mama, can I change, oh, my mind?'") in reference to Davis's 1968 top-five pop hit "Can I Change My Mind?"—one of the many moments where Hayes used his increasing cultural gravitas to celebrate his peers. Hayes's 1971 double album *Black Moses* found him acknowledging the work of Clifton Davis ("Never Can Say Goodbye"), Curtis Mayfield ("Man's Temptation" and "Need to Belong," which were originally recorded by Jerry Butler), and then-young songwriters and producers Kenneth Gamble and Leon Huff ("Never Gonna Give You Up"), and Thom Bell ("A Brand New Me," written with Gamble), just as the trio was launching the Mighty Three Music Group, whose catalog would dominate 1970s soul music. According to Hayes, "Although I was a songwriter, there were some songs that I loved, that really touched me. Came the opportunity, I wanted to record these tunes. I wanted to do them the way I wanted to do them."[14]

Davis's "Never Can Say Goodbye" was originally released by the Jackson 5 in the spring of 1971 (it had been intended for the post–Diana Ross Supremes) and was one of their last big pop hits at Motown, featuring some of Michael Jackson's most mature vocals as a child. In contrast, Hayes's version marked the distinctions between the sugary crossover soul of Motown and the increasing artistic seriousness of Stax, as embodied by Hayes. One of the highlights of *Black Moses* is Hayes's nine-minute version of the Carpenters' "white bread" pop hit "(They Long to Be) Close to You," which likely inspired Luther Vandross to tackle the group's hit "Superstar" a decade later. In fact, it's hard to imagine that Hayes's rearranging of the pop songbook didn't directly impact Vandross, who mined the catalog of 1960s soul-pop throughout his career. In this regard, *Black Moses* used the archive of Black music to make a larger cultural statement. Hayes might have been portrayed as the Black deliverer on the cover of *Black Moses*—an image the artist himself was never comfortable with—but the album's broader message was in the power of Black music and Black ownership in the pursuit of Black freedoms.

Who's Making Love . . . in the Archive?

Like Isaac Hayes's lyrical shoutout to Tyrone Davis on "By the Time I Get to Phoenix," Johnnie Taylor makes a similar gesture to Billy Paul. On the song "Careless with Our Love," a song about infidelity, Taylor sings,

> The rumors are spreading all over town
> And we don't wanna be like Mrs. Jones
> We can't meet at the same place

in reference to Billy Paul's "Me and Mrs. Jones," which topped the Billboard Hot 100 and Billboard R&B Singles charts in December 1972. Paul's song, which was the first number-one pop hit for the then-fledgling Philadelphia International Records, was itself an example of citational politics, as the song's intro features a melody from Doris Day's "Secret Love."[15] "Careless with Our Love" was the opening track of Taylor's 1973 album *Taylored in Silk*, which also illustrates Stax's commitment to exploring the archive.

Johnnie Taylor's career began in Chicago in the early 1950s as a vocalist in the Hi-Way Que C's, a sort of gospel finishing school: Taylor replaced Lou Rawls, who himself replaced Sam Cooke. Cooke departed the group to become lead singer of the Soul Stirrers, and when he left the

Soul Stirrers in 1957 to pursue what would become a landmark career as a secular artist, Taylor was hired to replace Cooke as lead singer. Taylor later joined Cooke at SAR Records, the label that Cooke had launched shortly before his murder. By 1966, Taylor found himself in Memphis, signing with Stax Records.

Taylor achieved minor success in his early days at Stax, landing on the upper tier of the R&B charts with tracks like "I Had a Dream" and "I Got to Love Somebody's Baby" in 1966. As talented as he was, at Stax he stood largely in the shadow of the legendary Otis Redding. It was in the context of Al Bell's now-famous rebuilding of the Stax catalog that Taylor recorded "Who's Making Love," which established him as a bonafide hitmaker. Taylor reportedly hated the song, which was written by Homer Banks, Bettye Crutcher, and Raymond Jackson, and referred to it as "the boogity boogity song" because of its fast pace.

In the aftermath of "Who's Making Love?," Bell fell into the grind at Stax, producing a string of solid albums including *Raw Blues* (1968), *Rare Stamps* (1968), and *The Johnnie Taylor Philosophy Continues* (1969), which included Taylor's cover of "(I Wanna) Testify," originally recorded in 1967 by the Parliaments before their re-formation as Parliament Funkadelic, and "I Am Somebody," drawing on a theme popularized in the speeches of labelmate Reverend Jesse Jackson. None of these recordings matched the success of "Who's Making Love?," yet this was a peak era for Stax, which entered into a new distribution deal with CBS in 1972. By 1971, when Taylor recorded *One Step Beyond* (easily his strongest recording to date, it cites Johnny Mathis's "Twelfth of Never"), the "soul man" might have been an afterthought at the label he helped to musically resuscitate. It was the same ballad-heavy formula found on *One Step Beyond* that Taylor and producer Don Davis chose to revisit on his 1973 release *Taylored in Silk*.

Released two years after Isaac Hayes's double-album masterpiece *Black Moses* and in an era where Black artists were encouraged to go large, *Taylored in Silk* features just eight tracks and logs in at thirty-five minutes. The album was launched by the lead single "I Believe in

You (You Believe in Me)," written by Don Davis, which became Taylor's highest-charting pop single since "Who's Making Love?" The nuts
and bolts of the song, as described by Rob Bowman, illustrate why the
song and the album register as a classic of the soul genre. According
to Bowman, "I Believe in You (You Believe in Me)" was "the first record on which Don Davis constructed the track via layered riffs instead
of functional chord changes. Davis referred to this as the "monolithic
approach." The next result was a more melodic, Sam Cooke influenced
Johnnie Taylor."[16]

The Cooke reference was not incidental; Taylor was one of the few
soul artists of the era who could legitimately bridge the sensibilities of
an older rhythm & blues (R&B) audience—the grits and gravy crowd—
and a younger soul audience that was becoming more attuned to the
slick production of post-1968 Stax and the emerging Philly Soul sound
of Kenny Gamble and Leon Huff—hence the opening reference to Billy
Paul. The album's self-awareness of the tradition that helped to produce
it stands out. For example, *Taylored in Silk* closes with a cover of "This
Bitter Earth" by Dinah Washington, who died a decade earlier, in what
is more than a musical tribute, but also a signpost of an artist whose
influence on R&B and soul cannot be overstated. Though much is made
of gospel singer Clara Ward's impact on Aretha Franklin, Washington's was just as pronounced on Franklin, if underappreciated. At the
time that *Taylored in Silk* was recorded, Franklin was, of course, the
standard-bearer of the soul tradition, and Taylor's version of "This Bitter
Earth"—which Franklin also covered in a tribute album to Washington
in 1964—restores Washington's role in Franklin's ascent for the benefit
of a younger audience.

The majority of *Taylored in Silk* was recorded at Muscle Shoals Sound
Studio in Alabama, with the exception of "Talk to Me," for which the
rhythm track was recorded in Detroit. "Talk to Me" was a cover of one of
the most popular songs by Little Willie John, whose brief career ended
with his death in a prison hospital in 1968 at age thirty. More than a
musical footnote, John was pound for pound one of the most impressive

performers of his generation; even "Godfather of Soul" James Brown was compelled to acknowledge the influence of his former labelmate with a tribute album shortly after John's death. As Gayle Wald writes, "Little Willie John was a small man with a big voice, an outsized talent who could croon and growl, sing ballads and rhythm and blues, dig deep into his lower register and hit high notes that took the wind out of lesser tenors . . . not even James Brown, the Hardest Working Man in Show Business, wanted to follow Little Willie John on a bill."[17]

While clearly acknowledging the importance of the soul tradition, *Taylored in Silk* also makes a claim for Taylor's place within that tradition. The haunting intro guitar riff from the opening track "We're Getting Careless with Our Love" is as recognizable as any Stax record intro save Hayes's iconic "Theme from *Shaft*." Like many of the songs on the album, "Careless" brings some nuance to the subgenre of "infidelity soul" that Stax promoted with Taylor, Luther Ingram, and the Soul Children. Taylor's take on Sir Mack Rice's classic strut "Cheaper to Keep Her," which updates Ray Charles's classic live rendition of "Makin' Whoopee," serves as a cautionary counterpoint for the very story that opens the album.

> When your little girl make you mad
> And you get an attitude and pack your bags
> Five little children that you're leaving behind
> Son, you're gonna pay some alimony or do some time

Side one of *Taylored in Silk* includes a cover of Mel and Tim's 1972 "Starting All Over Again," which was the duo's first top-ten Stax single after the success of their 1969 hit "Backfield in Motion" and was written by Prince Phillip Mitchell, who also penned Millie Jackson's 1973 breakthrough hit "It Hurts So Good." In softening the edges of the Mel and Tim version, Taylor's version offered a reminder of the "new" Stax's contribution to the soul tradition.

"The Hang-Ups of Holding On": Betrayal in the Archive

As part of Stax's earlier agreement with Atlantic Records, the duo of Sam & Dave (Sam Moore and Dave Prather), though signed to the latter, more established label, were loaned to the Memphis label, where they were produced by the duo of David Porter and Isaac Hayes. Sam & Dave enjoyed success between 1966 and 1967 with a string of crossover singles like "Hold On I'm Coming," "When Something is Wrong with My Baby," "I Thank You," and the classic "Soul Man." The end of Stax's relationship with Atlantic was also the end of Porter and Hayes's collaboration with Sam & Dave, who had to find new vehicles for their musical ideas. Porter and Hayes were not interested in replicating Sam & Dave or putting together another male vocal group, so they recruited vocalists Anita Louis, Shelbra Bennett, John Corbett (also known by his stage name, J. Blackfoot), and Norman West for a group they called the Soul Children.

Musically, the Soul Children combined elements of deep southern soul, blues, gospel, and even elements of the sermon; at times, their music might be described as capturing the "Holy Ghost." It was this element of the Soul Children that initially brought J. Blackfoot to the attention of Porter and Hayes, though at first they tried to record him as a crossover artist. Writing about one of the group's early singles, "I'll Understand," Bowman suggests that "what had not worked with Blackfoot as a solo artist is nearly too much to bear in the hands of The Soul Children."[18] According to Porter, "That was the reason for saying the Soul Children—take it all the way to church. We just got real with it."[19]

"Real with it," in the case of the Soul Children, often meant songs that dealt with the deep complexities of relationships, particularly in the realm of the illicit and forbidden. Throughout the Soul Children's four Stax albums, particularly their debut, *The Soul Children* (1969), *Best of Two Worlds* (1970), and 1972's *Genesis*, the theme of infidelity features prominently. More than simply songs about cheating, the Soul Children's music deeply probes notions of betrayal, hurt, and regret, speaking to deep fissures that can exist in families and communities around passion and desire. As Shelbra Bennett sings on the track "I'll Understand," a song in which a man and woman accept that their affair might be too difficult,

> While my sister call me low down, yes, she does
> And my brother won't even speak, no, he won't
> My daddy don't want me around
> But listen to this, my mama sayin',
> "Go somewhere else and eat."

Given the tenor of the times, such themes not only resonated with listeners' everyday lives, but also tapped into powerful feelings of grief and loss—particularly in light of what could still be lost—in the aftermath of the shootings of Medgar Evers, John F. Kennedy, Sam Cooke, Malcolm X, Robert Kennedy, and Martin Luther King Jr., iconic figures whose deaths, for many, tested faith in God and nation. The raw emotion of songs like "The Sweeter He Is (Parts 1 & 2)," "The Hang-Ups of Holding On" (which clocks in at over eight minutes), and "I Want to Be Loved," the opening track on the Soul Children's third album, *Genesis*, also capture broader emotions related to the failure of the State to adequately address the conditions of failing schools, poverty, and the lack of access to full citizenship.

On "The Sweeter He Is," the rich harmonies of the group, which boasted double male and female leads, creates a sense of multiple perspectives that mirrored a more democratic view experienced within Black communities. When the Soul Children sing the chorus, "The Sweeter he is, the longer the pain is gonna last," one hears, beyond the specific concerns of the song, resolve regarding both the allure and the price of freedom and justice. "The Sweeter He Is" captures some of the contradictions that Black Americans associated with such ideals of loving, symbolized by the nation-state, that were left unrequited. "The

Hang-Ups of Holding On" offers another version of this cautionary tale about love and nation:

> I keep seeing the bad in you
> So tell me why every night I pray you don't go? . . .
> When you've given all you got to give and you don't receive nothing
>   in return
> It's a hang-up.

The full power of the Soul Children is on display on the track "I Want to Be Loved," from *Genesis*. The album features their signature style, which elides the distinctions between gospel and soul music, the sacred and the secular; this is the music of a revival. "I Want to be Loved," another song that clocks in at over eight minutes, gestures toward vocalist Lorraine Ellison, who recorded the song in 1967 and came to some prominence in the 1960s while recording for the Gospel Chords—a group Al Bell was likely familiar with—before signing to Warner Brothers subsidiary Loma Records as a solo artist. Whereas Ellison's first album, *Heart and Soul* (1966), found her in the territory of soul-pop singers like Dionne Warwick and Nancy Wilson, her followup *Stay with Me*, on which "I Want to Be Loved" also appears, is more devoted to the gospel world that produced her. Still, "I Want To Be Loved" written by her manager, singer-songwriter Sam Bell, who recorded with Garnet Mimms and the Enchanters on their 1963 classic "Cry Baby," is a bit of an outlier, owing its sonic lineage to the gospel traditions of the 1950s.

In line with Stax's archival practices, the Soul Children's version of "I Want to be Loved" diverges from Ellison's original, save its the opening, and includes a dual sermon (or, rather, dueling sermons) between Shelbra Bennett and J. Blackfoot, before transitioning into an extended riff that briefly cites Simon and Garfunkel's "Bridge over Troubled Water" and repeats the "rainbow" riff made famous by Chicago vocalist Gene Chandler. Taken as a whole, "I Want to Be Loved" is a naked performance, exposing deep desires for love and affection that I argue transcend basic desires to just be with *someone*. The song issues a call for something larger than personal affection: for state redress and account-ability, with the moral power of the Black church called into service via the expression of carnal desire.

"I'll Take You There": Spirits in the Archive

If the Soul Children brought the church to the bedroom (or, more apro-pos, to the motel room), Stax also counted on a group like the Staple Singers to bring the church to the masses. The strategy of transformation and reinvention of the archive also applied to the Staple Singers, who began their career singing traditional spirituals and gospel songs behind a drum and guitar. Beginning in the early 1960s, the group, which initially featured patriarch Roebuck "Pops" Staples and his children, Cleotha, Per-vis, Mavis, and, later, Yvonne, reached for a wider audience, interpreting songs from the burgeoning folk music scene, including covers of Woody Guthrie's "This Land Is My Land" (1963), Bob Dylan's "Blowin' in the Wind" (1963), and Zilphia Horton's version of "This Little Light of Mine." Horton is most well known for transforming traditional gospel hymns into civil rights anthems, as part of her organizing at the Highlander Folk School, which served as a training ground for activists. The Staples' 1967 album *For What It's Worth*, one of their last for Epic Records, perfectly captures the group's relationship to the Black musical archive with covers of Pete Seeger's "If I Had a Hammer," (originally recorded as "The Ham-mer Song" by the Weavers in 1950), "Wade in the Water" (made famous by the Fisk Jubilee Singers at the beginning of the twentieth century), and Buffalo Springfield's 1966 recording "For What It's Worth" (written by Stephen Stills). With Mavis Staples as lead vocalist, coupled with their increasing use of electric bass on their recordings, the group was primed to reach a mainstream audience.

All of these dynamics likely informed Al Bell's interest in the Staple Singers. As an SCLC veteran who was familiar with the role of the Highlander School in the civil rights movement, Bell may have imagined taking the group's archival strategy even further by Stax-ifying their sound. The Staple Singers' first albums for Stax, *Soul Folk in Action* (1968) and *We'll Get Over* (1970), both produced by Steve Cropper, feature covers of Otis Redding's "(Sittin' on) The Dock of the Bay," The Band's "The Weight," and Joe South's "Games People Play," as well as takes on popular soul recordings like Sly and the Family Stone's "Everyday People" and "The End of the Road," which was released as a single by both Gladys Knight & the Pips and Marvin Gaye at Motown. With the exception of the reparations anthem "When Will We Be Paid," which was covered thirty years later by Prince and symbolically appears as the last track on *We'll Get Over*, the album's overall feel is one of ambivalence, occupying liminal spaces between folk and soul music, as well as secular and spiritual themes.

With Al Bell at the production helm, the Staple Singers found their literal groove on the albums *The Staple Swingers* (1971), *Be Altitude: Respect Yourself* (1972), and *Be What You Are* (1973). Leaving the relative comforts of Memphis, Bell took the Staples to Fame Studios in Muscle Shoals, Alabama (where Aretha Franklin recorded much of her genre-defining *I Have Never Loved a Man* in 1967), to record *The Staple Swingers* and *Be Altitude: Respect Yourself*. The first of those Bell-produced albums, which featured cover art of Roebuck "Pops" Staples pushing his adult daughters Cleotha, Yvonne, and Mavis on swings, encapsulates their new sound, now perfectly syncopated for the spiritual concerns of a secular world.

Even in this instance, the Staple Singers offered a productive trip into the archive. "You're Gonna Make Me Cry"—arguably the centerpiece of *The Staple Swingers*—is a cover of a song by the tragically underrated soul and blues vocalist O.V. Wright from 1965. Wright recorded for a short time on Goldwax, a Memphis-based label that also featured James Carr of "Dark End of the Street" fame. Though Wright's original background arrangements seem to have been inspired by what was even then the singular style of the Staple Singers—to which Anthony Heilbut notes the debt owed by Aretha Franklin's "Chain of Fools" and Gladys Knight and the Pips' "Freedom Train"—on the group's version the song is slowed down, and Mavis Staples's vocals largely stand alone, whose intervention, if you will, would be reflected in fellow Memphis artist Ann Peebles's own version of the song on her 1977 album *If This Is Heaven*.

As Bell later reflected, he had always imagined the Staple Singers as a three-for-one opportunity, hoping to establish Mavis Staples and Pops Staples as solo artists, alongside the group's recordings. It was a strategy used by Motown in the early 1970s to establish Michael Jackson and his brother Jermaine as solo artists with sustainable careers beyond the group. Beyond that, the group's cover of Wright signaled a bridge to a murkier generic area where artists like Wright, Bobby "Blue" Bland, James Carr, Little Milton (who signed with Stax in the early 1970s), and even Aretha Franklin trafficked easily in blues, traditional R&B, soul, and some gospel. Stax's excavation of the archive served as an attempt to render genre distinctions—at least as they related to Black music—obsolete.

While Bell valued the ability of the Staples Singers to push the boundaries of the archive, ultimately it was the vocal style of the group, and their brand of uplift politics, when secularized both thematically and musically, that helped to create a new, commercially viable, and unique archive for Stax. As Mavis Staple recalls in *Respect Yourself: Stax Records and the Soul Explosion*, "Pops would tell the songwriters. . . . If you want to write for the Staples, read the headlines—we want to sing about what's happening in the world today."[20] In *Country Soul*, Charles L. Hughes writes, "Al Bell saw the Staples as the cornerstone for reimagining Stax . . . the label marketed the Staple Singers as musical embodiments of the African American struggle for equality," adding that the Staples were more than compliant: "The group's commitment to the struggle was more than rhetorical. They were involved in black activist campaigns throughout the period, including regular association with [the National Association of Radio and Television Announcers]" (99).

"Up above My Head": Sanctuary in the Archive

Pops Staples was fifty-four years old when the Staple Singers signed with Stax, and lead singer Mavis Staples was in her early thirties when the group hit its commercial stride in the early 1970s. No matter how much Stax and Bell might have viewed the Staple Singers in the context of what Hughes refers to as "musical Blackness" throughout *Country Soul*, their core demographic was aging in comparison to young Blacks who were becoming enamored with groups like the Jackson 5, the Edwin Hawkins Singers, and Sly and the Family Stone.[21] Indeed even at Muscle Shoals, the sound of the Jackson 5 and their "corporation"-produced tracks was so palpable that Fame Studio head Rick Hall rescued the Osmonds from Disneyland and the barbershops of Utah with "One Bad Apple," a song straight from the Motown playbook.[22] Bell wasn't much interested in "bubblegum soul," but he did need to reach younger audiences, particularly in the wake of the success of the Edwin Hawkins Singers, whose "Oh Happy Day" was a major crossover pop hit in the spring of 1969. With the Rance Allen Group, Bell sought to bridge the gap.

Rance Allen was the lead vocalist of a trio of brothers, including Tom Allen and Steve Allen, from Monroe, Michigan, who recorded their first single in 1969. After winning a gospel talent show in Detroit in 1971, the trio came to the attention of veteran record promoter Dave Clark, who had joined Stax that year to launch the label's gospel subsidiary, the Gospel Truth. Prior to his move to Stax, Clark spent nearly twenty years at Duke/Peacock Records, where he worked with standout gospel acts such as the Dixie Hummingbirds and the Mighty Clouds of Joy. As a child, Rance Allen toured the Midwest as "Little Rance Allen, the Boy Preacher," much like a young James Cleveland, who first sang for Thomas Dorsey, the "father of gospel," when he was eight years old. Allen cited Cleveland as a primary influence; the elder Cleveland, who at the time of the Rance Allen's Group's emergence was simply known as the "King of Gospel," had come through the ranks apprenticing as Reverend C. L. Franklin's choir director in the late 1940s and serving as the primary accompanist for the Caravans, one of the genre's supergroups. Reverend Cleveland is largely credited with ushering gospel music into its modern period, centering large choirs in his productions, which augmented the communal sensibilities of Black music already heightened in the midst of the civil rights movement.

As soul groups like Curtis Mayfield and the Impressions sought to secularize the spiritual-uplift music of the era with tracks like "Amen" and "People Get Ready," Cleveland's success was grounded in rhythms that were attuned to the musical sensibilities of young Black Americans in the early 1960s. With regard to Reverend Cleveland's best-known recordings, the iconic "Peace Be Still," historian Claudrena Harold offers that "its unique time signatures represented a sonic departure from much of the music played on Gospel radio during the early 1960s, but its message was quite familiar to most Gospel audiences. . . . The words are familiar, but the delivery is not."[23] Music scholars Andrew Legg and Carolyn Philpott highlight Cleveland's influence in the context of performance practices in Black gospel music, noting that vocal "phrasing, for the gospel singer, is always subordinated to the expressive and rhythmic momentum and 'swing' of the song." In terms of Cleveland's vocal style, Legg and Philpott write, he "uses these African American concepts of rhythm and phrasing to communicate and express not only the music, but his character and his message with great intensity and depth of meaning."[24] These remarks capture the extent to which Reverend Cleveland, like his contemporary Ray Charles, demonstrated special interest in the role of gospel music, in terms of lyrical content, musical composition, and performance practices, in the secular world.

As part of a commentary on why she liked James Cleveland, Nikki Giovanni notes that "the church is a great archive of Black music."[25] To those ends, some of Cleveland's most popular recordings in the early 1960s were mined from the archives, including the aforementioned "Peace Be Still," which transformed Mary Baker's 1874 composition "Master, the Tempest Is Raging" into a gospel standard. On "I Can't Stop Loving God" from his 1964 album *I Stood on the Banks of Jordan*, Cleve-

land reworked Ray Charles's crossover classic "I Can't Stop Loving You,"
itself a cover of country singer Don Gibson's original. A decade later,
Cleveland covered Gladys Knight and the Pips' "You're the Best Thing to
Ever Happen" on his album *Jesus Is The Best Thing That Ever Happened
To Me* (1975). Connected to long-established practices of borrowing and
reanimation in Black music, it was also not surprising that one of Cleve-
land's breakthrough songs, "I Had a Talk with God Last Night" (1963),
would be secularized by Mitty Collier for her biggest hit a year later.
The Rance Allen Group borrowed Cleveland's practice on the group's
Stax debut when they recorded a version of the Temptations' "Just My
Imagination (Running Away with Me)," adding new sacred lyrics, for a
track they called "Just My Salvation." The Temptations original was the
last single from the group to feature their original falsetto lead, Eddie
Kendricks, and proved an ideal first single for the Rance Allen Group
and the Gospel Truth label to promote Allen's own use of the technique.

Even as the Rance Allen Group expanded the archive by pushing
the boundaries of the sacred and the secular, lead singer Rance Allen's
screaming falsetto created new ground on which to rebuild Stax's archive. On tracks like "If I Could Make the World Better" (1972), "Just
Found Me" (1975), "I Belong to You" (1978), and, especially, "That Will
Be Good Enough" (1972) and "Up above My Head" (1972), Allen's falsetto indexes notions of desire and transcendence that map onto abstract themes of queerness as sanctuary, or what ethnomusicologist
Alisha Lola Jones describes as a "dwelling place."[26] In the essay "'You
Are My Dwelling Place': Experiencing Black Male Vocalists' Worship
as Aural Eroticism and Autoeroticism in Gospel Performance," Jones
explores "the ways in which Gospel singing is understood as erotic and
sensual for nonheterosexual single believers, both performers and listeners," noting that "sexual abstinence discourses obscure the alternative forms of sensual and sexual exploration occurring in gospel music
participation."[27]

Writing about a tribute concert for Richard Smallwood that occured
in 2016, Jones reflects on the responses to two of the artists featured

in the concert: Charles Anthony Bryant and Anthony C. Williams (Tonex/B. Slade), both Black male vocalists who have publicly acknowledged their queer identity. Jones writes that Bryant was described as sounding "'like a real man,'" while B. Slade was "'just too much.'" As Jones explains, "B. Slade is a high-signing male vocalist with a range that spans literally 'whistle(d) tones' down to the baritone," whereas Bryant's "baritone sonic persona is less likely to signify his queer potential in predominantly black gospel music context."[28] While Allen has never identified himself as queer, I'd like to linger on this notion that his falsetto was "just too much" in the context of his early Stax performances, and that "just too much" more palpably mapped onto the desires for disruptive Black political and social movement in the period.

"Up above My Head," an early Stax single for the Rance Allen Group built around Rance Allen's falsetto, offers one of the best examples of a vocal style that might have been interpreted as excessive. Toward the song's end. Allen sings the refrain "I hear the music way up above my head" before engaging in a vocal break with his brothers that makes a clear reference to Sly and the Family Stone's 1967 breakthrough single "Dance to the Music." In signaling their artistic debt to Sly and the Family Stone, particularly Sly Stone's (Sylvester Stewart) own background in the sanctified tradition, the Rance Allen Group broadened the concept of what gospel could be. Allen's falsetto performance on "Up above My Head" also anticipates James Baldwin's *Just above My Head* (1979), the last of the author's novels to be published during his lifetime, which examines the life and death of the fictional Arthur Montana, the "Emperor of Soul" whose queerness was closeted in the worlds of Black gospel and soul music. The notion of singing "up above my head" or "just above my head" can also read as metaphors for queer or nonheteronormative desire, which would also apply to the Rance Allen song "That Will Be Good Enough for Me," which the group revived from the archive of Reverend James Cleveland and that New Orleans–based gospel artist Raymond Myles would revive again in the 1990s. In this sense, the refrain of "Up above

My Head" not only conceptualizes Rance Allen's vocal range, but also pivots to something otherworldly.

"Heaven, That Will Be Good Enough" was a James Cleveland composition, originally performed in 1964 by the James Cleveland Singers, a small ensemble with which Cleveland recorded in addition to his choirs. The Rance Allen Group covered the song as "That Will Be Good Enough for Me" on their Stax debut *Truth Is Where It's At*. Allen performs the song largely using Cleveland's original lyrics, though the end of the song takes a dramatic turn when Allen sings,

> Listen to the Lord talkin'
> So that's why I see you struggle
> A long, long, long time
> But I see here by your record
> You've been doing just fine
> I see the way you fought the devil on Ivory hill
> Say, listen here, man, you're what I call
> A good Christian man.

Allen's additional lyrics capture a vision of freedom—an aspirational insight, connected to actually conversing with "God"—that is not present in Cleveland's composition.

Allen's vocal range, particularly in the higher register, sharply contrasted with that of Cleveland, whose range was rather limited. I would argue, therefore, that Allen's performance of those lyrics in this higher register articulates a level of meaning that transcends Cleveland's original intent. Where song lyrics like the following (also from "Heaven, That Will Be Good Enough") imagine Black American bodies as transnational bodies, aligning with desires for travel and movement among the Black masses,

> I've never been to Paris in the spring or the fall
> I've never been to India, to the Taj Mahal. . . .
> I've never been to Switzerland, no, no, no, to see the winter games play

Ooh, I've never been to New Orleans on Carnival or Mardi Gras day, yeah

Allen's falsetto quite literally summons the power to *transform* Black American bodies into transnational bodies. Allen's open-ended and ethereal vocals change Cleveland's original lyrics from expressions of hope to expressions of possibility, as emblematic of the shifts that had occurred in Black politics between the time of Cleveland's original recording and Allen's cover.

The radical potential embodied in Allen's falsetto can be witnessed a generation later in the work of the late New Orleans gospel singer Raymond Myles. Like Cleveland and Allen, Myles was a child prodigy who by the early 1980s had formed his own group, the Raymond Anthony Myles Singers (or the RAMs). Myles was also openly gay, and, as record executive Leo Sacks explained, his queerness proved a challenge in pitching his music to a wider audience: "I told Raymond, '[Record labels] say you're too flamboyant.' . . . He knew it was code. But it was unfathomable to him that his artistry could be rejected because of the perception of his homosexuality."[29] After a series of stellar live performances, Myles was on the cusp of a commercial breakthrough with the album *A Taste of Heaven* (1995) when he was murdered in a carjacking in New Orleans in 1998.

Myles didn't leave a wealth of recorded music, but his live album *Heaven Is the Place* (1997) is notable for the title track "Heaven Is the Place I Want to Be," which reworks Cleveland and Allen's "That Will Be Good Enough." In a live setting, Myles's back-and-forth with the audience and choir, as well as the more personalized narrative ("The only thing Raymond Myles wanna do is just make it into heaven") provides a communal context that did not appear in Cleveland and Allen's version. Also, Myles's additional lyrics, such as "I ain't never been to New York City to see the famous Thanksgiving Macy's parade," highlight the spatial and political disconnectedness that a city like New Orleans, with its high rates of poverty and environmental threats, experiences in relationship to the rest of the United States—issues made even more apparent seven years after Myles was murdered, with Hurricane Katrina.

Whereas Reverend James Cleveland made no reference to political realities in his version of "Heaven, That Will be Good Enough," and, as I suggested, the Rance Allen Group's version gestures to a progressive politics, embedded in Rance Allen's falsetto, Raymond Myles and the RAMS' version of "Heaven Is The Place" makes an explicit political intervention in a spoken-word section toward the song's close. In what might be more technically described as a sermon, Myles draws the congregation in with "Can I tell you about . . ." and, after a few appeals to more traditional spiritual and everyday concerns, calls attention to both the random violence within Black communities and the media's depiction of anti-Black violence ("No drive-by shootings, and carjackings there. I won't have to see my brothers on the news anymore being shot down in the streets like animals"). Additionally, Myles makes connections to the realities of White supremacy, referencing former Ku Klux Klan Grand Wizard David Duke, who had run for the US Senate the year before ("There will be no David Dukes there. . . . There will be no segregation there, no racism").

Unspoken in Myles's sermon is any clear reference to a place where one could safely engage in safe-sex relationships, without fear of homophobic violence or sexually transmitted disease, yet he gestures to such a possibility in the song's closing section with the refrain "I'm on my way, to a better place, I'll take my rest, there I'll be blessed," which, in the context of the performance, is rendered as a Black or even afrofuturist utopia. Thus, "just too much" might also be read as the possibilities of a Black future that simply can't be contained in the contemporary moment.

Bell's efforts to rebuild the archive was tethered to an agenda to expand the narrative about and sonic ranges of Black music in the era. Isaac Hayes's contribution of what might be thought of a "symphonic soul" style—liberally borrowed in the 1970s by the likes of Marvin Gaye and Barry White, and in the production aesthetics of Kenneth Gamble and Leon Huff at Philadelphia International Records—is one example. The influence of the Rance Allen Group on a Raymond Myles long after their days at Stax is another example. And yet Bell's vision had a deeper meaning, as Robinson notes: "By the 1970s, the music industry was one of the largest employers of African Americans in the city of Memphis, contributing tens of millions of dollars annually to the local economy."[30] Bell's desire to add value to Stax and its archive was also embedded in the economic and cultural value of a city like Memphis, and its role as "a leader in the global music industry, recognized not only for its distinct contributions to sound but also for its prolific production of recordings at multiple iconic studios and labels across the city."[31] In under twenty years, Robinson writes, Stax had "created an iconic sound that temporarily transformed the neighborhood and forever transformed global music culture."[32]

2

"I Got the Blues of a Fallen Teardrop"

Erasure, Trauma, and a Sonic Archive of Black Women
Backwater blues have caused me to pack up my things and go
Backwater blues have caused me to pack up my things and go
'Cause my house fell down and I can't live there no more.
—Bessie Smith, "Backwater Blues"

Perhaps resistance to the violence of slavery is survival, the will
to survive, the sound of someone wanting to be heard, wanting
to live, or wanting to die. But the struggle against dehumanization is in the *wanting*. And sometimes we can hear it.
—Marisa J. Fuentes, *Dispossessed Lives: Enslaved Women,*
Violence, and the Archive

There's a certain haunting presence in the 2008 Academy Award–
nominated documentary *Trouble the Water*. It's a presence that is
immediately felt by anybody who journeyed to the city of New Orleans
in the years after Katrina. Tourists traveled through downtown New
Orleans and the French Quarter blandly commenting on the limited
hours of some of the city's more authentic haunts, as the Lower 9th
Ward, where portions of the city remained a decidedly barren reminder
of the vibrant living cultures that once existed there, continued to serve
as the most lasting monument of the destruction. If Hurricane Katrina
offered what might be the only contemporary example of ethnic cleans-
ing in the United States, then the power of *Trouble the Water* comes
from its brazen ability to summon the voices and spirits of those who,
by force or by choice, have not returned to New Orleans. As a visual
archive, *Trouble the Water* makes a striking intervention on the behalf

of a city that lacked the bodies and the political will to make that intervention itself.

The film tells the story of Kim Rivers Roberts, a twenty-four-year-old New Orleans resident and aspiring rapper, and her husband, Scott, as she documents their experiences before and after the hurricane. Roberts uses a handheld video camera that she purchased for twenty dollars on the street prior to the storm. Produced in collaboration with Tai Leeson and Carl Deal (*Citizen Koch*, 2013), it might be inaccurate to describe *Trouble the Water* as a film that tells the story of Roberts; rather, it depicts Roberts telling a story of loss, trauma, precarity, and resilience in New Orleans using archival footage that she herself shot. In this sense, *Trouble the Water* in some ways counters more official corporate media and government accounts of the hurricane and its aftermath, though Roberts's intent for the footage that she shot and its use by Leeson and Deal represent very different advantages of counternarratives.

When *New York Times* film critic Manohla Dargis writes, "Ms. Roberts is such a charismatic figure that she might have overwhelmed this movie. But Mr. Deal and Ms. Lessin have the big picture in mind, not just a personal portrait," the notion of Roberts's "charisma" might be read as a stand-in for her ingenuity during the disaster, an attribute that some critics might undervalue in stories about the victims of Hurricane Katrina and federal government malfeasance.[1] As Courtney R. Baker writes, "The victims of Katrina who acted on the part of their own survival were, in the eyes of the mass media and their public, altogether too capable to merit the status of 'victim.' If anything, Katrina survivors were victims of their own industry," which "actually mitigated their recognition as victims."[2] Lessin admits as much, telling the *New York Times*, "All we had been seeing in the media were images of helpless victims or of looters. . . . Those were the two archetypes. Kimberly and Scott were neither. They were survivors, and they were putting everything they had into protecting themselves and their community."[3]

Dargis's comments about Roberts' "big personality" also begs the question as to why a Black woman's survival and relative triumph can't be the "big picture."[4] Intentionally or not, Dargis speaks to the general devaluation of the stories of Black women and their archival work. *Trouble the Water* exists in part because of the economic hardships faced by Black women, as well as so many Katrina survivors. Kathleen A. Bergin notes that "gendered aspects of inequality endanger all women in a natural disaster. They cruelly intersected with race and class to particularize the danger for black women trapped in New Orleans during Hurricane Katrina and housed in Houston's shelters following the storm."[5] For those Black women, including Phyllis Montana LeBlanc, who was such a striking presence in Spike Lee's documentary *When the Levees Broke* (2006), precarity wasn't just the big story; it was the only story—an obsession, even. As Roberts told the *Brooklyn Rail*, "We'd run out of money. We had about a hundred dollars left, and we was like, 'We ought to try to see what we could do with this tape; we might find somebody we could give this tape to; well not give it, but either sell it, or license . . . you know, see what it's worth.'"[6] These comments reflect the do-it-yourself ethic of the hip-hop generation and the time-tested drive of African Americans to "make a way out of no way." Survival is, of course, a distinctly improvisational mode of navigating the world, and *Trouble the Water* harnesses the rhythms of Black improvisation via Roberts's audio and visual narration.

Trouble the Water stands in striking opposition to other popular representations of a contemporary and gentrified New Orleans, including the popular Hollywood film *Girls Trip*, which presents the city in a vibrant, celebratory light, despite the real-life trauma experienced by its Black women characters; the animated *The Princess and the Frog*; *The Curious Case of Benjamin Button*; and the television series *Treme*, which, despite its progressive political critiques, contributes to a nostalgic rendering of New Orleans that is dated, static, and believed authentic. As Roberts suggested in 2015, a decade after Katrina, "She's still interrupting quality of life for citizens of New Orleans who are not middle class and rich. For people in other neighborhoods it's still tough. The lower ninth ward didn't get enough help or money to rebuild . . . the kids don't even have access to bathrooms in a park here—that's Katrina in another form."[7] It is this notion of "another form" that lies at the heart of my interest in *Trouble the Water*: it serves as a metaphor for the tensions around, in this case, a Black woman's archive, her curation of that archive, and the question of what might get lost.

In one of the film's opening scenes, as Roberts and her husband Scott prepare to be interviewed by the filmmakers, Roberts clearly states that she wants "this" to go "worldwide," not remain merely "local." This statement serves as an early indication of Roberts's resistance to victimization and her exertion of agency, which nonetheless does not discount the fact that she and so many others fell victims to forces beyond their control. As Baker argues, Roberts's presence in the *Trouble the Water* counters corporate media attempts to "package scenes of atrocity to abet readings that condemn nature or the victims themselves for the tragedy."[8] Significantly, Roberts' own captured footage features her in the role of the "on-the-spot" reporter, interviewing neighbors, especially children, about their plans as the storm approaches: in utilizing this mode, Roberts anticipates loss that can still be documented as a form of condemnation of state-sanctioned neglect.

In one example, Roberts approaches a group of preteen Black girls, who all respond to the coming storm with a level of Black girl sass embodied by Roberts's own filmmaking. One of the girls introduces herself with "I'm from the uptown 3rd Ward, ya heard me," referencing a well-circulated New Orleans colloquialism. Yet the phrase "ya heard me" also holds relevance as the title of a song recorded by rap artists Soulja Slim on his 2001 album *The Streets Made Me*. Soulja Sim, who hailed from "the uptown, " is one of several New Orleans–based musicians who were born in the Magnolia Projects, including Juvenile and Jay Electronica, who contributed to the national relevance of New Orleans rap music via the labels Cash Money and No Limit Records. The young girl's affirmation of her origins may well have been emboldened by pride in the memory of Soulja Slim, who was murdered in 2003, and whose posthumous collaboration with Juvenile, "Slow Motion," topped the pop charts the year before Katrina's landfall.[9]

The video for "Slow Motion," which featured cameos by other New Orleans hip-hop dignitaries including Baby and Lil' Wayne, served as a memorial not only for the late Soulja Slim, but also, unwittingly, for the Magnolia Projects, and New Orleans public housing writ large, by wedding the city's musical traditions with a built-environment that, in the wake of the hurricane, would largely disappear. As art historian Amber N. Riley notes, "In New Orleans, music is a significant investigative lens because it is a place-based tradition that permeates every inch of the city." Though "architecture is not often considered a form of cultural production," Riley adds, it is a means to discuss the "social production of space, meaning in everyday life, and the power of public engagement with history. Built and natural landscapes contain a variety of narratives."[10] Journalist Brentin Mock, writing on the ten-year anniversary of Katrina, observes that the imagery of the Magnolia Projects and "other large public-housing developments mostly live on in the memories of those who once lived in them—and in the imaginations of those who didn't."[11]

Mock goes on to contend that the music videos shot by Cash Money and No Limit artists in New Orleans public housing developments oppose the "new urbanist" perception of such spaces as "dens of misery," adding that these artists "weren't afraid to show the worst of these conditions alongside the best . . . they were unconcerned with the white and middle-class gaze, and the judgement that comes with that."[12] Roberts finds her point of view as a filmmaker and archivist via her dismissal of the White gaze and rejection of the lens of so-called Black respectability. In the above example, Roberts privileges the worldview of a group of Black girls, generally dismissed both in Black and larger White communities as sources of knowledge. Given her sensibilities, it's not surprising that Roberts showcases this footage of a young Black girl, whose insight, implicit in her citation of Soulja Slim, offers a portal to acknowledging the physical and cultural communities that would be destroyed by Katrina.

Robert's strategy for representing New Orleans includes a key component: her sampling of Black cultural ephemera. A trip to the store on her bike to buy red beans and smoked neck bones—New Orleans staples—produces another series of interactions and reflections that contribute to Roberts's aim, in her own words, to show "the world that we did have a world" before the storm. For example, while sitting and joking with an uncle and his friends outside of the store, Roberts's singing of Patti La-Belle's "On My Own" serves as commentary on law enforcement officers who were themselves fleeing the city. Released in 1986, the duet "On My Own" between LaBelle and Michael MacDonald (he of contemporary "blue-eyed" soul lore) topped the pop charts that year and remains the most successful single for both artists. Roberts's citation of the song, which is ostensibly about an impending breakup, offers layered meanings, related to law enforcement's breaking of their oath to "serve and protect," her potential "breakup" with the city of her birth, and, more literally, her decision to wait out the storm "alone" with her husband, while so many of her neighbors chose to leave.

In another example, in footage that was shot by Lessin and Deal when Roberts and her husband, Scott, return to their neighborhood two weeks after the levees failed, the couple is confronted by one of their family dogs, who was left behind but survived the flood. The dog is named "Kizzy," a nod to *Roots*, Alex Haley's fictionalized account of his family's origin story. In the context of the book and, later, award-winning miniseries, Kizzy was the daughter of the main protagonist, Kunte Kinte, who is captured in the Gambia and transported to the United States. Given the series' popularity when it was broadcast in 1977, "Kizzy" became a primary way of referring to an enslaved Black girl, in the era before Harriet Jacobs's *Incidents in the Life of a Slave Girl* became more widely known, as a signifier of the impact of racialized sexual violence against Black women and girls.

In a naming ceremony after Kizzy's birth, Kunte Kinte describes her as one who "stays put," so there's no small irony that the family dog named "Kizzy" in fact, stayed put. Yet the naming of the dog is prescient, when considered along with earlier footage in the film, in which Roberts describes herself as "the only stupid nigga who stayed." Roberts's own affinity for "Kizzy" is important, as the character Kizzy plays a critical role in the miniseries in passing down the traditions and stories of Kunte Kinte and the people of the Gambia, particularly to her son Chicken George. In his cultural history of the groundbreaking miniseries, Matthew F. Delmont notes that many of the women characters in Alex Haley's original book were underdeveloped, writing that "Kizzy does not appear in Haley's early versions of his family history, and when she does show up in later drafts she is little more than a generational bridge to get from Kunte Kinte to Chicken George."[13] According to Delmont, "In the television series Kizzy has a character arc, and for a small measure of revenge, that she is denied in the book."[14] One of the most pivotal characters in the miniseries, Leslie Uggams, portrays Kizzy as a teenage girl, an adult and elderly woman over the course of three of the eight episodes, who in the end "becomes the matriarch for a community of enslaved people."[15] It is unknown how familiar Roberts might have been with *Roots* or the character of Kizzy. This example, though, as with others, highlights Roberts's deft use of Black vernacular to build a distinctly gendered metaphorical shelter from the winds of Hurricane Katrina and highlights sampling practices that exist beyond visual and sonic mediums.

In her short introductions and signoffs throughout *Trouble the Water*, Roberts refers to herself as "Black Kold Madina," her rap persona. Roberts's relationship to rap music and hip-hop culture illuminates the personal importance of archival practices to Roberts. She uses the decidedly male-centered cultural space of hip-hop as a vehicle for expressing the specificity of her life as a Black woman. Roberts's sampling of musical lyrics and referencing of popular culture, as in the naming of the family dog, serves as an archive of Black survival and Black female transcendence of trauma and tragedy. Roberts had believed that all of her own recorded music had been lost during Katrina, but when she and her husband landed in Memphis at the home of a cousin, she discovers a recording of her music that she had given to her cousin months earlier when he visited New Orleans.

Not surprisingly, Roberts's sampling practices are most evident in the creation of her own music. Arguably the centerpiece of *Trouble the Water* is Roberts's performance of the song "Amazing," which samples the beat from "You Got Me," the commercial breakthrough for the Roots in 1999 that featured vocals from Erykah Badu and earned the group a Grammy Award for Best Rap Performance by a Duo or Group in 2000. The song had been cowritten by a then–little-known Jill Scott, who originally intended to record the song with the group, but the Roots were encouraged by their record company to seek out a more established artist. The rapper Eve performs the song's second verse, but didn't appear in the song's music video. Scott does sing on a live recording of "You Got Me" that was released months later on the album *The Roots Come Alive* recorded at the Bowery in New York City. One hears on that version an almost mystical sense of perseverance from Scott, that foreshadowed her own breakthrough a year later with *Who Is Jill Scott? Words and Sounds, Vol. 1.*

The history of "You Got Me," in its various iterations, clearly illustrates the ways in which Black women's labor was subsumed in the context of the music industry in the late 1990s, although both Scott and Eve would ultimately use the song, and their relationship with the Roots ,as springboards for their own careers—in fact, Scott literally spells out her name in the live performance as a form of introduction. That Roberts would identify the song as an ideal platform for telling her own story of transcendence before Hurricane Katrina seems more than incidental. As David O'Grady writes, "In one of the more riveting and righteously fierce moments in recent documentary memory, Kim stares into the camera and raps along to the song."[16] In lyrics that detail the death of her mother from AIDS and Roberts's own turn to dealing drugs on the streets, O'Grady notes how Roberts's "perseverance and resilience . . . literally redirect the lens pointed at the storm to reveal instead an America languishing in the shadows cast by a country's shiny story of itself."[17] Roberts's lyrics ("I was just a little girl caught up in the storm") which were recorded pre-Katrina, makes the connection between the storm of poverty and the natural disaster that exacerbated it.

Trouble the Water, and Roberts's presence throughout, exemplify what the late historian Clyde Woods calls the "blues tradition of investigation and interpretation . . . a newly indigenous knowledge system that has been used repeatedly by multiple generations of working-class African Americans to organize communities of consciousness."[18] Roberts's narration draws on what Woods describes as "African-American musical practices, folklore, and spirituality to reorganize and give a new voice to working class communities facing severe fragmentation."[19] In and of themselves, those practices constitute ways of indexing, ordering, and archiving Blackness in the midst of material, spiritual, and, in some cases, physical loss. As Woods observes, "This tradition has been engaged in the production and teaching of African American history from its inception."[20] When queried as to why she decided to carry a handheld video camera during the storm, Roberts told the *Brooklyn Rail,* "I decided to film because I realized we weren't going to be able to leave—that was the fact . . . If I died, people gonna know how I died. So to some degree, I was feeling like my legacy should live on and people would know what had happened to us. "

Zu-Zu's Song: Trauma and Citation in *Five Days of Bleeding*

Kim Robert's citational creation of an archive throughout *Trouble the Water* finds a precedent in the experimental fiction of novelist Ricardo Cortez Cruz. *Five Days of Bleeding* (1995)—its title a reference to a woman's menstrual cycle—was Cruz's follow-up to his award-winning debut novel *Straight Outta Compton* (1992), which was described by *Kirkus*

Review as "a rap, jive, and video-inflected hallucination of the L.A. black ghetto."[21] Like *Straight Outta Compton, Five Days of Bleeding* traffics in rap lyrics, Black vernacular, and references to Black popular culture, creating a dense, insular archival project. Much of the novel's action centers on the experiences of a young homeless Black woman named Zu-Zu, who is pursued throughout by a group of young, presumably Black men, led by a nefarious figure named Chops. As a character, Zu-Zu makes plain—often in the form of song—the violence and trauma that she experiences throughout the novel, but she also labors on behalf of a sonic archive of Black women performers and as a caretaker of their legacies. Whereas Kim Roberts deployed a handheld video camera to tell a story, Zu-Zu's decidedly analog technology is the Black women's songbook.

Cruz's creative treatment of Zu-Zu raises questions as to both the history and present of the character: How does one imagine how Zu-Zu got to that place, in that time, and in that way? On the surface, Cruz seems unable or even incapable of answering these questions, at least to the extent that we believe that a Black male writer can fully experience or interpret the gendered and racialized existence of, in this instance, a young heterosexual Black woman. As the creator of Zu-Zu, and the world she inhabits, Cruz inhabits the ambivalent role of a male writer and archivist not dissimilar from the unnamed male narrator of the story, who, in his chaste romantic desire for Zu-Zu, also seems oblivious to the complexities of Black women's experiences with trauma and violence, as well as pleasure and desire. In a videotaped interview with Deborah Brothers at Lincoln Land Community College, Cruz admits that he works as a speculative thinker who, in his practice, views himself as functioning much like a turntablist or deejay, sampling language, gestures, emotions, and other ephemera to achieve an effect of intertextuality.

While Cruz gestures toward filling in the blanks of the archive via speculative thought, this vision would be fully realized almost two decades later in the work of Saidiya Hartman. Writing about young Black women, who, off the grid, "struggled to create autonomous and beautiful lives to escape the new forms of servitude awaiting them" in the early twentieth century, Hartman notes that "in writing this account of the wayward, I have made use of a vast range of archival materials to represent the everyday experience and restless character of life in the city", adding that "the aim is to convert the sensory experience of the city and to capture the rich landscape of Black social life." Hartman's theoretical contribution fleshes out a world that Cruz only hints at.[22]

I am particularly struck by Hartman's focus on the "sensory" aspects of the archive, to return to one of the epigraphs that opens this chapter. In her book *Dispossessed Lives: Enslaved Women, Violence, and the Archive*, Marisa J. Fuentes writes, "Perhaps resistance to the violence of slavery is survival . . . the *sound of someone wanting to be heard*, wanting to live, or wanting to die. But the struggle against dehumanization is in the *wanting*. And sometimes *we can hear it*."[23] This puts me in mind again of Zu-Zu from *Five Days of Bleeding*, who also wants to be heard, and who to this end makes use of a sonic archive of Black women. What is there to be heard in the music, lyrics, and voices of early Black blues women singers like Clara Smith, Victoria Spivey, Sippie Wallace, and Edith Wilson, and how does the archive of their work animate and inform the life of a late twentieth-century-character who is navigating much of the same terrain?

That the novel is set in Central Park in the early 1990s is not insignificant, as the relative obscurity of Zu-Zu's life and the level of violence that she negotiates within it stands in contrast to the highly publicized Central Park jogger case, which involved the rape of a young White woman in the park by Matias Reyes in the spring of 1989. Initially, five Harlem teens, the so-called "Central Park Five," were convicted of the crime, but exonerated years later when Matias confessed. Matias, a serial rapist nicknamed the "East Side Slasher," would be found reposnsible for the death of Lourdes Gonzalez and the rape of four other women, one of them only two days before the rape in Central Park, over a two-year period before police apprehended him in August 1989.[24]

The "Whiteness" of the Central Park jogger effectively obscured and overshadowed Matias's other victims, not to mention the many Black and Brown women and girls who were subjected to sexual violence, some of it unreported, in and around Central Park. Though fictional, the character of Zu-Zu illustrates the way violence against Black and Brown women fails to register in the public consciousness with the same urgency as sexual violence againt White women. Even when acknowl-edged, sexual violence against Black and Brown women and girls simply does not generate the degree of concern that would lead to actively ad-dressing such violence. Media scholar Marian Meyers makes a similar point in her study of the news coverage of "Freaknik," an annual spring break gathering of African American college students, in which Black women were subjected to forms of sexual assault and violence. As Mey-ers writes, "The news media's Freaknik coverage plan focused on traf-fic and potential property damage. . . . Significantly, the news did not warn women that attending Freaknik might put them at risk of physical harm, nor did it actively seek out stories that dealt with violence toward women. Only when the cameras just happened to be where a woman was being or had just been physically assaulted did the violence become news."[25] Like Kim Roberts, Cruz, via Zu-Zu, looks at the myriad forms of violence.

In Zu-Zu's male tormentors, Cruz references the phenomenon of "wilding," which was attributed to the unjustly accused Central Park Five, and became, in the years before notions of "superpredators," a public lexicon for describing unruly and dangerous Black youth. It goes without saying that the public imagination naturalized Black women and girls within the context of such violence and considered them com-plicit. Stephen J. Mexal troubles the term "wilding," suggesting that its usage can be traced to Black literary naturalism of the early twentieth century. He writes, "Properly understood, wilding acts as a site of her-meneutic confluence, illuminating the degree to which both the histori-cal language of wilderness and the contemporary cultural construction of postindustrial urban spaces inform American racialist discourse."[26] I cite Mexal here to illuminate the ways in which Cruz utilizes the rap lyrics of characters in "the wild" of Central Park—a space though to possess a "genteel, civilizing function"—to not only provide obvious commentary on forms of toxic masculinity that circulate within the genre, as well as the oncoming surge of gentrification in New York City, in collusion with the erosion of social and cultural space available to Black and Brown youth, that led them to the park in the first place.

With her additional ability to traffic in the discourses of late 1980s and early 1990s hip-hop, since she is in fact a product of that sonic moment, Zu-Zu's performativity might be viewed as dismissive of the rhetorical, emotional, and physical violence directed toward her, yet her deployment, in this instance, of the hip-hop archive best illustrates her acts of resistance. Zu-Zu uses her desirability as a sexual object as modes of both survival and pleasure to negotiate threats posed by the young men in the novel. In the words of Aimee Meredith Cox, Zu-Zu might be read as a "shapeshifter," who reveals the "destructive nature of normative ways of life that valorize white supremacy, patriarchy, and modes of production that render young Black women at best superfluous and at worst valueless" in ways that mirror the lyrics of early twentieth-century blues women.[27]

Zu-Zu primarily references lyrics associated with Black women blues artists, many of whom were obscure.[28] One example is Zu-Zu's referencing of the title of Sippie Wallace's "I'm a Mighty Tight Woman" (1929), in which Wallace sings, "I got all of them sayin' that I'm tight in everything I do / I got all the men cryin', I'm a broad that will never be blue." Indeed, Zu-Zu's own use of the archive of Black women's song suggests that the archive served as both a fictive and literal shield against the violence threatened by some of the men in the novel. In an interview late in her life, Wallace told *People Magazine*, "There isn't anything I sing about that hasn't happened to me."[29] In her case, Zu-Zu's use of the Wallace archive arguably allows her to tell her story in ways that Cruz himself might not have had the language to more fully explore.

Often, Zu-Zu's use of the lyrics of Black blues women does the additional work of recovery. Wallace, who died in 1986, has largely been overshadowed by her one-time mentee Bonnie Raitt, who covered Wallace's

"Woman Be Wise" and "Mighty Tight Woman" on her self-titled debut in 1971, and a year later began a friendship with Wallace that lasted until her death. According to Raitt, she discovered Wallace's music after being drawn to a photo of her on an album cover she saw in a record store in London in 1966. To Raitt's credit, her interest in recording songs from Wallace's catalog and her willingness to share the stage and recording booth with Wallace—Raitt appears on her last studio recording, *Sippie*, which earned the singer a Grammy nomination in 1983—helped Wallace live off of her art in her later years. As Raitt told *People Magazine* in 1982, "Sippie has always seen the struggle of the sexes with a sense of humor and compassion. . . . She knows that freedom is the name of the game even though women have always had to answer to men."[30]

Ironically, when Raitt achieved her biggest success, winning four Grammy Awards, including Record of the Year with *Nick of Time* in 1989, her triumph could have been read through the prism of the very generation of Black women blues singers embodied by Wallace. The album was released three years after Wallace's death and after a challenging period in Raitt's life and career during which she was dropped by her previous label and struggled with addiction. As one *New York Times* critic opined about Raitt's comeback, "Three years ago, I would have gone on to lament the injustice of the fact that Ms. Raitt, a first-rate folk-blues singer who exudes a special sort of true grit, never got the commercial recognition she deserved."[31] The writer's sentiment could have been arguably applied to virtually every Black woman blues singer from the 1920s (save the highly popular Bessie Smith). As such, Zu-Zu, in her way, recovers Wallace, among other underappreciated Black women blues artists, from obscurity.

A similar case can be made with Victoria Spivey, whom Zu-Zu also references, a longtime peer and collaborator of Wallace who may be best remembered for her role as Missy Rose in the 1929 film musical *Hallelujah*, directed by King Vidor, in his first "talkie." With its Black cast, led by Daniel L. Haynes and Nina Mae McKinney, "King Vidor's *Hallelujah!* of 1929 gave the folk musical genre its first masterpiece and major impetus."[32] Of Spivey's performance, the *Baltimore Afro-American* wrote, "Though new to the silver screen, Miss Spivey is by no means a stranger to the American public, especially the darker portion, as she is one of the featured singers on Okeh Records and her blues are known as the most typical, primitive on record."[33] What the newspaper calls "typical" and "primitive" likely refers to Spivey's "Black Snake Blues," a song cited by Zu-Zu in *Five Days of Bleeding.* Though Spivey's most well-known song from the 1920s, "Black Snake Blues" represents ground zero for the kinds of erasure that Black women performers both from that era and later have struggled against.

Recorded in 1926, a version of the song performed by Blind Lemon Jefferson was released by Paramount Records under the title "That Black Snake Moan," and a year later by Okeh Records as "Black Snake Moan," becoming Jefferson's signature tune and one of the iconic recordings from that era. Eighty years later, the song provided the title of a film starring Samuel L. Jackson and Christina Ricci and directed by Craig Brewer, which brought new attention to Blind Lemon Jefferson. In a 1966 interview with *Record Research Magazine*, Spivey recalled, "We were buddies and everything went along swell until I heard his recording of 'Black Snake Moan' on Paramount which came out some months after my original 'Black Snake Blues' on Okeh. It was so much like my 'Black Snake Blues' including the moan. I was really angry for a while knowing that Lemon and myself were like brother and sister in our jobs."[34] Robert Springer notes that it was "natural that reciprocal borrowings between traditional and 'classic blues' should occur," adding "both artists were in a position to claim as their own their respective versions of a song whose words and music were part of folklore."[35]

Spivey makes a finer point with regard to "reciprocal borrowings," recalling how she confronted Jefferson over his use of *her* song: "Lemon had made me recall one night at a party before he recorded 'Black Snake Moan' that he asked my permission, 'Hey, Vickie (that is what he used to call me!), I want to ask you something. Do you mind me using those snakes? I won't do it like you do. I mean the moan.' I said, 'Help yourself' not taking him seriously and not believing that he would or could do it."[36] Spivey's recollection highlights the fact that something in the exchange was *hers*—Jefferson couldn't sonically reproduce her signature moan—but she also makes clear the commercial and artistic stakes: "'Black Snake Moan' not only made Blind Lemon Jefferson but pulled him out of the sticks."[37]

After a successful career, Spivey settled into semiretirement in Brooklyn, New York, in the early 1950s, and began to take on a role as a caretaker of the blues legacy of the 1920s. Notably, she was included among a group of musicians and journalists who helped raise money for a headstone for Mamie Smith, whose songs "That Thing Called Love" and "You Can't Keep a Good Man Down" are considered the two recordings that launched the recorded blues era of the 1920s, and who was buried in an unmarked grave on Staten Island, New York, in 1946.[38] Spivey was also proactive in protecting both her own legacy and that of the blues tradition that produced her, founding Queen Vee Spivey Records in 1962 as well as her own publishing company, which was distinctive in an era when few Black artists owned the publishing rights to their songs. It was with Spivey's encouragement that Sippie Wallace agreed to tour Europe in the 1970s, after the two recorded an eponymous album in 1970 on Spivey's label.

Five Days of Bleeding was published before the Internet was widely available, and, as such, the lyrical references throughout *Five Days of Bleeding* function as analog era hypertext. In a 1990 essay on the phenomenon, Jakob Nielsen describes hypertext as "non-sequential writing: a directed graph, where each node contains some amount of text or other information."[39] James Joyce's *Finnegans Wake* (1939) is thought to be an early example of hypertext in literary form. As poet Billy Mills writes, "The book was, we can now see, crying out for the invention of the web, which would enable the holding of multiple domains of knowledge in the mind at one time that a proper reading requires."[40] Specifically, Mills cites an annotated version of *Finnegans Wake* that led him to believe that it, and other "difficult modernist texts such as Eliot's *The Waste Land* and *The Cantos of Ezra Pound*" were early iterations of the genre.[41]

Although Mills traces hypertext to a distinctly European Modernist tradition, it might also be identified in the context of what Henry Louis Gates Jr. calls the "trope of the talking book," where the "double-voiced text emerges as the text of ultimate critique and revision of the rhetorical strategies at work in the canonical texts of the tradition."[42] Hypertext might also be thought of in what Gates also identifies as the "speakerly text": "a profoundly lyrical, densely metaphorical, quasi-musical, privileged black oral tradition on the one hand, and a received but not yet fully appropriated standard English literary tradition on the other hand. The quandary for the writer was to find a third term, a bold and novel signifier, informed by these two related yet distinct literary languages."[43] In both instances, Gates alludes to a layering and unpacking that mimics early forms of hypertext, particularly as a gesture toward the musical and the sonic—we might think of Stevie Wonder's *Talking Book*, also. Zu-Zu's citational practices throughout the book are the embodiment of Cruz's use of hypertext.

In Zu-Zu's citation of figures such as Clara Smith ("Livin' Humble") Edith Wilson ("Vampin' Liza Jane"), and Bessie Smith ("I'm Going Back to My Used to Be") by Bessie Smith—who is perhaps more well known than her actual catalog of recordings—and the poetry of Angelina Weld Grimke ("I am the laughing woman with the black black face"), she not only utilizes their archive of cultural production to negotiate her own social condition; she also makes it visible to counter that archive's erasure more broadly. It is through the novel's narrator, who serves as intellectual and emotional kin to Zu-Zu, that the novels makes this issue of obscurity in the archive even more plain.

For example, the narrator makes reference to the legacy of singer-songwriter Syreeta Wright by citing the song "With You I'm Born Again," a major pop hit recorded by Wright and Billy Preston in 1979 and one of the most recognizable songs in the novel. It brought together two artists, who were born a month apart in 1946, with notable musical pedigrees:

Wright came up through the ranks at Motown in the 1960s as a secretary for A&R representative Mickey Stevenson and as a backup singer, who eventually signed to the label under her given name, Rita Wright. She recorded the single "I Can't Give Back the Love I Feel for You," which was written by Nick Ashford and Valerie Simpson with Brian Holland and initially rejected by Diana Ross & the Supremes, but eventually recorded by Ross for her third solo album, *Surrender* (1971).[44] The song would also eventually be recorded by Dusty Springfield for her album *Dusty . . . Definitely* (1968) and guitarist Jeff Beck in 1972.[45] "I Can't Give Back the Love I Feel for You" is among the more than twenty songs that Wright recorded for Motown between 1967 and 1969, many of which remained unreleased for more than forty years.[46] Among those songs were the demo vocals for Diana Ross & the Supremes' "Love Child" (1968). Berry Gordy was enamoured enough of Wright's voice, which was reminiscent of Ross's, that she was among those considered to replace Ross when she left the Supremes in 1969, at which point Gordy came up with the more exotic stage name "Syreeta."[47]

Preston had been part of Little Richard's touring band as a teen, provided accompaniment on some of James Cleveland's iconic 1960s recordings with the Angelic Gospel Choir, and later in the decade joined Ray Charles's touring band—a musical apprenticeship few artists could claim. An organist by trade, Preston released several instrumental recordings in the 1960s, including *The Wildest Organ in Town* (1966), which was arranged by a then-unknown Sly Stone. He came to prominence for his contributions to the Beatles' final studio albums *Abbey Road* (1969) and *Let It Be* (1970), on which he played electric keyboard and the Hammond B3 organ, most notably on the track "Get Back." During this period, Preston recorded two albums on the Beatles' Apple label, *That's The Way God Planned It* (1969) and *Encouraging Words* (1970), both coproduced with George Harrison. The latter album featured original recordings of "My Sweet Lord" and "All Things (Must) Pass," both of which appear on Harrison's first post-Beatles solo project, *All Things Must Pass* (1970).

Preston's Apple recordings offer early examples of the ways that his music, like that of Rance Allen and Donny Hathaway, often straddled diverse musical genres grounded in Black gospel traditions. Moving to A&M Records, Preston's first four albums for the label—*I Wrote a Simple Song* (1971), *Music Is My Life* (1972), *Everybody Loves Some Kind of Music* (1973), and *The Kids & Me* (1974)—all spawned top-five pop singles, including "Will It Go 'Round in Circles" and "Nothing from Nothing," which topped the POP charts in 1973 and 1974, respectively. *The Kids & Me* also featured the original recording of "You Are So Beautiful," which became the biggest hit of British vocalist Jim Cocker's career when he recorded it in 1975. Preston's *It's My Pleasure*, released in 1975, included the obscure single "Fancy Lady," which didn't crack the top forty and was Preston's highest-charting single until "With You I'm Born Again" was released four years later. "Fancy Lady" was the first pairing of Preston and Wright, who wrote the song together.

At the time of "Fancy Lady," Wright was still relatively unknown, except as the ex-wife and muse of Motown legend Stevie Wonder. One early profile of the singer-songwriter describes her as Wonder's "protégé," apparently subscribing to the notion that the success of women in the industry—think Carole King (Gerry Goffin), Laura Nyro (Felix Cavaliere), and Roberta Flack (Donny Hathaway)—was largely the product of their professional, and sometimes personal, relationships with more powerful and even talented men.[48] "With You I'm Born Again," which peaked at number four on the pop charts, was Wright's only single to break into the top forty (it charted eighty-six on the R&B charts) in a career that spanned nine full-length albums between 1972 and 1983. That "With You I'm Born" would be included on the soundtrack for a largely forgettable Gabe Kaplan film, *Fast Break* (1979), only enhances what some might interpret as Wright's one-hit-wonder status. Yet in the very way that *Five Days of Bleeding*'s narrator cites the Preston and Wright song, in tune with other citational moments throughout the novel, Wright herself offers a portal into a richer and more complex narrative. In her case, the literal hypertext links, if you will, animate a creative life and impact that has been, at best, forgotten, and, at worst, usefully obscured.

Born in Pittsburgh, --Wright moved to Detroit with her family at age eleven. She was interested in ballet, but when the cost of following that path proved prohibitive, Wright turned to singing and songwriting. In 1968 Wonder and Wright met at Motown, where Wonder began to set Wright's lyrics to music. Their first collaboration was "It's a Shame" (1970), cowritten with Lee Garrett, which was the breakthrough hit for the Spinners. "It's a Shame" was followed by Stevie Wonder's *Signed, Sealed, Delivered* (1970), the title track of which Wright cowrote (with Garrett) and later served as election anthem for President Barack Obama in 2008. To my mind, a scan of Wright's partnership with Wonder in that period challenges the notion that he was her Svengali and even suggests that Wright herself played a more pivotal role in their careers.

Wright and Wonder were married in 1970, and although the marriage only lasted eighteen months, their romantic and professional union produced Wonder's *Where I'm Coming From* (1971), in which Wright and Wonder cowrote all of the album's tracks, including the iconic "Never Dreamed You'd Leave in Summer." Though Wright and Wonder's collaborations are often read through the context of their marriage, Wright's contributions on Wonder's *Music on My Mind* (1972) and the landmark *Talking Book* (1972), including her role as a featured background vocalist, occurred after their marriage had effectively ended. The duo also contributed two tracks, "I Am Yours" and "Something Lovely," to the Main Ingredient's Wonder tribute album *Afrodisiac* (1973). Indeed, Wright's Wonder-produced solo albums, *Syreeta* (1972) and *Stevie Wonder Presents: Syreeta* (1974), appear after their divorce. All told, Syreeta Wright earned thirteen songwriting credits on four Wonder albums between 1970 and 1972. Ironically, even the simple act of reading the liner notes from Wonder albums in the period creates a context in which Syreeta Wright's own obscurity further obscures that of fellow songwriter Yvonne Wright (no relation), who emerged as a new Wonder collaborator in the period.

Yvonne Wright first appeared on Wonder's *Music on My Mind* as a cowriter of "Girl Blue" and "Evil" (later featured on a standout episode of the Emmy Award–winning series *Atlanta*). "Girl Blue" would be covered a year later by the Main Ingredient on *Afrodisiac*. Yvonne Wright also contributes songwriting on "You've Got It Bad Girl" and "I Believe (When I Fall in Love It Will Be Forever)" on *Talking Book*, as well "They Won't Go When I Go" on *Fulfillingness First Finale* (1974), a song later covered by George Michael, and, much later, "Black Orchid" from *The Secret Life of Plants* (1979). "Take a Little Trip" from *Perfect Angel* (1974), the breakthrough album for former Wonder backing vocalist Minnie Riperton, was also cowritten by Wright with Wonder.

Throughout this period, Wonder earned three Grammy awards for his albums, leading to his elevation as one of the most critically acclaimed pop music artists of the 1970s. Indeed, *Innervisions* (1973) and *Fulfillingness First Finale*, the albums that follow *Talking Book*, both won Album of the Year in 1974 and 1975, and Wonder remains the only artist to achieve that feat (he would make it three of four with *Songs in the Key of Life* in 1977). It was at this point that Wonder was largely viewed as a singular genius, and to the extent that his work was perceived as collaborative, it was in the context of the contributions of Robert Margouleff and Malcolm Cecil, who introduced Wonder to the possibilities of electronic music via their use of the Moog synthesizer. Rarely was Wonder's output considered a byproduct of his collaborative relationships with Yvonne Wright and Syreeta Wright. Yet it is not too far to reach to suggest that it was in fact Wonder who served as a songwriting apprentice under Wright.

Wright and Wonder's partnership did produce two breathtaking and vastly overlooked albums, *Syreeta* and *Stevie Wonder Presents: Syreeta*. With songs like the original "Black Maybe," later covered by jazz trumpeter Freddie Hubbard, and covers of Lennon and McCartney's "She's Leaving Home" and the Smokey Robinson–penned "What Love Had Brought Together," Wonder's production of Syreeta claims the singer's voice as a template for his own writing: he literally works his own songwriting talents through her voice. Yet it is Wright's own songwriting that anchors the album, notably on the Wright-penned "Happiness" and "To Know You Is To Love You," cowritten with Wonder, who also joins Wright on lead vocals. A year later B. B. King would record a version of the song, backed by the famed Philadelphia International house band MFSB and Wonder, that became one of a handful singles by the blues legend to break into the pop top forty.

The followup album *Stevie Wonder Presents: Syreeta* offers more of an accounting of the couple's frayed romantic relationship. In an interview, Wright recalled that "we got married at a very young age and no one gave us a manual. Going through a divorce at the same time we were making that album, songs like 'Heavy Day' have something to do with what we were going through."[49] Wright suggests that the song "Spinnin' and Spinnin'" was about another woman Wonder was dating—perhaps Yvonne Wright, with whom he was also romantically linked. According to Wright, she "felt he would get emotionally injured by that situation and he did."[50]

Syreeta Wright died in July 2004, Yvonne Wright in January 2016. Both were integral collaborators of Stevie Wonder in the period in which he transitioned from a child star into a fully fledged musical genius, although their influence has largely been erased from that narrative. Such erasure does not take place suddenly, but constitutes the process that visual artist Carrie Mae Weems rightly describes as a "slow fade to black" in the title of her 2010 exhibition.

Slow Fade to Black: Linda Jones, Carrie Mae Weems, and Obscurity in the Archive

One of Zu-Zu's contributions to *Five Days of Bleeding* is the recentering of Black women's trauma within a broader narrative of Black marginalization, and the recognition of the role of Black musical traditions in the mediation of and resistance to trauma and violence. In mainstream culture, more often than not, the lives of Black women are reduced to their anger and style. For example, in February 2016, *T: The New York Times Style Magazine* featured a group of then relatively unknown and largely independent Black female R&B vocalists in a piece entitled "The Season's Most Seismic Earrings, on R&B and Hip-Hop's Rising Stars" featuring artists Lord Narf, Abra, Dej Loaf, Empress Of, Jean Deaux, SZA, and Tinashe and accompanied by a short behind-the-scenes film. Director Florida Naitijo presents several of the artists in a way that finds the camera constantly trying to pull them into focus, a tactic that recalls the work of artist and MacArthur "genius award" winner Carrie Mae Weems, whose 2010 exhibition *Slow Fade to Black* deliberately presents a generation of early to mid-twentieth-century century Black women artists in a manner that might be described as shadowed echoes of themselves, or what Emily J. Lordi might recall as resonances: knowable to those who might know, but are unaware of the stories of those women, and largely unknowable to a generation that doesn't care to know.

The short film shows the young women singing the Charles Fox and Norman Gimbel composition "Killing Me Softly (With His Song)," chosen likely in homage to Lauryn Hill and the Fugees, whose breakthrough album *The Score* (1966) is anchored by a version of the song, which is best known for Roberta Flack's version, which was the title track of her 1973 Granny-nominated album and would earn Flack the Grammy for Record of the Year. The lyrics have long been the source of discussion, though for my purposes I'd like to explore the meaning of the opening lines in particular—"Strumming my pain with his fingers / Singing my life with his words"—as means to explore the ways that Black female pain and trauma serves as an erotic source for Black male intellectual and artistic production, often at the expense of the visibility, and at times audibility, of Black women.

This claim about the productive uses of Black women's pain and trauma, in the form of their art, by Black male writers and scholars, is one made by scholar Emily J. Lordi in her book *Black Resonance: Iconic Women Singers and African American Literature*. Writing initially about the work of Bessie Smith, Lordi states that "ever since Bessie Smith's improbably powerful voice conspired with the emerging 'race records" industry to make her "the first real 'superstar' in African-American popular culture, black writers have memorialized the sounds and detailed the politics of black women's singing." Citing James Baldwin's essay "The Uses of the Blues," Lordi writes, "Baldwin figures Black female musicians in particular as embodying a material, extratextual reality that his writing must validate (or make legible?). . . . The effort is to cast [Bessie] Smith and [Billie] Holiday as embodied "others" to and enabling forces for the more "cerebral" art of black men."[51] Providing some context to my earlier conversation about Stevie Wonder's collaborative relationships with Syreeta Wright and Yvonne Wright, Lordi notes that "Baldwin's essays and fiction consistently repeat this structural logic: in several works, the telos of Black female singers' testimonies to suffering is a Black male's creative breakthrough."[52]

Baldwin's own conceit here, made explicit by Lordi, can also be identified in the myriad ways that the artistic labor of Black women has been exploited for more direct political designs. Consider the moving scene in the film *Selma*, when Martin Luther King Jr. (David Oyelowo) calls Mahalia Jackson (portrayed by the vocalist Ledisi) in the middle of the night, to essentially calm his nerves and serve as his personal music streaming service. The music of Aretha Franklin and Nina Simone, for instance, is regularly interpreted as responses or reactions to the racial politics of the era, rather than as indexes of the abuse and betrayal that occurred at the hands of Black men in their own personal lives. Despite our official remembering of that era, Franklin's passion in "Respect" could have easily been reserved for her philandering husband/manager Ted White, or Simone's subtle rage on "I Wish I Knew How It Would Feel to Be Free" could conceivably have been directed at her own abusive husband, Andy Stroud.

I'd like to shift, though, to an artist who is far less known and knowable than Franklin and Simone, but who utilized her art most directly to speak to her own pain. In his book *In the Break: The Aesthetics of the Black Radical Tradition*, Fred Moten describes Billie Holiday's *Lady in*

Satin as a "record of a wonderfully articulate body in pain."[53] Recorded as Holiday's body was literally failing, *Lady in Satin* lacks the robustness and sass that mark so many of her earlier recordings. Here, though, Holiday is defiant, embracing death in the full bloom of her imperfection. As Moten writes, Holiday "uses the crack in the voice, extremity of the instrument, willingness to fail, reconfigured as a willingness to go past."[54] The same could be said for Soul singer Linda Jones, who recorded her most famous tune, "Hypnotized," eight years after Holiday's death. What links Holiday and the largely obscure Jones is the violence they enacted both lyrically and musically within the realm of their vocal performances—a violence that, in large part, was a response to their own physical suffering. To echo the words of Elaine Scarry, how does one sing of a body in pain?

Born in Newark, New Jersey, in 1944, Jones spent much of her childhood and early adulthood struggling with a debilitating case of diabetes. The disease led to Jones's early demise at the age of twenty-eight, in the midst of successful week-long engagement with Joe Tex at the Apollo Theater in Harlem in 1972.[55] Vocally, Jones's style can best be described as "fits of melisma": that particular style of vocal performance marked by the singing of single syllables across several pitches, likely one of the reasons, in addition to lack of national distribution of her records, Jones never found a mainstream audience for her music. Though some found her performances as overwrought, that was exactly the point; Jones performed songs like "That's When I'll Stop Loving You" or "For Your Precious Love" not simply as performative gestures, but as if she was singing for her life.

Jones's music demanded an emotional investment, specifically in the lives of Black women, that mainstream audiences, I'd like to argue, were at the time likely incapable of making. Jones's performances were inspired by a depth of pain that the music of Aretha Franklin, who attracted a broad mainstream audience in the late 1960s, more actively attempted to transcend. While Jones had peers in this regard—the tragic career and life of Esther Phillips being a prime example—few could match her vocal calisthenics. As *Rolling Stone* critic Russell Gersten once commented, Jones sounded like "someone down on her knees, pounding the floor, suddenly jumping up to screech something, struggling to make sense of a desperately unhappy life."[56]

What distinguishes Jones from a figure such as Holiday was the extent to which Jones made palpable the influence of the Black church on her vocal style. An early profile in the *Baltimore Afro-American* notes the "ease with which she sings comes directly from singing in the church choir for 15 years in Newark, NJ."[57] As such, Jones hailed from a generation of vocalists who were making the transition from the gospel choirs of their youth to the secular music charts. In this regard, Sam Cooke served as a tremendous influence, which can be clearly heard on Jones's soul-stirring performance of "That's When I'll Stop Loving You" on the live recording *Never Mind the Quality . . . Feel the Soul*, released posthumously in 1997. Cooke's singing was a model of control and restraint, performed under the guise of aesthetic risk-taking, arching to reach that high note only to float seamlessly across a phrase. Jones, in comparison, had no interest in playing to the fiction that she was in control of anything: the music, her voice, and, at times, her own body. Both artists conveyed an aura of vulnerability that made their music so moving to audiences—Cooke's emotiveness was particularly striking for a male singer—but in Jones's case she *was* vulnerable, and each performance functioned as an attempt to grasp the humanity slowly slipping away from her.

Like Cooke, Franklin, and Sly Stone, among others, Jones helped to secularize African-American gospel ritual in the late 1950s and 1960s. In his work on the tradition of African-American gospel quartets, the specific tradition that helped produce Cooke, Ray Allen writes, "In its ritualized context, gospel performance promises salvation for the believer in this world as well as the next. Chanted narratives remind listeners of their past experiences, collective struggle, common southern and familial roots, and shared sense of ethnic identity."[58] By enacting these rituals, Jones likely provided her audience with some language to better interpret the aspects of her performance that were simply beyond language. In this regard, Jones literally had to talk through those aspects of her pain—testifyin', as it were—in order to better galvanize her largely African American audience around her pain, and, by extension, the pain uniquely experienced by all African-American women.

Jones's desire to give tangible meaning to her pain can be seen in her performance of "Things I Been Through." Ostensibly a song about a woman surviving the infidelity of a partner, Jones's sermonic break midway through the song transforms it into a performance of Black women-centered resistance in which Jones seemingly relishes her literacy of African-American church traditions. Speaking directly to her audience, Jones says, "I don't believe you people out there no what I'm talking about. I hear people say that it's a weak women that cries. But I do believe that there are very few women that can stand up under all of this pressure without out at least shedding one tear. I do believe that some of you out there have had heartaches and pain of some kind. . . . Now if you have, I just want you to raise your hand and say with me just one time . . . now mercy, mercy, mercy, mercy, whoo, whoa."

The irony for Jones is that it was never about simply "shedding one tear," but a cavalcade of shrieks, screams, and cries that found its place in the violence she did literally to each note she sang. As Elaine Scarry observes in her now-classic book *The Body in Pain* (1985), one of the dimensions of physical pain is "its ability to destroy language, the power of verbal objectification, a major source of our self extension, a vehicle through which the pain could be lifted out into the world and eliminated."[59]

"Things I Been Through" highlights the intonations of Jones's music, particularly with regard to the connections it makes between the Black preacher and African American musical idioms. According to jazz scholar Robert O'Meally, the "black preacher presents a rhythmically complex statement in which melisma, repetition, the dramatic pause, and a variety of other devices associate with black music are used," noting that the "man or woman of the Word," often "drops words altogether

and moans, chants, sings, grunts, hums, and/or holler the morning message in a way that one of [Ralph] Ellison's characters calls the 'straight
meaning of the words.'"[60] Writing in the late 1980s, O'Meally captures in
his analysis a progressive notion of the gender politics of the Black pul-
pit, but when Jones was recording in the late 1960s, the idea of a Black
female preacher (and there were many) was still a fairly radical concept,
especially during an era when many still presumed Black men of the
cloth to be the logical public voices of Black communities; think here
of James Brown's deliberate marketing of Jones's contemporary Lynn
Collins as "the female preacher." "Things I Been Through" stands out
because it exemplifies Jones's employment of the Black preacher tradition, historically one of the most prominent sites of Black patriarchal
power and privilege, in the service of addressing Black female pain and
struggle. Consider how, for example, Jones disturbs assumptions about
the relationship between physical emotiveness and weakness by stating
that there are "very few women that can stand up under all of this pressure without at least shedding one tear."[61]

Jones's music can also be considered transgressive because of the way
that it exploited African-American religious rituals for distinctly secular
concerns. The same could be said about the Black liberation struggle of
her era, which consciously utilized the discourses of Christianity to address the political and social realities of the Black masses. In this regard,
Jones's music was focused on the more immediate concerns of pleasure
and joy amid the physical pain that largely defined her life as exemplified
by her rendition of "For Your Precious Love," popularized by Jerry Butler and the Impressions in 1958. Like "Things I've Been Through," Jones's
version of "For Your Precious Love" features a sermonic break, while
also providing a spoken introduction. Midway through the song, Jones
specifically addresses the women in her audience directly: "Sometime I
wake up in the midnight hours, tears falling down my face. And when
I look around for my man and can't find him, I fall a little lower, look a
little higher, kind of pray to the Lord, because I always believe that Lord
could help me if nobody else could. But sometimes I think that he don't

hear me, so I have to fall a little lower on my knees, look a little higher, kind of raise my voice a little higher." Here Jones suggests that the "Lord" has not been fully attentive to *her* needs. Though this could be read as a rejection of religious practice, I'd like to suggest that, given her use of African American gospel ritual, that here Jones instead rejects the distinctly masculine concerns ("*he* don't hear me") that often frame such practices. In other words, Jones suggests that if such practices were fully cognizant of the lives of Black women, as embodied in her own voice, the emotional and sexual desires of Black women would be addressed. In her case, the desire for companionship in the midnight hour was infused with the knowledge that any midnight could be her last.

Akin to the musical performances of Linda Jones, the photography of visual artist Carrie Mae Weems expresses visual cognizance of the lives of Black women. Weems is most well known for *The Kitchen Table Series* (1990), a series of domestic photographs depicting her situated at a kitchen table. Though the series frames the lives of Black women—and Black life more broadly—within a context of intimacy and interiority, Weems has offered another view about her motivations in making it: "To place a woman boldly front and center in the work and have her look back at the audience. There was a time in the '50s, '60s, and '70s when women didn't really know how to present themselves before the camera."[62]

Linda Jones does not appear among the Black women that Weems includes in her 2010 series *Slow Fade to Black*, which features blurred publicity photos of iconic Black women performers from the mid-twentieth century such as Marian Anderson, Dorothy Dandridge, Abbey Lincoln, Dinah Washington, and Mahalia Jackson. The series served as an extension of Weems's career-long practice of forcing viewers to grapple with the intricacies of Black womanhood. As fellow photographer Deborah Willis notes, "Weems uses publicity stills of universally known black actresses and vocalists to remember and reevaluate these stars from the past. Weems reimagines their images through the soft-focus representation of their sensual, iconic, and constructed poses, evoking the past."[63]

That these women are in fact iconic, albeit via a decidedly civil rights movement–era Black gaze that saw many of them as pantheons of Black respectability, offers the potential for misreading Weem's intent—for instance, in Robert Storr's reading of Weems's photos, where he suggests "the partial obliteration of detail renders them more obviously theatrical than the originals, while it disperses their mythic qualities into an effervescent aura of untouchable fabulousness."[64]

Storr's comments, however favorably intended, flatten Black women's identity into a form of performativity that obscures more complicated realities of pain, trauma, and struggle. The obscurity of many of these women, in comparison to their Black male peers and White female counterparts, highlight a general lack of attentiveness to the specificity of their lives. In a review of a 2014 presentation of *Slow Fade to Black*, critic Maurice Berger notes that the photos "play on the concept of the cinematic fade, the transition of an image to or from a blank screen. The freeze-frame makes it impossible to tell whether the scenes are fading out or fading in—whether the women themselves are disappearing or materializing."[65] As such, *Slow Fade to Black* offers a view of the liminality of Black women in the archive, always already in the processes of being found or being erased—processes that are heightened by the failure to adequately curate their presence in the archive. As Weems told Berger, "I started to realize that I rarely heard mention of these women. . . . Unless, I was playing them on CDs in my own home, I didn't hear them or see them much anymore. This saddened me."[66] Weems added, "They are disappearing, dissolving before our eyes."[67]

Slow Fade to Black speaks specifically to Weems's practice as an artist, and more broadly to the idea of Blackness in the archive. In an exchange with photographer Dawoud Bey, Weems asserts, "It's fair to say that black folks operate under a cloud of invisibility—this too is part of the work, is indeed central to the work."[68] Weems's work visually addresses notions of Black female invisibility, just as Zu-Zu and Linda Jones countered such invisibility via literature and music, respectively. To Weems's point that "Black people are to be turned *away* from, not turned toward—we bear the mark of Cain. It's an aesthetic thing," there is the question of what there is in the archive to be *turned away from*. What are the connections to be made between the trauma found in the archive and the shame associated with the acknowledgment of that trauma ("the mark of Cain")? The autobiography of yet another icon of soul and R&B provides some insight.

Whose "Danny Boy"? Trauma, Betrayal, and Loss in the Archive

Though less remarked upon than his contemporary James Brown, the so-called "hardest working man in showbiz," Jackie Wilson (also known as "Mr. Entertainer") literally worked himself to death, collapsing on-stage in 1975 and remaining in a semicomatose state until his death in 1984.[69] Wilson's catalog includes classic oldies such as "Lonely Teardrops" and "(Your Love Keeps Lifting Me) Higher and Higher." Though he was from Detroit, and Berry Gordy penned some of his early hits, Wilson never recorded for Motown, which became associated with any upbeat tracks recorded by African Americans in the 1960s. Ironically, a track like Martha and the Vandellas' "Dancing in the Street," which sonically epitomizes the Motown sound, was as much about taking it to the streets politically as it was about happy Negroes dancing their troubles away.

In the late 1950s, before the watershed moments of the civil rights movement and the emergence of Black Power discourses, distinct political commentary by artists and in the music was often muted. Yet there is no denying that Black performers, regardless of gender, were subjected to often-inhumane logics of legal segregation that denied them access to food, lodging, and other facilities while traveling on the road, as well as threats and acts of anti-Black violence. Yet women and transgender performers were themselves subjected to gender violence by the proverbial "soul men" of the era. If those men had few outlets for publicly complaining about how they were treated, what, then, were the circumstances for women performers, who not only risked their livelihood and safety challenging White supremacy, but also the retribution of their males peers and the broader Black community for holding Black men accountable for sexual violence?

These questions could be raised in light of singer Patti LaBelle's revelation in her 1996 memoir *Don't Block the Blessings* that Jackie Wilson and a friend tried to rape her when she was a young performer with the Bluebelles in the 1960s. If we are to consider the point of James "Thunder" Early, a fictional Marvin Gaye–like figure from the stage production and later film *Dreamgirls*, that mid-twentieth-century R&B was shorthand for "Rough and Black" rather than "Rhythm and Blues," then it's reasonable to believe that many Black women tethered to the economy of the Chitlin' Circuit were literally made black and blue by acts of sexual assault perpetrated by Black male artists. Wilson himself is no outlier; even his biopic *Get On Up*, James Brown admits as much, while consigning the relevant events to off-screen.

Labelle made her claim in print more than thirty years after the fact; she told the *Washington Post* that she hadn't even shared the story with her husband until she began working on the book.[70] LaBelle's unwillingness to share the details of her attempted rape is not unusual for victims of sexual violence. Yet when she does tell her story, that story evokes a sense of betrayal. As Black music and culture became more popular in the 1950s and 1960s, particularly among White American youth, Black performers stood at the forefront of the racial uplift project, aimed to humanize African Americans for Whites. As such, Black men and women shared the risk associated with traveling on the Chitlin Circuit, yet for some Black women performers the threats existed both in the literal landscape of anti-Black racism and in the intimacies of shared racial struggle. Given the history of lynching, for example, and the centering of Black male life in the discourses of Black resistance, many Black women felt compelled to remain silent in response to sexual violence by Black men.

Though Jackie Wilson is remembered for his radio-friendly hits, he is also renowned for his interpretation of a composition that some might read as a direct response to trauma and loss: "Danny Boy," written in 1910 by British songwriter Frederic Weatherly and set to the music of the Irish song "Londonderry Air." Generally regarded as an anthem of Irish Americans and often sung at the funerals of law enforcement officers, "Danny Boy" might seem an odd choice for Wilson to record. But his connection to "Danny Boy" was personal: it was his first recording under the nickname of Sonny Wilson in 1953, before he replaced Clyde McPhatter as lead singer of the Dominoes. As Susan Whitall writes in her biography of Wilson's Detroit friend and sometimes nemesis Little Willie John, "Danny Boy" was a sentimental favorite that both singers included in their repertoires. As Wilson's first wife, Freda, recalls, "He'd always win amateur nights doing 'Danny Boy,' and when he recorded it, he did it the same way."[71]

In the same period, "Danny Boy" was also covered by Sam Cooke and Patti Labelle and the Bluebelles. But it was not, however, some novelty song explicitly utilized by Black performers to cross over to White audiences; it was a song that resonated among *Black* audiences. "Danny Boy" would become, in fact, Wilson's signature tune; he often closed his shows with it. As music critic Don Walker notes in Tony Douglas's *Jackie Wilson: Lonely Teardrops*, "By the time Wilson hit the final cadenza in which he wrings 23—count 'em—notes out of the word 'therefore,' I was convinced there wasn't a pop singer alive who could stretch such a thin piece of material into the aural equivalent of an Armani suit."[72]

I surmise that LaBelle's own earth-shattering version of "Danny Boy," recorded with the Bluebelles for the Parkway label in 1962, was at the root of Wilson's assault as an attempt to "discipline" her for challenging *his* ownership of the song, particularly in distinctly Black performance spaces. This was part of the reality of the Chitlin' Circuit, where money was tied to the billing of the artist on the marquee: if somebody out-sang an artist one night, the more effective singer might appear higher on the marquee the next. The struggle for "top billin'" stands among the myriad of reasons why singers of less stature than Labelle might get lost in the archive.

But let me make the claim that Labelle also owned that song, in the way that Black performers have often created an intimacy with pieces of art never intended for their use or consumption. Wilson and Labelle transform "Danny Boy" into something that Weatherly never intended; ain't nothin' "Irish ballad" about the song the way they sing it. Wilson's second version appears on *Soul Time*, an album that finds him between the successes of the early 1960s and his commercial resurrection later in the decade. Released in April 1965, *Soul Time* may be one of Wilson's most accomplished recordings, featuring "Danny Boy" as well as the opening track "No Pity (in the Naked City)."

"Danny Boy" began to circulate among Black performance publics during the historical moment in which Paul Robeson reimagined "Ol' Man River," a song written by Jerome Kern and Oscar Hammerstein II and featured in their musical *Show Boat* (1927), in which Robeson starred. As Shana Redmond writes of Robeson's revisions in the post–World War II period, "Robeson infused the song with the contemporary currents and political of the struggles for civil rights and self-determination in the workplace . . . . 'Ol' Man River' was Robeson's clarion call in Robeson's crusade for civil and human rights."[73] As Redman further notes, per the work of Bernice Johnson Reagon, a significant amount of Black protest anthems from the first half of the twentieth century can be described as "adapted songs with a new purpose." Citing another example from that period, Redmond writes of "We Shall Overcome" that the song "rose to prominence as the anthem of the Civil Rights Movement but began its political life as a freedom song in a labor battle on the southeastern seaboard."[74]

In Wilson's hands, "Danny Boy" is performed as nothing less than a dirge. Like so many of the hymns that Black Americans transformed into anthems of loss, resistance, and resurrection—for example, Alfred E. Brumley's "I'll Fly Away" or Civilla D. Martin and Charles H. Gabriel's "His Eye Is On the Sparrow"—Wilson's 1965 version of "Danny Boy" indexes the immediate losses of his contemporaries Sam Cooke and Malcolm X, the ongoing drama that was the Selma campaign, and also the bombing of the 16th Street Baptist Church. Though "Danny Boy" never rose to the level of national recognition of "We Shall Overcome" or Robeson's "Ol' Man River," it was a Friday and Saturday night anthem for those whose most accessible freedoms might be the time they spent at the Apollo in New York or Chicago's Regal Theater.

"Danny Boy" no longer forms part of the live repertoire of Black performers from the generation in which Wilson and Labelle made the song most famous for Black audiences. The version recorded by the Bluebelles was one of the group's most successful during the 1960s, before their transformation into the proto-Black feminist funk group known simply as Labelle. Yet the title track of the Bluebelles' first album for Atlantic would provide Patti Labelle with another anthem. The studio version of "Over the Rainbow" was hit for the Bluebelles in 1966 and, like "Danny Boy," became a feature of their live performances.

In the national consciousness, "Over the Rainbow" remains tethered to Judy Garland's performance of the song in *The Wizard of Oz* (1939), though for more than fifty years after the Bluebelles' studio recording, the song remains a centerpiece in Patti Labelle's live performances. A version appears on her 1981 studio album *The Spirits in It*, as well as at least two of her live recordings: *Patti Labelle Live!* (recorded at the Apollo Theater in 1991) and *Live! One Night Only*, from the Hammerstein Ballroom in New York City in 1998. In the light of the song's original popularity, Labelle's performance of the song might be misread, but considered in the context of songs like "Danny Boy" and "Lift Every Voice and Sing," it might be seen instead as aspirational, an effort to transcend the traumatic circumstances of aspects of Black life in the 1960s and beyond. Given *The Wizard of Oz*'s relation to the fantastic, and the futuristic garb worn by Labelle, Sarah Dash, and Nona Hendryx wore as the group Labelle in the 1970s, "Over the Rainbow" might even be thought of as an example of Afrofuturism.

"Over the Rainbow" is not the only anthem that has become a fixture of Labelle's concert performances. "You Are My Friend," cowritten by Labelle, her then-husband Armstead Edwards, and her musical director Charles "Budd" Ellison, appears on Labelle's first solo album *Patti Labelle* (1977). A modest R&B single, the song was transformed two years later when it appeared on disco icon Sylvester's live album *Living Proof* (1979). In Sylvester's hands, the song transformed into an anthem for the Black LGBTQ community and its allies. During the course of the eight-minute performance, recorded at the War Memorial Opera House in San Francisco in March 1979, four months after the shooting death of Harvey Milk, the first openly gay elected official in the state of California, Sylvester shares the spotlight with Izora Armstead and Martha Washington, his backing vocalist known as "Two Tons O' Fun" and later member of the Weather Girls and "It's Raining Men" fame. The gesture was important because it highlighted the shared fate of a queer Black man and two Black women—notably two plus-sized Black women, invisible in their excessiveness—and while obvious critiques can be made about possible gender appropriation on Sylvester's part and the economic and power dynamics of his relationship with backing vocalists, the gesture spoke to their mutual marginalization in Black communities and virtual silencing on Black radio.

In the aftermath of Sylvester's death from complications of AIDS in 1988, Patti Labelle's performance of "You Are My Friend" (which, increasingly, more closely resembles Sylvester's cover than her original) represents a larger gesture of alliance with Black LGBTQ communities, and those living with HIV. In this way, Labelle's channeling of trauma in her life could be said to illustrate the broader concerns of those marginalized in Black communities via sonic interventions that challenge the invisibility of Black women in the same context.

3

"Promise That You Will [Tweet] about Me"

Black Death in the Digital Era

In July 1979, Edward Hope Smith and Alfred Evans, both aged fourteen, disappeared within four days of each other in the city of Atlanta, Georgia. Their dead bodies were discovered later that month. In September and October, two other Black children, Milton Harvey and Yusef Bell, aged fourteen and nine, respectively, also disappeared and were found dead. These deaths would be the first known of what came to be referred to as the Atlanta child murders, in which close to thirty Black children and teens were found dead over a two-year period. Wayne Williams was tried and convicted of the last two murders—notably, of the oldest of the victims. Williams was never charged with the other murders, which remain unsolved, though conventional wisdom attributes them to him. The belief that Williams was a scapegoat occasioned James Baldwin's last original work before his death in 1987, the book-length essay *The Evidence of Things Not Seen* (1985).

Easily one of Baldwin's most overlooked works, the literary icon wrote the book after covering the Wayne Williams trial on assignment for *Playboy* in 1982 and was most remarkable at the time of its publication for Baldwin's expressed belief in Williams's innocence. Yet *The Evidence of Things Not Seen* also provided insight into the contradictions of Black American life in an era that many interpreted as a pinnacle of twentieth-century Black aspiration, considering the increased visibility of Black public figures in entertainment, sports, and politics. As Baldwin writes, "The missing, menaced, murdered children were menaced by color and locality; they were—visibly— Black, which in this republic, is a kind of doom, and actually poor—

which condition elicits from the land of opportunity and the work ethic a judgement as merciless as it is defensive."[1]

Baldwin also captures an awareness of dread among Atlanta's Black youth, quoting one teen, "I'll be coming home from (baseball or football) practice and somebody's car will come behind me and I'll be thrown into the trunk of the car and he'll drive the car away and I'll never be found again."[2] In this instance, what Baldwin records is the sense of precarity that working-class and poor Black youth began to associate with their daily experience, in strong contrast to the guarded optimism of, say, the Black middle class. As Baldwin writes, "The usefulness, however, of the Black "middle class" to the southern city— that is, to the maintenance of the White *status quo*—was, and had to be, so dubious a matter, that is is fair to say that it existed, principally, in the imagination of the White South," adding that "this 'class' was not created by the White imagination, but by Black apprehension of their Black history, and by those institutions that their ancestors had forged."[3] In light of perceptions of and by Atlanta's Black middle class, Joe Vogel reminds us, such precarity was generally viewed "in the eyes of many white Georgians and white Americans [as a] black problem. Black parents didn't watch out for their children; black police botched the investigation; and black leaders proved unable to govern and make the city safe."[4] Many in the Black middle class agreed, mirroring yet another iteration of respectability politics.

A week after the bodies of initial victims Smith and Evans were found in July 1979, Michael "Wonder Mike" Wright, Guy "Master Gee" O'Brien, and Henry "Big Bank Hank" Jackson walked into a New Jersey recording studio to lay down tracks for what would become "Rapper's Delight." The release of "Rapper's Delight" in early September 1979 is generally recognized as the moment when hip-hop culture ascended to mainstream consciousness. Though seemingly disconnected from the Atlanta child murders, throughout the 1980s and into the early 1990s hip-hop culture emerged as one of the primary locations where Black American youth articulated *their* political concerns, aspirations, and social criticisms, allowing them to bear witness to the circumstances of their lives in ways that were unprecedented at the time.

For the generation of Black youth who grew up on hip-hop culture, in both local and national iterations, the Atlanta child murders may have also informed their identity. Vogel notes that "it is not mere coincidence that the Terror of Atlanta (1979–1981) coincided with the birth of cable news. CNN launched in the summer of 1980."[5] The new media platform contributed to what became a spectacle of Black death in the city of Atlanta: "With each new headline—'They found another body'—the plot continued and the media was on the scene, snapping pictures of lifeless children."[6] By the early 1990s, hip-hop had emerged not only as a vehicle for Black youth to address their political and social positions in the United States (and, increasingly, globally), but also as a space for exercising their agency in mourning rituals.

The widely circulated footage of the police beating of Black motorist Rodney King in 1991 also had a significant impact on the media landscape, as the footage easily mapped onto narratives that had been widely circulated in hip-hop lyrics, particularly in the subgenre of "gangsta" rap. As Vogel highlights, the emergent new platform of CNN and the introduction of the twenty-four-hour news cycle found resonance in the two events, observing that "CNN reached the second highest ratings in its history in 1982, the year of the Wayne Williams trial and the network's peak ratings came in 1991, the year of the Rodney King beating and the Gulf War."[7] Often overlooked amid the grand narratives of Rodney King's beating and the community outrage over the acquittal of the police officers charged with it was the shooting death that year of fifteen-year-old Latasha Harlins, who would be among those rescued from the obscurity and mundaneness of Black death by hip-hop culture and the Black digital publics of the early twenty-first century.

A Fallen Black Girl

Latasha Harlins would not live to see the birth of Twitter, but it is difficult not to summon her name among hashtag memorials for any number of dead Black youth: Aiyana Stanley-Jones, Renisha McBride, Jordan Davis, Hadiya Pendleton, Michael Brown, Trayvon Martin. Two weeks after the Rodney King beating in 1991, Harlins, aged fifteen, was shot in the back of the head by Soon Ja Du during a dispute in Du's grocery store in South Central Los Angeles. Harlins would be found dead on the ground with two crumpled dollar bills in her hand, a $1.79 bottle of orange juice on the counter above her. Much about Harlins's life and death is all too familiar: another Black girl denied girlhood while still recovering from the murder of her mother—herself denied a Black girlhood—a few years earlier.

As Du testified during her trial, when she saw Harlins in her store, see didn't she a Black girl who loved Bell Biv Devoe (BBD)—a "round the way girl" with the "New Edition Bobby Brown button" on her sleeve once lovingly described by LL Cool J. Rather, Du saw,on the basis of her teenage son's "expertise," a "gang member"—a perception that evacuated Harlins's identity as a young Black female.[8] Conventional wisdom has it that the dramatic deaths of Black women and girls simply don't inspire the agitation invoked by the names Emmett Till or Trayvon Martin; to be sure, we'd be hard pressed to think of a Black woman or girl who resonates in our collective psyche the way Till and Martin do.

Yet my interest here is not simply about indexing perceived gender divides in Black public mourning, let alone for Black bodies that don't fit into neat gender categories. Harlins's murder stands as a marker for a generation of young Blacks who, at the dawn of the digital era, living in homes wired for twenty-four-hour cable television, publicly expressed their mourning for her death. Videos of Harlins's shooting and King's beating circulated on local and national news broadcasts in ways that carried the gravity of Lee Harvey Oswald's murder on live television or the televised images of young civil rights activists being hosed on southern streets. For many, this served as an introduction to media going "viral"; the reality of anti-Black violence had literally "bled" into the living rooms of America, courtesy of handheld cameras and enhanced security technology. As then–Deputy District Attorney Roxane Carvajal asserted opening arguments, "This is not television. This is not the movies. This is real life. . . . You will see Latasha being killed. She will die in front of your eyes," her comments anticipating reality TV and social media. (In fact, MTV's *The Real World* launched weeks after the 1992 LA riots.)[9]

Before broadband, digital social media, and public access to the Internet, the relative availability of this footage gave both events a sense of immediacy matched only by the sight of Emmett Till's bloated and mutilated body in the pages of *Jet Magazine* in 1955. I'm certainly not suggesting that Black folk in the 1950s experienced anti-Black violence in any way other than immediate; rather, that the real-time dynamic in which they watched Harlins's shooting and could organize accordingly was pronounced. The tragic shootings of Latasha Harlins and Trayvon Martin a generation apart provide useful framing for the roles that handheld technology, digital culture, and social media have played in the lives of Black youth in mourning, protesting, and responding to scenes of violence and trauma.

Using the video footage of the 1991 shooting of Latasha Harlins as a signpost for the beginnings of the digital age, I will explore how Black youth have utilized digital and other forms of new media to negotiate violence. Harlins's shooting at the hands of a Korean shop owner in a largely Black neighborhood has been viewed as the catalyst in a series of events that culminated in a week of violence in Los Angeles in 1992 after the acquittal of four police officers accused of assaulting Rodney King. The outpouring of digital mourning in the aftermath of Trayvon Martin's death in 2012 at the hands of an unofficial neighborhood watchman might be read as the logical product of a generational shift in expressions of public grief. But I'd to suggest that Black folk—in this instance, Black youth in particular—have often navigated the dynamics of mourning with an attentiveness to Black archival ephemera, or what we might think of as ritual, while making creative use of available technologies, as an attempt to subvert the invisibility and silencing embedded within spectacles of Black death and pain.

Who Got the Camera

In the opening scene of the 1993 film *Menace II Society*, directed by Albert and Allan Hughes, characters Caine (Tyrin Turner) and O-Dog (Larenz Tate) are thrown into a confrontation with two married Korean American store owners, who are eventually shot and killed by O-Dog. The killing of the couple would lead to Caine's now-famous deadpan comment: "Went in the store to get a beer, came out an accessory to armed robbery and murder. It was funny like that in the 'hood sometimes." The film's opening, which lasts less than three minutes in real time, reflects a microhistory of stereotypes projected onto the bodies of Black youth, including that they are always thieves, even when they clearly indicate their intention to pay for goods and services ("Hey, man, I said I'm gonna pay you, won't you calm your motherfuckin' nerves"). The violence in the encounter pivots on a classic insult in African American vernacular: the male store owner comments, "I feel sorry for your mother," and the relative decorum of their verbal exchange gives way to a rage that ends in the unwarranted shooting deaths of the two store owners. There is no small irony in the fact that mundane activities like simply going to the store to get a (nonalcoholic) beverage, as Latasha Harlins and Trayvon Martin did, could end in acts of violence and even death, though they would never be able to convey their experience from Caine's perspective as the shooter and not the victim.[10]

The shooting death of Latasha Harlins can be considered a primary referent in the opening scene of *Menace II Society* in the sense that it reflects grocery stores as microcosms for the tensions between the Korean American store owners and Black customers. The real and fictional tensions mirrored conflicts then taking place in major American cities and historical incidences of new immigrants opening businesses in historically Black communities where Black residents were often denied access to capital to do the same, a dynamic also addressed in Spike Lee's 1989 film *Do the Right Thing*. In New York City, for example, fights broke out between Black women customers and Korean American store owners at the Tropic Market in the Bedford-Stuyvesant section of Brooklyn and the Red Apple Market in Flatbush. Both incidents produced public boycotts, that in the second instance, to the dismay of some Black residents, necessitated mediation by New York City's first Black mayor, David Dinkins.[11]

In *Menace II Society*, the privileging of what the Hughes brothers might have presumed as the more universal narrative of trauma and violence directed against Black men marginalizes the experiences of Harlins and the women in the New York City, ironically as Harlins was a source of inspiration to flip the script, if you will .Indeed the directors give Caine the agency to pull the trigger before having the trigger pulled on him. In her book *The Contested Murder of Latasha Harlins: Justice, Gender, and the Origins of the L.A. Riots*, Brenda Stevenson suggests that victims of racialized State violence like Harlins and or even King were seen by some Black citizens as "symbols of a community's savaged past and fragile future," adding that, as a relative youth (King was only twenty-five years old at the time of his beating), "the black community viewed both Rodney and Latasha as victims whom the criminal justice system had not just failed to protect, but that had indeed contributed to their brutalization."[12] Whatever trauma Caine and O-Dog avert (and King, for that matter, in surviving his attack), Harlins was afforded a very different and tragic fate, unlike that of Caine later in the film, one that was not of her own making. Yet it is also the issue of hypervisibility, rendered as new technological forms of surveillance of Black bodies, that bind Harlins's shooting death to that opening sequence in *Menace II Society*.

Stevenson recalls that "the image of Du shooting Harlins, available because the Empire Liquor Market's anti theft video camera captured

the event, was on a constant loop, along with the Rodney King beating video."[13] As Mike Davis writes in his classic *City of Quartz: Excavating the Future in Los Angeles*, emergent technologies "established a
new epistemology of policing, where technologized surveillance and
response supplanted the traditional patrolman's intimate 'folk' knowledge of specific communities."[14] In Los Angeles, such surveillance was
provided an additional sheen of insidiousness with the use of what Ice
Cube described in his song "Ghetto Bird": "French Aerospatiale helicop-
ters equipped with futurist surveillance technology."[15] The emergence
of the kinds of affordable cameras found in community groceries and
handheld video cameras like the one used to capture the Rodney King
beating (or that LL Cool J used in the video for "Round the Way Girl"),
in addition to the embrace of advanced surveillance technology by law
enforcement, coincided with a renaissance of Black filmmaking in the
post–civil rights era.

While Spike Lee was the most famous of this generation of Black
filmmakers, with his signature films *Do the Right Thing* (1989) and *Malcolm X* (1992), others like John Singleton, Robert Townsend, Julie Dash,
and the Hughes Brothers were also critical to the moment. If the use of
surveillance and handheld cameras could not always be counted on to
render the truth of experience—as suggested by the not guilty verdict
of Rodney King's assailants and the guilty-with-no-jail-time outcome
for Harlin's shooter—young Black filmmakers offered another version
of the truth, replete with humanizing backstories, on behalf of Black
bodies, which were subject to the whims of the criminal justice system.
In the best instances, these films addressed similar challenges as hip-hop
culture in rendering Black life. As S. Craig Watkins notes in *Representing: Hip Hop Culture and the Production of Black Cinema*, "Black youth
believe that the popular mediascape functions as an all-important site
for giving voice to their ideas," a role currently played by social media.
Watkins adds, "Whereas producers of rap music have struggled to articulate the lived experiences of poor youth, filmmakers likewise waged
a similar struggle."[16]

The challenges that Black filmmakers also posed to official narratives of Black criminality and lawlessness are powerfully captured in Ice Cube's song "Who Got the Camera?," where the rapper reenacts a police stop:

> No lights, no camera, no action
> And the pigs wouldn't believe that my slave name was Jackson
> He said, "Don't lie to me, I'm looking for John, Matty, or Spike Lee."

In the lyric, Ice Cube specifically references directors John Singleton (*Boyz n the Hood*), Matty Rich (*Straight Out of Brooklyn*) and Spike Lee. The song was featured on his 1992 album *The Predator*, released months after the violence in in Los Angeles following the acquittal of the officers in the Rodney King beating, on which many of the tracks, including "When Will They Shoot," "Wicked," and "We Had to Tear This Motherfucka Up," served as sonic documentaries of the LA riots, their origins, and their aftermath.[17] Indeed, Ice Cube's cinematic career began with John Singleton's portrait of South Central Los Angeles *Boyz in the Hood* and achieved some gravitas in his star turn in Charles Burnett's *The Glass Shield* (1994), a film that openly indicted one LA police precinct for abuses against Black and Brown citizens.

In *Menace II Society*, it is a surveillance camera that becomes central to the action. Shortly before shooting the second store owner, O-Dog demands that she provide him with the videotape; her actual shooting occurs off-screen, and presumably off-camera, in a back room, where the tape recorder was housed. For O-Dog, much less than Caine, who functions throughout the film as a voice of reason and reflection, taking the video was not just an attempt to stay ahead of law enforcement, but an opportunity to provide evidence of his notoriety among peers. Throughout the film, O-Dog screens the video for others, not unlike the sharing of digital content that has become the foundation of contemporary social media. Indeed, the actual video of the store owner's shooting circulates throughout the film as an early form of spreadable media, which creates the "potential—both technical and cultural—for audiences to share content for their own purposes, sometimes with the permission of rights holders, sometimes against their wishes."[18] In *Menace II Society*, the video is tethered to O-Dog's own social capital, which it enhances, much like word of mouth.[19]

When Ice Cube queried, "Who got the camera?," he referred not only to cameras found in convenience stores, but also those belonging to professional filmmakers (which Ice Cube would himself eventually become) and to passersby like George Holliday, who filmed the infamous Rodney King beating on his Sony Handycam.[20] For some, the ability of Black film to represent the truth of the Black urban experience became a form of social activism, linking it to the image production and politics of earlier eras, notably during the reign of filmmaker Oscar Micheaux. With the emergence of personal digital assistants (PDAs) and smartphones, the power of representation shifted to a broad public, members of whom could deploy it to capture the everydayness of aggressive policing, particularly in urban communities. In the context of a surveillance society, affordable handheld technology allowed the public to, in effect, "watch the watchers."

One could argue that the hypervisibility of hip-hop and Black popular culture since the mid-1990s has, in the context of celebrity culture, functioned as a form of surveillance, diverting attention away from the ways in which power and finance have been consolidated. There is a generation of Americans more knowledgeable about the net worth of Lebron James, Shawn Carter, Beyonce, Cardi B, and the stars of *The Real Housewives of Atlanta* than they are about the board members of this country's most powerful financial institutions, many of whom were complicit in, if not direct agents of, the financial collapse of 2008.

Projects by artists like B. Dolen and Pharoahe Monch repurposed the very technological platforms that have increased the surveillance of American citizens and literally adjusted the frame to offer countersurveillance and critique of American institutions like law enforcement. The presence of social media and accessible technology has allowed such projects to circulate in ways unimaginable two decades ago. B. Dolen's song and video for "Film the Police" (2010), featuring Toki Wright, Jasiri X, Buddy Peace, and Sage Francis, updates N.W.A.'s classic "Fuck tha Police," which addressed the visible abuses of law enforcement at the time of its production. Yet there is a more specific context for "Film the Police": the efforts of law enforcement organizations to criminalize the filming of police officers, which came to the forefront of public attention when Simon Glik, an immigration attorney, videotaped with a cell phone Boston police officers beating a man in 2007. Police officers arrested Glik and charged him with an obscure wiretapping statute, which was quickly thrown out of court. Glik and the ACLU filed a countersuit against the police department, and in August 2011, the First Circuit Court of Appeals concluded "that Glik was exercising clearly established First Amendment rights in filming the officers in a public space, and that his clearly-established Fourth Amendment rights were violated by his arrest without probable cause."[21] Propelled by a documentarian sensibility, "Film the Police" as much offers evidence of police brutality and misconduct as it issues a call to "point and shoot": an open declaration of the right of American citizens, in the midst of militarized crackdowns on public dissent, to hold their institutions accountable.

Concerns about police misconduct also inform the short film for Pharoahe Monch's "Clap (One Day)," the featured single from Monch's stellar 2011 release *W.A.R. (We Are Renegades)*. Directed by Terence Nance, who also shot the short film *Native Son* for Blitz the Ambassador (2011), and starring Gbenga Akinnagbe (*The Wire*'s Chris Partlow), "Clap (One Day)" takes place in Brooklyn on the morning after a cop shooting. In a cash-and-carry exchange, an informant provides a detective with the shooter's family's address, cautioning that the shooter is rarely there, and presumably wouldn't be now, if he is suspected of the shooting. A SWAT squad is dispatched to the apartment complex, and though the officers rush into the wrong apartment (1B instead of 1D) and accidentally kill a Black child who was using the bathroom, there is every indication that such a fate would have been met by the family of the cop shooter if the mistake had not been made. In either instance, the confrontation draws attention to the general lack of regard for Black life by law enforcement officers charged with policing (or occupying) Black neighborhoods; the death of the young boy would be viewed by some law enforcement officials as simply collateral damage.

"Clap (One Day)" resonated in the aftermath of the accidental shooting death of seven-year-old Aiyana Stanley-Jones, who was sitting on the couch with her family when members of a Detroit SWAT team bumrushed their apartment, with reality TV cameras in tow, and officer Joseph Weekley fired a single shot to Stanley-Jones's head. Weekley was indicted on charges of involuntary manslaughter, but after two hung juries in 2013 and 2014, charges against him were eventually dismissed.[22] The family and neighbors in "Clap (One Day)" would not have such recourse, so they take retribution into their own hands. Whereas a term like "clap" invokes gunfire in many urban communities, Monch uses it as a metaphor for the deep archival knowledge that many residents in Black communities possess regarding the misconduct and abuse of law enforcement officers: in "Clap (One Day)," community members literally break out into rhythmic clapping when they confront the offending officer, who, not surprisingly, lives in the very neighborhood where the killing occurs. That the officer (portrayed by Akinnagbe) lives in a working-class community serves as a subtle reminder of the economic status of many officers as municipal employees.

What You Mean, Forever?

In an early scene in the 2013 film *Fruitvale Station*, Oscar Grant III, portrayed by Michael B. Jordan, tells Sophia Mesa (Melonie Diaz), his partner and the mother of his daughter, in an intimate moment, that he was committed to her for "forever," to which Mesa responds, "What you mean, forever?" *Fruitvale Station* is a biopic that depicts the last day of Grant's life, New Year's of 2009, on which Grant was shot and killed by a Bay Area Rapid Transit (BART) police officer. Grant's death, which occurred only weeks before the inauguration of Barack Obama as the first Black president of the United States, registered the contradictions between the reality of anti-Black State violence and the discourse of hope represented by Obama's election. Grant's death also marked a rupture: unlike the shooting deaths of Trayvon Martin in 2012 and Mike Brown in 2014, and five years before the Eric Garner choking death by New York City police officers was captured on video, the shooting that led to Grant's death was documented by several BART passengers.

Like the beating of Rodney King nearly eighteen years earlier, the shooting of Oscar Grant III offered visual confirmation of the frequently excessive use of force in interactions between law enforcement and Black and Brown people. In fact, the stimulus for many of the BART riders who pulled out their phones to film the unfolding events was the use of excessive force on Grant and his friends prior to the shooting itself. With Twitter not even five years old when Grant was shot, and the phenomenon known as #BlackTwitter still a few years away from being acknowledged as a social force, footage of Grant's death began to circulate in ways that would seem redundant by the time Philando Castile was shot on camera, in his car, by a law enforcement officer in Minnesota in 2016. As such, Grant's shooting became ground zero for renewed organizing around anti-Black State and extralegal violence, serving as a precursor to the founding of Black Lives Matter in the summer of 2013 by Alicia Garza, Patrisse Cullors, and Opal Tometi after the acquittal of George Zimmerman in the shooting death of Trayvon Martin.

Written and directed by Bay Area native Ryan Coogler, *Fruitvale Station*—which was released the day before Zimmeran's acquittal—served not only as a memorial to Grant, but as a counter to the quotidian dehumanization of men like Grant by the State. In its opening scenes, the film features original footage of Grant's shooting and later re-creates the incident with graphic and dramatic intensity, including Jordan's depiction of Grant's cry to officers, "You shot me! I got a four-year-old daughter." As critic Stephane Dunn writes, "The humanization of Oscar Grant, both a gift of Coogler's direction and Michael B. Jordan's perfectly pitched performance as the young victim, is one of the great achievements of this difficult dramatization. Grant is neither neatly hero or anti-hero but a young man who alternately has failed to make sound choices but desires to do right, to do better."[23] Importantly, Grant is depicted in a manner that troubles general narratives regarding whether those Black men who are killed by state-sanctioned violence are sinners or saints, making the claim that such men should be memorialized regardless.

Coogler's *Fruitvale Station* also serves as a call to action to those armed only with handheld devices in their battles against excessive policing. By the time of the film's release in 2013, camera phones had been in production for generations, and the technology had not only improved, but, because of increased affordability, become more accessible as a tool in documenting the everydayness of Black trauma. As Usame Tunagur notes about Coogler's cinematic representation of the cell phone user's point of view, "Coogler is replicating the angle of the cell phones that taped the moment–which then went viral on the internet and which motivated him in the first moment to write and direct this film. This also forces the audience to be on the field, almost feeling like we are witnessing this event here and now, providing a close proximity."[24] Notable is a young White woman character who has already been established as a figure of trust after an earlier interaction with Grant, who makes the point of capturing the shooting on camera, thus embodying the passerby who captured Rodney King's beating almost twenty years earlier. Closing footage of a Bay Area protest in response to Grant's killing doubles down on the the film's call to action.

In a similar of sense of being "on the field," a scene from the film *The Hate U Give* (2018), based on the debut novel by Angie Thomas, depicts the character Maverick Carter (Russell Hornsby), who is the father of the protagonist, Starr (Amandla Stenberg), being harassed by police officers outside of a soul food restaurant where he was dining with his daughter, her mother (Regina Hall), and her two brothers. The number of handheld devices wielded by eyewitnesses in the film to capture the moment seem almost redundant in an era in which virtually every anti-Black microaggression becomes an Internet meme. It has come to the point that, when such incidents occur, one can almost anticipate bystanders pulling out their phones to record the action: life imitating art imitating life.

While *Fruitvale Station* won the Audience and Grand Jury Prizes for Drama at the 2013 Sundance Film Festival, it was ignored by the Academy of Motion Picture Arts and Sciences in a year in which another historical Black film, *12 Years a Slave*—which featured several prominent White characters—was nominated for nine awards and won three, including Best Picture. Commenting on the discrepancies the academy's assessment of two versions of Black suffering, Tunagur writes, "Could this omission stem from the fact that even though both films are based upon true stories of racial inequality and injustice, that *Fruitvale* does not offer a final redemption or relief to its audience in the face of such obvious contemporary violation of rights?"[25] Jordan's invocation of "forever" earlier in the film is important here, as memorializations are not necessarily resolutions, but actionable remembrances, which are critical in the context of a larger societal view often blind to Black death beyond its spectacle. In this way, the original footage of Oscar Grant's shooting and Coogler's memorialization of his death award Grant eternity in ways that exist well beyond the affirmation of the Academy of Motion Picture Arts and Sciences.

Sing about Me

In 2011, two years after the death of Oscar Grant III, and two decades after the death of Latasha Harlins, Compton-born rap musician Kendrick Lamar released his debut studio recording, *Section.80*. Generally regarded as one of the best hip-hop storytellers of his generation, Lamar displays his considerable narrative skills throughout the album, notably on the tracks "No Makeup (Her Vice)" and "Keisha's Song (Her Pain)," which introduced listeners to the figure of Keisha, a local sex worker from Lamar's community. On "No Makeup (Her Vice)," Lamar highlights Keisha's natural beauty, somewhat chastising her for what he perceives as an overreliance on makeup. The song's narration ends abruptly with the suggestion that Keisha has become a victim of domestic violence, though Lamar signals that the story will be picked up later on track 11 ("To be continued . . . 11").

What "Keisha's Song (Her Pain)" reveals is that Keisha's use of makeup helped cover up the bruises inflicted on her during sexual assaults by her mother's boyfriend, a "daddy" figure who had her working the streets as an underaged teen. With Keisha's death by stabbing at the end of the song, it is revealed that the song essentially serves as a memorial for her, as well as a cautionary tale. Shana Redmond observes that music is the "perfect technology through which blackness is animated, even that of presumed dead and gone . . . sonic memorials intended as life support for the memories and visions of loved ones as well as hopes of and for communities who face ongoing structural and physical brutalities."[26] Lamar has admitted to immediately playing the song for his eleven-year-old sister after recording it.

The figure of Keisha appears again on Lamar's commercial breakthrough album, *Good Kid, M.A.A.D City* (2012), on the track "Sing about Me, I'm Dying of Thirst," which logs in at more than twelve minutes and serves as the album's thematic centerpiece. The song's opening verse acknowledges two dead friends, who are brothers, and the desire of one of the brothers that they both would be remembered in one of Kendrick's songs. The second verse captures the challenges of such memorialization, as Keisha's younger sister confronts Lamar over sharing her sister's stories ("How could you ever just put her on blast and shit? / Judgin' her past and shit?") on the previous songs "No Makeup (Her Vice)" and "Keisha's Song (Her Pain)." Keisha's sister is defiant about the life choices that both she and her dead sister had to make to survive, as well as the health risks associated with her life on the streets ("I'll never fade away, I'll never fade away, I know my fate"), her voice literally fading as the verse comes to an end. When Lamar picks up the narrative in the third verse, he acknowledges his own anxieties about dying ("And I'm not sure why I'm infatuated with death") and how he would be memorialized himself, which he attaches to his own thoughts about self-worth ("And hope that at least one of you sing about me when I'm gone / Am I worth it? Did I put enough work in?").

Referring to Lamar's query "Am I worth it?," Matthew Linder writes, "Taken on its own, Kendrick's question is of his existential value and purpose in the world. Within the context of the song and album's narrative, the question becomes whether life has meaning in the brutalized urban environment of Compton, CA."[27] The trauma and precarity of life in Compton might explain the shift that occurs in the song's second movement, "I'm Dying of Thirst"; with its faster-paced rhythm, the song transforms from an interior reflection to a literal act of survival, as if Lamar was literally running from death, with the refrains "I'm tired of running" and "I'm dying of thirst."

Rachel Kaadzi Ghansah notes that "Lamar is equal parts oral historian and authorial presence . . . he has captured all the pathos and grief of gun violence, poverty and families who carve out their lives out amidst all of that chaos."[28] Ghansah's comments accentuate Lamar's role and status as one of the critical archivists working within contemporary hip-hop discourse. Lamar builds on his own narrative archive in a collaboration with musician Flying Lotus on the Flying Lotus album *You're Dead!* (2014), where, in the track "Never Catch Me," he returns to the theme of running. With the lyric "I can see the darkness in me and it's quite amazing / Life and death is no mystery and I wanna taste it," Lamar seems to embrace the inevitability of his own demise, to find freedom in it. The album and song was released only months after the shooting deaths of Michael Brown, which generated the hashtag #handsupdontshoot, and Laquan McDonald, who was shot sixteen times by the Chicago Police department. As such, "Never Catch Me" indexes some of the spiritual and emotional fatigue of those who live with the realities of anti-Black death and violence, who are often left to wonder if the next death will be closer to home, if not the heart.

One can't be sure that there are any more killings now than there were in the past, or are experienced as any more real than they were before the Chocolate Supa Highway, to use a distinctly postanalog but not quite digital reference: the killings are what they are, and as African Americans learned three generations ago, protest and organizing function as much as demands to simply get up in the morning as they are a clarion call to take to the streets in protest. Flying Lotus's "Never Catch Me" disrupts Black protest narratives within the realm of dance (movement) and visual culture. Directed by Hiro Murai, best known as the visual curator of the arresting television series *Atlanta*, the music video for "Never Catch Me" stands in visual conversation with another Lamar and Flying Lotus collaborator, filmmaker Kahlil Joseph, who directed short films for Flying Lotus's "Until the Quiet Comes," and as well as the short film "M.A.A.D.," which features music from Lamar's *Good Kid, M.A.A.D. City.*

"Never Catch Me" could be said to answer Lamar's earlier query "Will you sing about me?" with "We will *dance* for you." The video opens with a view of a casket in the back room of a church, perhaps awaiting the *next* homegoing ceremony. The opening frame of "Never Catch Me" visually cites a section of Joseph's "M.A.A.D." film where Lamar's "Sing About Me, I'm Dying of Thirst" is introduced with images of a dead body on a cooling board, as it awaits a move into a nearby casket. The scene that immediately follows is as familiar as it is unremarkable: a minister eulogizing the death of dreams, ministering to the scattered bodies of the barely living, each of them counting down until their own demise, as if to confirm that life, promise, and aspiration had long left these pews. The actually dead two bodies, even in their miniaturized caskets, seem more alive than the parishioners, a point the film emphasizes when both of the dead—a young man and a young woman—emerge to dance the dance electric. Speaking to Black traditions of funeralizing, it all begs the question: Is it still a second line if the dead are more free to dance than the living?

The fact that a Black community is burying children seems not to be the video's point. In the moment of Renisha McBride and Trayvon

Martin, who were killed in 2013 and 2012, and whom the teenage danc-
ers in "Never Catch Me" best approximate, we're all innocents—ain't
no saint and sinners in this, only more dead Black bodies. As Karla F.
C. Holloway writes in her book *Passed On: African American Mourning Stories*, "The death of children should be unexpected events in the
life-death cycle. But, from the fact that such occasions had become
familiar—and even anticipated—emerged a perspective of black community life that told a larger story than the single, pitiful event of one
child's dying and burial."[29] Yet the video importantly disrupts popular
narratives about the deaths of Black children in the era of hip-hop with
the inclusion of a Black girl and boy, presumably kin, thus linking Black
girls to storytelling usually reserved for the deaths of Black boys. In the
aftermath of President Barack Obama's My Brother's Keeper initiative,
launched in the midst of numerous shooting deaths of Black youth and
effectively Obama's de facto response to those deaths, the experiences of
young Black males were seemingly singled out at the expense of young
Black females, who shared in the precariousness of contemporary Black
life.[30] In "Never Catch Me," these children are collateral damage in wars
never undertaken to save their lives, even had they lived, which provides some clarity regarding whose precarity takes precedence in Black
communities.

The duo dances in death because it is the only place where they are allowed to live, their actual lives constrained as they are by the infrastructures of anti-Black racism, White supremacy, toxic masculinities, and
(dare I suggest) Black respectability politics, recalling Laurence Fish-
burne's comment in his performance as Ellsworth "Bumpy" Johnson in
the film *The Cotton Club* (1984): "The White man ain't left me nothing
but the underworld, and that is where I dance." The teens' sprint through
the church amid soul claps of praise reminiscent of Richard Smallwood's
iconic "Praise Break" and out into a world of others living and playing as
they never could in life and to the awaiting hearse where the girl takes
the wheel recalls earlier traditions. In death, the teens exhibit an agency
over the meaning of their lives not unlike that of Black youth who also

plan for the inevitable. As Karla F.C. Holloway notes, "Many African American children anticipated their own deaths and dying and participated in the adult ritual of planning their funerals"—a ritual that "Never Catch Me" stages.[31]

Nevertheless these rituals are tied to much older traditions. In the introduction to *Passed On*, Holloway writes, "The twentieth century rehearsed, nearly to perfection, a relentless cycle of cultural memory and black mourning."[32] In her work, Soyica Diggs Corbett addresses the phenomena of "Flying Africans," which began as "a tale circulated among enslaved black people in the Americas that depicted Africans who, tired of the oppressive conditions of chattel slavery, used metaphysical powers and flew back to Africa."[33] Diggs Corbett argues that "flight is a paradigm of black performance precisely because it communicates an ongoing life-and-death battle in black culture,"[34] adding that "the Flying Africans offered hope for freedom and transcendence, even though that flight might mean physical death. In its most recent articulations, the narrative provides temporary relief to struggle as it continues to invoke death as a mode of deliverance."[35] The awaiting hearse that the teens mount becomes their chariot—or, to use Diggs Corbett's own logic, their spaceship, in reference to the cultural contributions of George Clinton and Kanye West—that delivers them to freedom in death.

Hashim Khalil Pipkin makes a corollary point in relation to the ways that Black art stages such deliverances, noting that "Never Catch Me" serves as a "testimony for the urgency to make our art now. Our creative locus can be our mourning. Our confusion can be our canvas. Our art is our protection from the rambunctiousness of normative time and hegemonic history."[36] Pipkin highlights the way that Black art has historically staged Black trauma and mourning and takes a step further to suggest how the production of art might be an act of mourning in and of itself. Indeed jazz musician Robert Glasper, a frequent Lamar collaborator, added a coda to Kendrick Lamar's "Sing about Me, I'm Dying of Thirst," with an acoustic trio version of the song, which closes his 2015 album *Covered*. The album was notable for its acoustic covers of contemporary pop and R&B songs, including Radiohead's "Reckoner," Joni Mitchell's "Barangrill," Musiq Soulchild's "So Beautiful," and John Legend's "Good Morning." "Unbound by word count," Redmond notes in response to the limitations of mourning via social media, "contemporary Black musicians translate IP addresses into time signatures in order to organize the 'noise' of the Twitterverse into a unique repertoire of continued debate and rebellion."[37] Glasper offers such examples throughout *Covered*.

Glasper's *Covered* finds its political grounding in the closing suite, which includes a rendition of Bilal's "Levels"; "Got Over," a brief spoken-word collaboration with Harry Belafonte; and a moment-defining cover of Lamar's "I'm Dying of Thirst." Bilal's afrofuturistic "Levels" is literally brought back down to earth and into the present via Glasper's trio, resisting the impulses of imagining beyond this moment by asserting the urgency of this moment. The sonic space created by "Levels" offers a glimpse into a past/present of Blackness captured in "Got Over," where in just over two minutes Harry Belafonte provides brief insight into a career of defiant vision that at once reflects his genius and highlights his ordinariness. As Belafonte simply states, "I'm one the ones of color who got over / I'm one of the ones your bullets missed." The album closes with Glasper's treatment of Kendrick Lamar's "I'm Dying of Thirst," which could serve as a definitive response to Lamar's original question: "Will you sing about me?" Sing they do, as the voices of young children remember out loud those who have been lost in this particular moment of assault on Black bodies. Like the generation that came of age with the image of a brutalized Emmett Till, and Mamie Till Mobley's refusal to let them forget, the young folk who perform on *Covered* will find their inspirations in the names—oh, so many—that they, too, will refuse to forget.

Dirges for a King

James Brown's appearance at the Boston Garden on April 5, 1968, in a concert televised on Boston's WGBH, has become part of the lore associated with the aftermath of Martin Luther King Jr.'s assassination on April

4, 1968. The proverbial "soul man" helped avert a riot by encouraging Black youth to stay off the streets and watch his concert on TV instead. Less remarked upon is Nina Simone's April 7 concert at the Westbury Music Fair on Long Island, which is notable for producing one of the first recordings to mourn King, as well as one of the most affecting dirges from that period that addresses not only the loss of King, but of so many others in the Black freedom movement.

Simone opens the concert with the statement that "we hope that we can give you something," highlighting for her audience their shared awareness of the events that had taken place just days before. The Westbury concert was captured on an album titled 'Nuff Said (1968), which includes eight tracks recorded from it, along with three studio tracks overdubbed with audience applause, including the album's one hit, "Ain't Got No, I Got Life" from the musical Hair. The self-awareness of the moment shifts quickly into protest mode with Simone's "Backlash Blues," a song that had appeared on the album Nina Simone Sings the Blues (1967), which featured lyrics from Langston Hughes, who had died a year earlier. Where the studio version is performed as a traditional barrel-fisted blues number, the Westbury version picks up the pace, animating a sense of defiance, particularly with additional lyrics in which Simone recalls Hughes imploring her to resist: "When Langston Hughes died, he told me many months before / 'Nina, keep on working until they open up the door.'" Broadly viewed, Simone's live rendition of "Backlash Blues" stands as one of her most political performances, performed within the context of real-time political retribution.

In the centerpiece of the concert, "Why? (The King of Love Is Dead)," Simone appends a poignant introduction to the song, acknowledging that "we want to do a tune, written for this day, for this hour," adding, "We had yesterday to learn it," in reference to her bassist Gene Taylor, who had written the song two days earlier. As Simone's brother and organist, Samuel Waymon, recalled to NPR's Weekend Edition Sunday in 2008, "We learned that song that [same] day. . . . We didn't have a chance to have two or three days of rehearsal. But when you're feeling compassion and outrage and wanting to express what you know the world is feeling, we did it because that's what we felt."[38] The song is performed as a dirge as timely as it is telling, given the gravity of a moment when death was not singular, but communal, as Simone emphatically sings, "Will the murders never cease? / Are they men or are they beast?" With more than a hint of resignation, she asks, "And Did Martin Luther King just die in vain?" As that lyric registers with the crowd, the song picks up into a strut, more like a reserved second line, with the reminder that King "had seen the mountaintop / And he knew he could not stop," a lyric that aligns with Diggs Corbett's notion of "flying Africans."

We might think of Simone's performance as an act of building an archive of protest music at a time when such protests have been and will continue to be met with anti-Black violence. One of the most powerful moments in 'Nuff Said is Simone's spoken monologue at the end of "Why? (The King of Love Is Dead)," where she reminds the audience of the literal bodies that had been lost in the field: "Lorraine Hansberry left us. . . . Langston Hughes left us, Coltrane left us, Otis Redding left us. You can go on. Do you realize how many we have lost. . . . We can't afford any more losses, oh, no, oh, my God. They're shooting us down one by one." Here Simone recalls not only the losses of that moment, but the impact of previous losses, like those of Malcolm X, Medgar Evers, and others in the five years prior to King's death.

Many pop songs tried to lend significance to the nation's experience of loss experienced in that historical moment, including the Rascals' "People Got to Be Free" and Dion's (of Dion and the Belmonts) "Abraham, Martin, and John," written by Dick Holler before the assassination of Senator Robert Kennedy in June 1968. "Abraham, Martin, and John" would be covered by many artists and become a standard of the era, particularly among folk music audiences. A version appears on Marvin Gaye's 1970 album *That's the Way Love Is*, and, as expected, Gaye's treatment, with its touch of longing, resonates within the context of the Black freedom movement. Yet it is another song from that period that appears on the album, Lennon and McCartney's "Yesterday," that more fully captures the era's collective mourning, audible in Gaye's humming of the song's bridge, as if unable to utter the lyrics due to grief.

Whereas as Gaye ultimately relied on wordless expression to acknowledge the grief of the moment, instrumental jazz music, dating back to the emergence of second lines, has long figured in the practice of Black mourning. Jazz drummer Max Roach was one of the young guns of the bebop movement in the late 1940s, and by the early 1960s was a leading voice of jazz's revolutionary wing, largely on the strength of his collaboration with vocalist Abbey Lincoln on *We Insist! Freedom Now Suite* (1960). The centerpiece of the *Freedom Now!* suite was the song "Triptych: Prayer/Protest/Peace," which prominently featured Lincoln's vocals and now-iconic screeching. The song, originally intended as a ballet, sonically reproduced both the trauma and possibilities of Black life in an era overwhelmingly defined by protest and threats of violence. As Roach reflected decades later on the occasion of the beating of motorist Rodney King, "I have pictures of black men hanging from trees, tarred and feathered, barbecued. . . . This kind of thing, I'm afraid, is part of the fabric of this country, and I'm not sure when it's going to stop."[39]

When Roach went into the studio to record *Members Don't Get Weary* in June 1968, his goal seemed to be reminding folks that there was no time to mourn; indeed, Roach's "Equipoise," written by pianist Stanley Cowell, literally exhorted listeners to find the balance of the moment.[40] The title track, "Members, Don't Git Weary," featuring Andy Bey on vocals, drew a line in the sand in this regard, with Roach's insistent drumming throughout, alongside Bey's "voice of God." But, yes, there would be time to mourn, and Roach does just that on his 1971 outing, *Lift Every Voice and Sing*, where he is joined by the J. C. White Singers. Recorded only days after the third anniversary of King's death, the album opens with a rendition of "Motherless Child" and closes with "Joshua," a song that reminds the congregation, if you will, that others have to pick up the mantle.

When, on the album's penultimate song, the J. C. White Singers bravely ask, "Were You There When They Crucified My Lord?," they did more than make just another memorial gesture to mark the passing of the greatest symbol of the Black liberation struggle. "Were You There?" is a timeless "Negro" spiritual, lamenting the death of a "messiah," but at the moment that the J.C. White Singers performed the song, it resonated as a defiant response from a culture by now very much aware that filling the air with the sound of Black grief might be the most defiant act possible. "Were You There?" begins as a death march, musically transporting listeners back to the horse-driven carriage behind which so many boldly walked on the day Martin Luther King Jr. was laid to rest in April 1968.

Just as you could imagine the collective Black body kneeling at yet another grave for yet another murdered soul and succumbing to an unfathomable despair, the song's tone changes. Like the phoenix, the collective Black body musically rises, and when the J. C. White Singers ask the question "Were you there when they rolled away the stone?," as in the Resurrection, they transform the place and space of physical and psychic death into something like a freedom—not in the traditional sense, but more philosophical, as simply represented in a phrase like "I'm—We're still here." The power of these dirges, cultivated in the darkest and most dire moments of Black life in America, is that they are so easily recalled at a moment of great distress. They were not simply emotional responses to loss, but intellectual responses as well—the way in which Blackness thinks life through death.

To Holloway's earlier point, the twentieth century seemed to serve as a rehearsal for the staging of Black mourning in Black art in the twenty-first century, particularly in the case of Black music. In the years before King's assassination, the deaths of Black musical icons resonated among Black musicians. At a time when there was no guarantee that the mainstream White press would treat those icons with the care they deserved, Black musical artists created their own pathways of tribute to mainstream audiences.

You're Nobody 'Til Somebody [Sings] You: Tributing Blackness

"Boy, you sound like Nat King Cole": this remark by Gregory Porter's mother is the way the Grammy Award–winning singer remembers being introduced to the figure of Nat King Cole as a child.[41] Porter reflects, "I remember thinking how strange that name was . . . seeing his image: this elegant, handsome, strong man sitting by a fire," while promoting an album of songs recorded in 2018 associated with the legendary vocalist and musician, who died of lung cancer in 1965. Porter is, of course, not the first artist to record a collection of Nat King Cole standards; Cole's late daughter, Natalie Cole, had her biggest commercial success in 1991 with the Grammy Award–winning album *Unforgettable . . . with Love*, anchored by the then-groundbreaking digital duet between father and daughter on the title track. A second duet with her father, "When I Fall in Love," also earned Cole a Grammy Award in 1996, and she won the last Grammy of her career for *Still Unforgettable* (2008), a deep dig into the American Songbook, that was, in part, inspired by her father's music.

Cole's tributes to her father are, of course, deeply personal, and so is Porter's tribute, which he suggests was inspired by his *hearing* of Cole as a father figure: "I put the vinyl on the player and out of those speakers came that voice, that *nurturing* sound. It filled a void in me. My father wasn't in my life."[42] Porter's performance of his music also came at a time, more than fifty years after Cole's death, when Cole's repertoire represented an untapped resource for a generation of young jazz audiences, who, though familiar with Porter, are largely unfamiliar with Cole's catalog, save for his songs "Unforgettable" and "The Christmas Song," which Porter also covers on his tribute album. While I do not mean to question the sincerity or legitimacy of Porter's connection to Cole's music—you can hear the influence in his voice—the fact that such a recording might have also been prompted by the commercial considerations of Porter's label, Blue Note Records, regarding Cole's catalog cannot be dismissed either; both Blue Note and Cole's longtime label, Capitol Records, are owned by the Universal Music Group. *Nat King Cole & Me* was Porter's fifth album and his third for the "major" label, after beginning his recording career with two stellar and underappreciated albums on the independent Motéma Music label.

The tensions at play in the impetus for releasing tribute albums can also be discerned in an earlier tribute recording to Cole. Less than ten months after Cole's death in February 1965, Motown released Marvin Gaye's *A Tribute to the Great Nat "King" Cole*, between Gaye's *How Sweet It Is to Be Loved by You* (1965) and *Moods of Marvin Gaye* (1966), albums that produced four top-fifteen pop singles, and Gaye's first number-one R&B singles ("I'll Be Doggone" and "Ain't That Peculiar"). *A Tribute to the Great Nat "King" Cole*, in contrast, produced no singles and was generally overlooked. Yet Motown's desire to market Gaye as an heir to Cole's legacy—even before Cole's death, Gaye had recorded several Cole-like pop standard albums such as *The Soulful Moods of Marvin Gaye* (1961), *When I'm Alone I Cry* (1964), and *Hello Broadway* (1964)—was also a major reason for the album's relative fast-tracking. Additionally, in the 1960s, Gaye was rumored to be slated to portray Cole in a biopic of his life.

The genius of Berry Gordy and Motown Records can be attributed to Gordy's ability to be self-reflexive about commercial opportunity while remaining attentive enough to the everyday within Black culture to know when to give pause to those ambitions, given the tenor of the era. Certainly this was the case with Motown's Black Forum label, which issued performances of spoken-word poetry and political speeches, as well as the more obscure tribute album *We Remember Sam Cooke* (1965), recorded by the Supremes. To be sure, many tributes to Sam Cooke appeared after his death; friend and roadmate King Curtis, for instance, recorded an album of instrumental covers. Otis Redding, in many ways Cooke's heir apparent, recorded versions of Cooke's songs throughout his career, beginning with his debut album *Pain in My Heart* (1964), which included a version of Cooke's pop breakthrough single "You Send Me." It was with his signature album, *Otis Blue: Otis Redding Sings Soul* (1965), that Redding paid fitting tribute to Cooke, recording versions of "Shake," "Wonderful World," and a rendition of "A Change Is Gonna Come" that would have made Cooke proud.

We Remember Sam Cooke would seem an odd choice for the Supremes. Indeed, "Stop in the Name of Love," the trio's fourth number-one pop single, topped the charts only a month before its release. But it spoke broadly to Gordy's intent to establish the group as a premiere pop entity, and Cooke, as both a musical and cultural icon, represented a model that Motown and its artists admired very much. As the Supremes charted a path that would lead them to Las Vegas only a few years after venues on the strip had been desegregated, as well as high-end supper clubs like New York's Copacabana—a venue long craved by Gordy for the label's flagship act—and concert spaces like the Philharmonic Hall at Lincoln Center, they looked up to a figure like Cooke, whose own ability to break through in such spaces created opportunities for groups like theirs. In fact, the trio's *The Supremes at the Copa* (1965) came out a year after Cooke's own Copa recording was released.

The commercial aspects of tribute recordings notwithstanding, within the economies of Black cultural production, particularly in an era when Black artists were largely marketed to segregated Black audiences, such recordings took on greater significance and relevance. In his book *Soul Covers: Rhythm and Blues Remakes and the Struggle for Artistic Identity*, while examining Aretha Franklin's tribute to Dinah Washington, Michael Awkward notes that Dinah Washington had anointed Aretha Franklin as the "next one." But, Awkward writes, "having failed to that point to produce recordings that proved indisputable that she was worthy of such praise, Franklin's remakes of songs associated with the recently deceased Queen of the Blues can be seen as her attempt to demonstrate that she was indeed ready to wear her idol's crown."[43] According to Awkward, Franklin's *Unforgettable: a Tribute to Dinah Washington* (1964) stands as a "compelling manifestation of this singer's early attempts to master the nuances of black vocal traditions."[44]

At the time of her death, Dinah Washington might have also felt the pressure to fill the stilettos of the previous "one." When Billie Holiday died in July 1959, Washington was the most natural heir to her legacy, and thus that of a broader tradition of Black vocalists. That Franklin's tribute to Washington was called *Unforgettable* indicates that even Nat King Cole cast a shadow over Washington, as *Unforgettable* was also the title of a 1961 album of pop standards by Washington that included covers of Cole songs such as the title track and "When I Fall in Love." The album, Washington's second for the Mercury label after a string of recordings on Mercury's jazz subsidiary, made a deliberate attempt to cross her over to a pop audience. Indeed, Washington recorded her best-known songs, "What a Difference a Day Makes" and "This Bitter Earth," for Mercury in this period.

In 1957, Washington recorded tribute albums for Bessie Smith and Fats Waller, twenty and fourteen years, respectively, after their deaths. Performing signature tunes like Waller's "Tain't Nobody's Biz-ness If I Do" and "Ain't Misbehavin'" and Smith's "Backwater Blues" with a restraint that suggests the singer's and the record company's angling, seems to exemplify Washington's apprenticeship within the Black Blues Songbook that was yet to be correctly associated with *the* American Songbook—the kind of apprenticeship that may have been what Sam Cooke had in mind when he recorded a tribute to Billie Holiday in 1959, shortly after her death.

Tribute to the Lady is easily the most obscure of Cooke's recordings as a pop singer, and his stilted execution of Holiday's catalog only adds to the oddity of the recording. Yet what Cooke reminds us is that for the generation of Black artists prior to the incorporation of independent Black music into the popular music mainstream, the politics of cross-over had less to do with an individual performer's access to a larger audience, and more with a communal ethic to broadly share the aesthetic and spiritual practices of Blackness, or what might more applicably be described as Negro-ness. This is what you hear in Cooke's tribute album to Holiday: clean, smooth, even playful, Cooke's covers of Holiday's classics don't attempt to overshadow the spirit, the darkness, or the trauma of her own recorded history, but aims to make the genius of Holiday palatable—even legible—to an audience that could never see, hear or feel Holiday's genius for what it was. Cooke offers his versions of "God Bless the Child" (arguably the most covered of Holiday's songs, and thus the safest), "Good Morning Heartache," and "Lover Girl," which adapts the gender pronoun to reflect the gender normativity of the time. Given Cooke's later reputation as an activist artist, largely on the strength of "A Change Is Gonna Come," noticeably absent from his tribute is a cover of Holiday's overtly political "Strange Fruit."

That Cooke largely fails in his endeavor—that he is indeed still finding his voice is not lost here—only highlights the difficulties of refracting such brilliance, and, by extension, the brilliance of the archive. As Peter Guralnick writes in his biography of Cooke, *Dream Boogie*, Cooke's tribute album is "overwhelmed by the impatient need, bred in him since childhood, to have a seat at the table."[45] Perhaps the challenge would be best met by one of Cooke's own pupils, who, in the context of a nearly six-decade career, would make the American Songbook her own.

4

"I'll Be a Bridge"

Black Interiority, Black Invention, and the American Songbook

In April 2011, Aubrey Drake Graham went into the studio to record the lead single to his second studio album *Take Care*, produced by 40 (Noah James Shebib). The song, "Marvin's Room," was, in fact, recorded in Marvin's Room, a refurbished recording studio built in 1975 by the late Marvin Gaye. Though Gaye was forced to sell it in 1979 because of debt, the studio was purchased and restored by former record company executive John McClain in the late 1990s, and since that time has served as a recording home for Usher, Mariah Carey, Yolanda Adams, Lenny Kravitz, and Mary J. Blige. Luther Vandross recorded some of his final sessions there.[1]

There's no small irony in the fact Marvin Gaye was shot to death by his father, Marvin Gaye Sr., in "Marvin's room," in his parents' home, which he had built for them. After a period of exile in Europe, Gaye lived in his parents' home in the year before his death, in part because he no longer had the studio, which served for periods during the late 1970s as his home. As David Ritz writes, "In addition to a spacious control room and a studio large enough to contain Marvin's eighteen-piece band during rehearsals . . . a loft bedroom with a one-way window looking into the studio below. Gaye's mini-apartment had a small refrigerator, stove, large closet, bath, and shower. The centerpieces were Marvin's custom-made king-size waterbed and Jacuzzi big enough to accommodate a dozen consenting adults."[2] Gaye's second wife, Janis Gaye, recalls, "This was always like a second home for Marvin, me and the kids. . . . He fancied himself an architect, an antiques dealer, and he oversaw everything, from the colors to where the seats would go. This place became alive. It was a part of him."[3] Plainly stated, Marvin's Room was a domesticated space in which Gaye found the freedom to explore both sonic and emotional interiority.

In Marvin's Room, Gaye constructed a layered and complex soundscape. Some of Gaye's landmark artistic achievements were realized there, including *I Want You* (1976) and *Here, My Dear* (1978), the latter of which Ritz describes as "an explosion of feeling, a composition unique in the annals of American pop in which Marvin used the medium of music . . . to explore the dark side of a male-female conflict. On a personal level, it was a work every bit as powerful as *What's Going On*, and proof of Gaye's artistic courage."[4] According to longtime Motown archivist Harry Weinger, "*I Want You* is Marvin's many voices, and that's where he really developed that ability to overdub himself in all the different harmonies. . . . It's just extraordinary. There are four, five, maybe six voices and they are all Marvin."[5] It was at the intersections of emotional and sonic interiority, as experienced in Marvin's Room, that Gaye faced the career-long challenge of the American Songbook.

In April 1955, some twenty years before Gaye built Marvin's Room, Frank Sinatra released *In the Wee Small Hours of the Morning*, an album of torch songs and ballads arranged by Nelson Riddle. The songs had been written by some of the giants of Tin Pan Alley, including Hoagy Carmichael ("I Get Along without You Very Well"), Richard Rodgers and Lorenz Hart ("Glad to Be Unhappy," "It Never Entered My Mind"), Cole Porter ("What Is This Thing Called Love"), and even Duke Ellington ("Mood Indigo"). The title track, which featured lyrics from Bob Hilliard ("Our Day Will Come"), was composed by David Mann, whose only other notable song was Bobby Vinton's "There I Said It Again" (1964). The album was disparaged by some at the time as "Ava's songs," in response to Sinatra's breakup with his second wife, actress Ava Gardner. But, as Matt Micucci writes, *In the Wee Small Hours of the Morning* "marked the beginning of Sinatra's 'mature' singing style, defined both by a depth of expression and rhythmic experimentation."[6]

Sinatra's desire to bring some gravitas to his music—he openly admitted his debt to Billie Holiday—would have more ramifications for popular music than introducing the so-called pop "concept" album.[7] According to music critic Stephen Holden, with *In the Wee Small Hours of the Morning*, "Sinatra gave men license to cry without shame. Sanctioned by a tough guy who consorted with mobsters, behavior once synonymous with cowardice and weakness became noble suffering."[8] As Micucci further explains, "All of its tracks are introspective Great American Songbook compositions dealing with lost love, failed relationship, depression and loneliness."[9] Sinatra partnered with arranger, orchestrator, and composer Nelson Riddle during the period, and that partnership proved invaluable to Sinatra's artistic ambitions at the time with regard to the musical qualities of his records. Bandleader Count Basie would play a similar role for Sinatra in the 1960s.

Marvin Gaye was sixteen years old, and six years away from recording his debut album for Motown, *The Soulful Moods of Marvin Gaye* (1961), when Sinatra released *In the Wee Small Hours of the Morning*. Gaye admitted to David Ritz, "My dream . . . was to become Frank Sinatra. I loved his phrasing, especially when he was very young and pure. He grew into a fabulous jazz singer and I used to fantasize about having a lifestyle like his—carrying on in Hollywood and becoming a movie star."[10] The allure of Sinatra and the torch songs that he made famous in the late 1950s and early 1960s can be discerned in Gaye's first recordings for Motown; three of his first four albums with the label—*The Soulful Moods of Marvin Gaye*, *When I'm Alone I Cry*, and *Hello Broadway*— were collections of ballads, torch songs, and show tunes. Gaye included on those albums several songs associated with Sinatra, including the swaggering "Witchcraft" (released as a single by Sinatra in 1957) as the clear standout. Beyond his performance of masculinity, what Sinatra and those songs seemed to offer Gaye was an aesthetic and professional gravitas that was not granted to gospel or R&B performers in that era.

Sinatra wasn't the only artist that inspired Gaye. Like Sinatra, he was also drawn to Billie Holiday, who died two years before the release of *The Soulful Moods of Marvin Gaye*. "Her pain is what got to me," Gaye told David Ritz in *Divided Soul*. "She was deeper than sex. The hurt she felt was the hurt of all humanity. Great artists suffer for the people." Of Miles Davis, Gaye tells Ritz, "Somewhere in the fifties I also got hooked on Miles Davis, especially the way he played ballads through his mute . . . Miles cried like a singer, and Billie sang like an instrumentalist, and everything they both did was wrapped in the blues."[11] Gaye covers both "My Funny Valentine," one of Davis's standards from the period, and "You Don't Know What Love Is," which appears on Holiday's final session, *Satin Blue* (1958). Nothing on those recordings reflect what audiences would come to know and expect from Marvin Gaye, who is, quite frankly, overmatched by the Holiday material. As Ritz writes, "Emotionally, he distanced himself from these songs; his performance lacked the impassioned sincerity of his soul hits. He became a cold observer, studying rather than feeling the music. His intention, he told me, was to interpret the tunes 'correctly.'"[12] Here we might think of Gaye consciously reigning his more natural musical sensibilities, in lieu of performances that conjured the respectability of peers who had crossed over, such as Nat King Cole and Sam Cooke.

After his R&B breakthrough with *That Stubborn Kinda Fellow* (1963), which generated three top-fifteen R&B hits, including the title track and "Hitchhike," Gaye returned to Sinatra, *In the Wee Small Hours of the Morning* in particular, on his third album, *When I'm Alone I Cry*. Gaye is more assured on Sinatra's "I'll Be Around," which Sinatra first recorded in 1943 and later in 1955, and indeed the subtle but substantial differences in Sinatra's performances of the two versions—the saccharineness of the first version versus the aching of the second—might have been a signpost for Gaye, whose R&B vocals had not yet developed that level of nuance. The revelations on *When I'm Alone I Cry* are "If My Heart Could Sing" and the title track, which were written by Motown staffers William Stevenson (under the pseudonym Avery Vandenberg) and Morris Broadnax, who would later work with Stevie Wonder ("Until You Come Back to Me," "All I Do").[13] Gaye sounds more comfortable singing pop ballads most likely custom-fitted for him, though the development of his own vocal style, as heard on *That Stubborn Kind of Fellow*, may have also had something to do with Gaye's increased confidence.

1965 proved to be an important year in Gaye's commercial develop-ment. In January 1965, Gaye's "How Sweet It Is to Be Loved by You" be-came his highest-charting pop single, peaking at number three. It served as the title track of his next album, the first of Gaye's to appear on either the pop or R&B charts. By the end of 1965, Gaye had also released his tribute to Nat King Cole, who died in February 1965 at age forty-five (incidentally, Gaye was killed on the eve of *his* forty-fifth birthday.) A fine tribute to Cole, which featured more than a few credible takes on Cole standards including "Straighten Up and Fly Right" and "Unforget-table," the album was largely overlooked, given the string of hit singles that Gaye released throughout 1965. Two of them, "I'll Be Doggone" and "Ain't That Peculiar," were Gaye's first to top the R&B charts, and both were top-ten pop hits. His next album, *Moods of Marvin Gaye* (1966) contained six singles, five of which were top-ten R&B hits. Marvin Gaye had become a bonafide soul hitmaker, and much of what one hears on *Moods of Marvin Gaye* is his signature vocal style.

Curiously, Gaye wouldn't record another solo album for two years. That album, *In the Groove* (1968), featured his most recognizable single from the 1960s, "I Heard It Through the Grapevine," as his first number-one pop single and one of Motown's biggest hits of the era. In the in-terim, Gaye recorded three duet albums, *It Takes Two* (1966) with Kim Weston, and *United* (1967) and *You're All I Need* (1968), both with Tammi Terrell. The iconic Terrell and Gaye pairing generated five top-five R&B singles, including "Ain't Nothing But the Real Thing" and "You're All I Need to Get By," both of which topped the R&B charts in 1968. Gaye's career arc suggests that his interest in the American Songbook was well behind him, but the archive—both hidden and hidden in plain sight—suggests otherwise.

Other songs on *Moods of Marvin Gaye*, an album of R&B and soul "bangers," would be overshadowed by the success of Gaye's singles. Norman Mapp's "I Worry 'Bout You," was originally recorded by Arthur Prysock and Sinatra collaborator Count Basie in 1965, and George Benson recorded an instrumental version of the song in 1969 that wouldn't be released until 1984. While Gaye's version is largely forgettable, the same cannot be said for his cover of Willie Nelson's "Night Life." The Nelson cover is important because, as Gaye is trying achieve some mastery of the American Songbook, and perhaps failing in his efforts, the American Songbook itself was going through some revision.

Released by Nelson as a single in 1960, "Night Life" was a hit for country singer Ray Price in 1963 and later appears on Nelson's 1965 album *Country Willie: His Own Songs*. The song proved a challenge for Nelson, as it was thought to be not "country" enough, perhaps pivoting too closely toward the blues. The same could be said about Nelson's "Funny How Time Slips Away," which also appears on *Country Willie* and was later covered by a who's who of soul and R&B acts, including Joe Hinton, for whom it was a top-fifteen pop hit in 1964; Joe Tex on his 1968 album *Soul Country*; in the mid-1970s by Dorothy Moore of "Misty Blue" fame; and Junior Parker on his posthumously released *I Tell Stories Sad and True, I Sing the Blues and Play Harmonica Too, It Is Very Funky* (1968). The song would also be covered by Parker's more famous cousin Al Green, who performed the song on his 1973 album *Call Me*.[14] At Motown, the Supremes included the song on their *The Supremes Sing Country Western & Pop* album from 1965, and a studio version recorded by Stevie Wonder in 1965 would remain shelved for decades.

Nelson was part of a generation of country artists, among whom he and Waylon Jennings were two of the most prominent, whose "incorporation of black influences . . . became coded as a broader rebuke of the South's racist past."[15] The so-called "Outlaws," as Charles Hughes writes, "sought to shake up the country establishment and offer an antidote to both the musical and political conservatism of the Nashville sound."[16] Nelson's "Funny How Time Slips Away" is easily his biggest contribution to the American Songbook, though it overshadows his equally impressive "Night Life."

With "Night Life," Gaye begins to find some clarity about those songs, and what his contribution to them could be. The assertiveness that Gaye projects vocally on *Moods of Marvin Gaye*—this sense that he could sing *anything*—can be heard in his performance of "Night Life," and yet the song's fade, where Motown producers clearly felt the need to bring the song to a close, Gaye's improvisational riffs and moans suggest the blueprint from where Gaye would find his voice in the American Songbook, by not playing it straight and embracing the gospel, jazz, R&B, and soul influences that influenced his style.

Gaye closes *Moods of Marvin Gaye* with a four-plus minute rendition of "One for My Baby (and One for the Road)," a song written by Harold Arlen and Johnny Mercer and initially performed by Fred Astaire in musical comedy *The Sky's the Limit* (1943). Sinatra first recorded the song in 1947 and reprised it for the 1954 film *Young at Heart*, in which he starred opposite Doris Day. He recorded the song on several other occasions, but it is his 1958 version from *Frank Sinatra Sings for Only the Lonely* that became his signature version. One could suggest that the differences between Sinatra's 1958 version and his earlier version can be attributed to his hearing Billie Holiday's 1957 rendition on her album *Songs for Distingué*. Like his performance of "Night Life," Gaye pushes past the limitations heard on his previous efforts at singing standards and torch songs, and it's clear that he had spent some time with the Sinatra and Holiday versions from the late 1950s.

What is also clear is that Motown still had no interest in enabling Gaye's desire to be a pop balladeer, especially since Gaye had finally broken through as a "soul man," establishing himself alongside standard-bearers like James Brown, Otis Redding, and Wilson Pickett, and as an artistic heir to the late Sam Cooke. The archives of unreleased recordings from 1964 and 1965 evidence an album's worth of torch songs, pop ballads, and show tunes that would only be issued well after Gaye's death in 1984, including "(I'm Afraid) This Masquerade Is Over," which had been recorded for Gaye's 1961 debut, and Nat King Cole's signature songs "When I Fall in Love" and "Autumn in New York," which was also associated with Holiday and Sinatra. A discerning listener can understand Motown's reluctance to release some of the material; the songs simply weren't up to the standard that Gaye had set for himself as an emerging pop star.

Yet there are surprises in the archive. Included among the tracks recorded and unreleased from the sessions for Gaye's Nat King Cole tribute album were several songs arranged by noted jazz trombonist and arranger Melba Liston. Best remembered for her work with big band luminaries such as Gerald Wilson, Dizzy Gillespie, and Quincy Jones and her long-term collaborations with pianist Randy Weston, Liston arranges "Good-Bye," "So In Love," "If I Had to Go On," and "You're All That Matters" for the Cole sessions, and additionally arranges "Quiet Nights of Quiet Stars" and "Maria" from sessions in 1965 that remained in the can for at least a generation. Stephen Sondheim's "Maria" from *West Side Story* was recorded as part of a \album of Sinatra music that was abandoned as an album project with Cole's sudden death in 1965 and the label's pivot to the Cole tribute album. In his exhaustive work on Gaye's balladry, Andrew Flory notes that when Gaye recorded the Cole sessions, Motown was embarking on a major tour of Europe, leaving Gaye, who was "sick," behind: "With the majority of the company's most prominent artists and background musicians, as well as many of its executives, out of town for several weeks, Gaye and producer Harvey Fuqua must have had the run of the Motown facilities."[17] Flory adds of Liston's work with Gaye, "In her scores, the instrumental group is treated more like a nimble big band than an orchestra . . . leaning heavily on interplay between winds, horns, and strings, and moving instrumental voices deftly between these sections to create extremely vivid coloristic textures."[18]

The tracks Gaye made with Liston for the Cole sessions were not released for decades, and even then there was little comment, save for Flory's, on the remarkable nature of the sessions, particularly from the standpoint of musical and cultural history. The fact that Gaye recorded these sessions when left to his own devices, with the additional privilege of being the boss's brother-in-law, suggest that he was looking beyond his comfort zone as an artist and was paying attention to musical explorations taking place in other cities such as New York, with artist like Liston, Randy Weston, and Miles Davis. Gaye's work with Liston predates by two years his collaborative efforts with Tammi Terrel, and it's reasonable to think that the magic of the pairing might have found some of its own inspiration in the early collaborations between Liston and Weston, whose efforts have been likened to the celebrated work of Billy Strayhorn and Duke Ellington.[19]

Though Gaye did not release a solo album between 1966 and 1968, he was working on album-length material, essentially contributing to the archive of the American Songbook, with composer and arranger Bobby Scott, without the full support of Motown. Gaye began working with Scott, known for his composition "A Taste of Honey," in early 1966; Scott also arranged "Night Music." In Scott, Gaye found his Nelson Riddle—a departure from Motown practice, which liked to keep production in-house. As Gaye confided to Ritz, "I hadn't given up. In the late sixties, when I was trying to figure things out, I had Bobby Scott, the jazz pianist, write arrangements on a group of pop songs. . . . His arrangements were absolute genius. There were four ballads and two jazzy big-band numbers, and never before had I been so excited about music."[20] Of the 1967 Scott recordings, several were first recorded for the sessions that were canned in 1965, including "More" and the Sinatra standard "Fly Me to the Moon." Four of them—"This Will Make You Laugh," "She Needs Me," "The Shadow of Your Smile," and "Funny"—comprise part of what would become known as Gaye's "vulnerable" sessions.[21] Flory notes that "Gaye's first documented use of expanded vocal composition techniques occurred during these 1967 ballad sessions."[22]

When placed alongside Gaye's earlier attempts at the American Songbook, the Bobby Scott sessions are fairly extraordinary. Had Gaye the benefit of working with Scott's (or even Liston's) arrangements earlier in his career, he might be remembered as one of the last great interpreters of what was at the time a dying tradition of pop standards. Yet the stakes had changed, even for Gaye, and, in the end, he and Scott agreed to scrap the project. "It was as though the arrangements were too deep for me. Maybe I froze up thinking that the ballads would flop like all the ballads I'd sung before," Gaye explained to Ritz. "Later I learned that it wasn't really a block. I couldn't sing the songs because I wasn't old enough. I didn't know enough. I had more suffering to do before I could get to the feelings."[23] Gaye was a year short of thirty when he gave up on the American Songbook.

The early 1970s proved a transition period for Gaye. His popular re-cording partner Tammi Terrell died of a brain tumor in 1970. Gaye, who was also deeply impacted by the Vietnam War and the increasing tenor of the civil rights and Black Power era, began to look inward. This intro-spective turn ushered in the most sustained period of creativity in Gaye's career, in which a succession of commercially and artistically successful recordings including *What's Going On* (1971), *Let's Get It On* (1973) and *I Want You* (1976) helped to establish him not just as a pop star, but one of the iconic geniuses of late twentieth-century Black music. Whereas *What's Going One* offered Gaye's very personal and spiritual views on social and cultural issues such as the Vietnam War, the environment, urban life, and religion, *Let's Get It On* and *I Want You* found Gaye ex-ploring the emotional contours of sex and eroticism, largely light of the end of his marriage to Anna Gordy Gaye and his burgeoning relation-ship with Janis Hunter, whom he would marry. For Gaye, part of this process included remixing some of his previous efforts. "In a number of cases," Flory writes, "Gaye used advanced vocal composition techniques to create new songs from old ballad tracks," citing Gaye's "Just to Keep You Satisfied" as an example of a song that went through several itera-tions with different vocalists before it appeared on Gaye's *Let's Get It On*.

With Marvin's Room up and running and on the heels of his own set of "Ava songs," on the album *Here, My Dear*, Gaye turned back to the Bobby Scott sessions in 1977–78. Gaye was on the brink of his fortieth birthday, just like Sinatra when he recorded *In the Wee Small Hours of the Morning*, and, to be sure, with his divorce to Anna Gaye finalized and his relationship with second wife Janis Gaye fraying, Gaye had achieved some of the emotional gravitas he believed he needed to record the Scott tracks. "In the midst of one of my worst depressions over Jan, I went into my studio and recorded them," Gaye tells Ritz. "I had the tracks for years, but it took me only a single night to sing all those songs . . . and a lifetime of pain to gain the wisdom."[24]

Yet Gaye's increased emotional maturity and his willingness to explore the inner workings of his domestic life only tell part of the story; just as significant were the advancements that had been made in recording studios, including the emergence of multitrack studios, which allowed Gaye to layer his vocals. Gaye transferred his late-1970s ballads from sixteen-track to twenty-four-track tapes, which, Flory writes, "collated nearly all of the ballad performances dating back to the original 1966 Scott sessions, with tape transfer groups mostly intact."[25] Hearkening back to a point made earlier by Harry Weinger about "Marvin's many voices," Michael Eric Dyson explains that "there are few artists who are superb in the art of vocal layering: Al Green and The Beach Boys—especially Brian Wilson."[26] Dyson adds, "By the time [Gaye] did *I Want You*, the first of his albums completed in Marvin's Room, he had "mastered the technique. It's all the more remarkable when one realizes that Gaye didn't have forty-eight digital tracks to work with. He had had sixteen tracks."[27]

Armed with a sense of interiority literally cultivated in Marvin's Room and aided by recording technology, Gaye finished seven tracks, including the four of those previously mentioned from 1967, and three new ones: "I Won't Cry Any More," which Scott himself recorded in 1967, "I Wish I Didn't Love You So," and "Why Did I Choose You?" A stunning achievement vocally, technologically, and artistically, the album was not released during Gaye's lifetime. His relationship with Motown and its founder, who had been Gaye's brother-in-law, was always challenged by the label's bottom line and Gaye's own desire to trample the commercial boundaries set for him. Gaye, who scored only his third number-one pop hit with the disco-tinged "Got to Give It Up" and then followed it up with *Here, My Dear*, in which the highest-charting single, "A Funky Space Reincarnation," didn't break into the top-100 pop chart, was, from Motown's vantage point, in no position to be "experimental," particularly in a vocal genre that had been largely dormant for a decade.

In the aftermath of Gaye's death in 1984, versions of the Bobby Scott sessions surfaced on compilation albums like *Romantically Yours* (1985), which fulfilled Gaye's contract to his last label, Columbia, and at least two Motown box sets, *The Marvin Gaye Collection* (1990) and *The Master: 1964–1984* (1995). The best representation of the Bobby Scott sessions can be found on *Vulnerable* (1997), which included the seven tracks from 1967 as well as alternate takes of "I Wish I Didn't Love You So," "I Won't Cry Anymore," and "Why Did I Choose You?" Flory cites "Funny," in particular, as representing "the distance that Gaye had traveled, personally, professionally, and artistically, since recording with Bobby Scott in New York in 1966."[28] Released almost fifteen years after his death, *Vulnerable* was treated more as an afterthought than as the revelation it was. As Ritz acknowledges, "In singing achingly slow ballads . . . [Gaye] achieved the mastery of Sinatra's *Wee Small Hours* or Billie Holiday's *Lady in Satin*."[29]

Aretha Franklin's American Songbook

Marvin Gaye spent nearly his entire professional career trying to achieve mastery of the American Songbook, the canon of the most influential American pop songs, which at the beginning of Gaye's career in 1961 was a virtual all-White male collective of lyricists and composers. In Gaye's case, pursuit of that mastery—and to what end?—might have seemed a flight of fancy, but that was not the case for one of his most significant contemporaries, Aretha Franklin, who began her career as a pop music vocalist a year before Gaye, in 1960. And although Franklin lived in Detroit, and her family was cordial with the Gordy family, she eschewed the hometown label to sign with Columbia Records and to work with legendary producer John Hammond. Unlike many of her Detroit friends who signed with Motown, Franklin wasn't saddled with the pressure of building a brand at Columbia, whose roster in the late 1950s included Frank Sinatra, Miles Davis, Billie Holiday, and later included Barbara Streisand, who signed to the label in the early 1960s.[30] Franklin recorded with Columbia until late 1966, when she signed with Atlantic Records and established herself as one of America's most significant vocalists.

Through Franklin's Columbia archive, a portrait of her early career has been curated by the label that easily distinguishes those recordings from those made during the Atlantic years, which clearly overshadow the work she made for Columbia. Perhaps Columbia prefers Franklin's earlier records to be set apart in this way, since it provides the label with a distinct Franklin brand, that, while less commercially successful than the body of work Franklin produced with Atlantic from 1967 to 1978, positions her as a separate, distinct artist. Franklin's primary repertoire at Columbia was comprised of torch songs, 1960s-style pop ballads in the vein of Dinah Washington and Dionne Warwick (Franklin covers songs by both), show tunes, and what might be described as "turntable" hits. The dominant narrative suggests that, in her Columbia recordings, Franklin was not gritty enough, not soulful enough, not Black enough, and that the Aretha Franklin that literally *Arrives* in 1967 is the real, authentic Franklin. As Daphne Brooks writes, "Skeptics who stereotype Aretha as the 'earthy,' 'natural' woman who only connected with her 'soul' on Atlantic Records conveniently forget the active role that she played in developing her own virtuosic talents as a musician. . . . Calling Aretha a 'natural' diminishes our appreciation of the ways that she worked hard at cultivating her craft."[31]

Brooks's point about Franklin's attention to craft is borne out in both her direct relationship with the American Songbook, as well as the artists whose work she covered and whose careers were aligned with the American Songbook and other songs from that era. Franklin's covers seemed to be inspired by several dynamics: to work through a style in an effort to achieve mastery, to pay tribute to an artist, and to do something different (or better, shade being shade) with a song. Therein lies

Franklin's genius—she didn't cover a song; she made it something new, something distinctly Aretha. Franklin, for all intents, invented her own personal American Songbook and, in doing so, raised questions about the validity of an "American Songbook" absent of the sonic contributions of Black American singers and songwriters.

Franklin's 1960 debut, called simply *Aretha*, paired her with the talents of pianist Ray Bryant, who also served as the session's musical director, and was produced by John Hammond, whose résumé at the time included work with Bessie Smith and Billie Holiday. At eighteen years old, Franklin's signature talents were already on display on tracks like "Maybe I'm a Fool" and "Today I Sing the Blues." Revelatory from that first session is Franklin's rendition of "Over the Rainbow." The song, performed by Judy Garland in *The Wizard of Oz*, had generated renewed interest when the soundtrack was released to coincide with the film's television premiere in 1956. In the 1960s, "Somewhere Over the Rainbow" became a favorite tune for a young Patti Labelle, then fronting the Bluebelles. Though the song still remains Labelle's signature, resonances of Franklin's early version can be heard on that original Labelle cover, which in many ways erases Garland's singular imprint on the song—at least for Black audiences—save the cultural significance of *The Wizard of Oz*.

Franklin's recordings *The Tender, the Moving, the Swinging Aretha* (1962) and *Laughing on the Outside* (1963) find Franklin coming into her own as a vocalist. Together, the two recordings should have made Franklin a star on the level that Streisand achieved in the mid-1960s. Though Frank Sinatra and Barbra Streisand were giants in their own right, neither could sing "Amazing Grace" like Franklin, yet Franklin could have sung anything on *In the Wee Small Hours of the Morning* and indeed in 1964 recorded Streisand's "People" from the musical *Funny Girl*, the same year as her labelmate, though it wouldn't be released until 1969, three years after Franklin left Columbia. The career trajectory of Franklin's labelmate Streisand offers an instructive view of the limits placed on Franklin during her time there. Throughout the 1960s, Streisand could be Streisand, without the pressures of placed on pop top-forty artists, while also being presented with opportunities in film and television, and on the stage, where she first established herself, that Franklin would never have. "[Franklin] wanted to be a movie star," filmmaker Alan Elliott recalled on the occasion of the 2019 release of Franklin's Sydney Pollock–directed documentary film *Amazing Grace* after a forty-year delay. "Which is something I don't think [Franklin] ever really got over," Elliott adds. "That same year, Barbra Streisand got to make *The Way We Were* [ironically with Sydney Pollack]. Diana Ross got to make *Lady Sings the Blues*."[32] While Franklin's work in this period didn't grant her the artistic cache of Streisand, it offered the opportunity for something more sustainable.

Laughing on the Outside (1963), released the same year of Streisand's debut with Columbia, *The Barbra Streisand Album*, in retrospect represents Columbia's most successful attempt to package Franklin as a song stylist, with brilliant interpretations of Johnny Mercer and Hoagy Carmichael's "Skylark"; "If I Ever I Would Leave You," from the 1960 Tony Award–winning Broadway production of *Camelot*, in which the song was performed by Robert Goulet; and "For All We Know," later covered by Donny Hathaway and Roberta Flack for Atlantic. Among the songs included on Franklin's 1962 and 1963 Columbia releases, Lil Hardin Armstrong's "Just for a Thrill" is a telling choice. Hardin, who was married to Louis Armstrong in the 1920s, is credited with mentoring him when they met as members of King Oliver's band. A pianist by trade, Hardin, who led several all-women orchestras, was one of the few Black women musicians to work among early jazz musicians. "Just for Thrill" was covered by Ray Charles on his album *The Genius of Ray Charles* (1959), which signaled his move to more mainstream pop music, and as such was an ideal song for Franklin to cover. Yet Hardin's song, which is followed on the album by Billie Holiday's "God Bless the Child," is a bit of an outlier, given Hardin's obscurity, her career overshadowed by that of her former husband, and the scarcity of songs by written by women on the two albums. Franklin's performance of "Just for a Thrill" figures as an early effort by the singer to reimagine the American Songbook.

Officially, Franklin's next release was *Unforgettable* (1964), a collection of songs recorded by Dinah Washington, and in tribute to Washington, who died in December 1963. Perhaps her most remarkable achievement at Columbia, *Unforgettable* is also Franklin's most well-known collection of covers, characteristic of the dynamics that compelled Franklin to record songs previously performed by others. Washington, the "Queen of the Blues," was a family friend and mentor of sorts to Franklin. More important, Washington's ability to straddle genres such as the "ballsy" blues, hard-driving R&B, and pop jazz standards made Franklin her logical heir apparent. On *Unforgettable*, Franklin paid fitting tributes to some of Washington's most popular mainstream hits, including "What a Difference a Day Makes," "This Bitter Earth," and the title song, a hit for Washington, who updated Nat King Cole's signature version by mostly playing it straight.

On tracks like "Drinking Again" and Washington's early hit "Evil Gal Blues" (1944), recorded two years after Franklin was born, you can hear the singer working toward mastery of a style most associated with the back rooms of the Chitlin Circuit. But it is with "Cold, Cold Heart," a piece of classic Americana originally written and recorded by rockabilly legend Hank Williams in 1950, that Franklin finds her voice. Known for songs like "Hey Good Lookin'" and "Your Cheatin Heart," released after his death at age twenty-nine in 1953, Williams, as Richard Leppert and George Lipsitz write, "presented a masculine voice that longed for reconnection with the feminine" that was in contrast to the "masculinist rhetoric of Mickey Spillane novels and John Wayne films . . . and paternalistic pressures of outer-directed corporate culture to the hedonistic appeals of *Playboy* magazine all encouraged men to widen the distance between themselves and women."[33]

Leppert and Lipsitz's comments illuminate why a Black woman artist like Dinah Washington would choose to cover Williams, whose sense of emotional interiority in his singing offered emotional access for Washington's interpretation. Indeed Washington had a major hit in 1951 with "Cold, Cold Heart," transforming the country blues into a strutting, mid-tempo R&B track. When Washington moved to the Mercury label in the late 1950s and found success as a crossover pop singer, she recorded a second version of "Cold, Cold Heart." Franklin's version of the song is unrecognizable from the original Williams version as well as both of Washington renditions. Accompanying herself on piano, "Cold, Cold Heart" is, for all intents, an original composition, and the prototype for the style of soul that Franklin would revolutionize in the late 1960s. One might say the "Queen of Soul" was born on that track.

But *Unforgettable* only tells part of the story of Franklin's ascendance as an interpreter and emerging arbiter of the American Songbook. In 1963, between the releases of *Laughing on the Outside* and *Unforgettable*, Franklin recorded an album-length session with the same Bobby Scott who, four years later, would curate an American Songbook session for Marvin Gaye. Franklin's Scott sessions raise questions about Gaye's level of awareness of Franklin's work with the arranger, particularly since the sessions where canned by Columbia before resurfacing on the 2002 collection *The Queen in Waiting* and later given a more formal release as *Tiny Sparrow: The Bobby Scott Sessions* in 2011. "I Won't Cry Anymore," the only track that both Franklin and Gaye recorded with Scott, appears on the 1952 debut *Because of You* (along with "Cold, Cold, Heart") of Tony Bennett, whose career has largely been defined by his interpretation of the American Songbook. The album's track listing, which, in addition to "I Won't Cry Anymore," includes tracks like Henry Mancini's "Moon River" from *Breakfast at Tiffany's*, Billy Strayhorn's "Little Brown Book" (which was given legendary treatment on the only album-length collaboration between Duke Ellington and John Coltrane in 1962), and a simply breathtaking version of "Tiny Sparrow," the American folk ballad that appeared on Peter, Paul, and Mary's second album *Moving* (1963), speaks to the eclecticism of Franklin's session with Scott and also likely explains why it was shelved at the time.

Like Marvin's session from Scott, which remained in the archive for decades, Franklin's Scott sessions provide a fuller view of her career designs and the wide range of material she felt comfortable or even worthy of recording. At the time that Franklin recorded *Unforgettable*, neither Hank Williams nor Dinah Washington would have been considered natural interpreters of the American Songbook, yet Franklin's recordings of "Cold, Cold Heart" and Washington's "This Bitter Earth" highlight the ways that a new generation of artists in the 1960s helped to redefine the canon of American song, particularly at the intersections of music made by African Americans and working-class ethnic Whites.[34] Williams's "I'm So Lonesome I Could Cry" (1949), a song credited to both Williams and Paul Gilley, has become a standard, recorded by a wide array of artists including Al Green, who covered the song on *Call Me* (1973), the same album where he tackles Willie Nelson. The same can be said about Washington's "This Bitter Earth," which was written and produced by Clyde Otis and covered by a litany of Washington's contemporaries, such as Big Maybelle, Nancy Wilson Brook Benton, and Etta James (forty years after Washington's original), and, years later, by Johnny Taylor, Lou Rawls, Gladys Knight, and Jimmy Scott.

Not surprisingly, given the artistic accomplishment of *Unforgettable*, Columbia turned to Clyde Otis himself to produce Franklin's next two albums, *Runnin' Out of Fools* (1965) and *Yeah!!!* (which was originally released with a canned audience track). The Otis sessions also yielded material that was included on *Soul Sister* (1966) and *Take It Like You Give It* (1967), the albums that fulfilled Franklin's contractual obligations to Columbia before her move to Atlantic. *Runnin' Out of Fools* might have been Franklin's most important Columbia album, not just because of it was her first commercial success for the label, having reached the R&B charts, but because it hinted at the way Franklin began to imagine herself in a pop music world that was exploding in the midst of anti–Vietnam War demonstrations, the civil rights movement, and the death of Camelot. At least from Columbia's standpoint, Clyde Otis seemed the perfect musical interlocutor for Franklin: *Runnin' Out of Fools* included covers of the R&B hits of Inez and Charlie Foxx ("Mockingbird"), Brenda Holloway ("Every Little Bit Hurts"), Brook Benton ("It's Just a Matter of Time"), Mary Wells ("My Guy"), Dionne Warwick ("Walk on

By"), Barbara Lynn (You'll Lose a Good Thing") and Betty Everett ("The Shoop Shoop Song"), though it was the title track, an original from Kay Rogers and Richard Ahlert, that became a hit single. The covers on the album were important because they exhibited Franklin's literacy with the music of young Black America—something that might not have been presumed, given her lifelong connections to the gospel music establishment and the adult pop she previously recorded at Columbia.

Otis also produced the session *A Bit of Soul* (1965), which Columbia chose not to release, deciding to issue a series of singles instead, the most famous of which is "One Step Ahead," which formed the basis of Mos Def's "Ms. Fat Booty" thirty-five years later. On those sessions with Otis in 1964 and 1965, Franklin also recorded Barbra Streisand's "People," in addition to "Cry Like a Baby," an early composition by Ashford and Simpson, who would become iconic songwriters in their own right with their popular collaborations with Marvin Gaye and Tammi Terrell. She also recorded the Otis original "Take a Look," a subtle protest ballad that further evinced Franklin's interest in the social and political world evolving outside of the recording booth. The song, which was later covered by Martha and the Vandellas on the 1970 album *Natural Resources*, would become the title track of Natalie Cole's 1993 collection of standards.

It would be an overstatement to say that Franklin's ability to add nuance to tracks like Holloway's "Every Little Bit Hurts" or Warwick's "Walk on By" created the context in which such songs might be viewed as canonical (Warwick could do as much in her own right); Franklin had neither the artistic inclination nor the commercial gravitas to do so in the mid-1960s. Yet the unreleased recordings that remained in Columbia's archive for years suggest that Franklin had her own mind about how to interpret songs that belonged in both the American Songbook and in a canon of jazz, R&B, and soul, and that such categories were not mutually exclusive. The situation was quite different when Franklin covered Warwick in 1968 on her fourth album for Atlantic. "I Say a Little Prayer" was written by Hal David and Burt Bacharach for Warwick, the duo who penned most of Dionne Warwick's hits during the 1960s. Warwick scored a top-five pop hit a year before Franklin's version, which hit the top-ten charts but was a bigger hit than Warwick's on the R&B charts. To say that Franklin's version, which featured her on piano, backed by the Sweet Inspirations (including Warwick's cousin Cissy Houston), is better than Warwick's—the most successful Black female solo vocalist of that era, until Franklin's ascent—is unfair; it's a fundamentally different song.

By the time Franklin walked into the Atlantic studios in April and September 1968 to record *Soul '69*, she was unquestionably the "Queen." Franklin's first four albums for Atlantic were all top-five pop hits, and all of them topped the R&B charts, generating eight top-ten pop singles and six number-one R&B singles. With so much ahead of her, Franklin chose to look back on *Soul '69*, covering a group of soul and R&B classics, many of which would be noted in contemporary conversations about the American Songbook. Some of the choices were obvious nods to the moment, such as a cover of her Detroit homeboy Smokey Robinson's "Tracks of My Tears" and Sam Cooke's "Bring It On Home To Me" (she had covered Cooke's "You Send Me" and "A Change is Gonna Come" on previous albums). There were inspired choices as well, like Big Maybelle's "Ramblin' (Blues)"; "River's Invitation" by Percy Mayfield, known for penning Ray Charles's "Hit the Road Jack"; "Crazy He Calls Me," a hit for Billie Holiday in the late 1940s; and "So Long," one of Franklin's best performances, and a song most famous as a hit for Ruth Brown, also covered by R&B stalwarts Big Maybelle and Charles Brown. The irony of many of the covers on *Soul '69* is that Franklin paid tribute to artists that her successes had, to some extent, made irrelevant to mainstream pop audiences. That includes Franklin herself: *Soul '69* also features a version of "Today I Sing the Blues," which Franklin recorded in 1960 on her first album with Columbia. With the latter version of the song, listeners can literally hear the changes that Franklin had wrought on Black music.

Some of Franklin's most inventive covers would be found on a string of studio albums that she released between 1970 and 1974—albums that did not match the commercial success of her earlier Atlantic albums, but may represent her best, if not most underrated, work. *This Girl's In Love with You* (1970)—the title a riff on Herb Alpert's *This Guy's in Love with You* (1968), written by David and Bacharach—is most remembered for a composition by Franklin, "Call Me," one of the few originals on the album. The single for "Call Me" was backed by what the Reverend C. L. Franklin might have called a "stone cold" take on Dusty Springfield's "Son of a Preacher Man." To the uninitiated, one might have thought that Springfield must have been covering Franklin; in fact, Springfield recorded the song, which was produced by longtime Franklin collaborators Jerry Wexler and Tom Dowd, after it had been turned down by Franklin, who took a second look at the song after Springfield's success with it. Franklin also paid tribute to the "death" of the Beatles, with a faithful cover of "Let It Be" and gave "Eleanor Rigby" a bath in the mythical lake of Muscle Shoals.

Culling her roots, Franklin also recorded a version of "Share Your Love with Me," the first single from *This Girl's in Love with You*, an R&B hit for Bobby "Blue" Bland six years earlier, as well as of James Carr's "Dark End of the Street," a song that would inspire the title of historian Danielle McGuire's book on sexual violence against Black women in the early twentieth century. Franklin went deeper with the follow-up album *Spirit in the Dark* (1970), the biggest hit from which was her fresh cover of labelmate Ben E. King's "Don't Play That Song." On the follow-up studio album *Young, Gifted, and Black* (1972), she reimagined King's "Spanish Harlem." After this, Franklin returned to the Carole King songbook—one of her signature recordings "(You Make Me Feel Like) A Natural Woman" was penned by King—with a cover of "Oh No Not My Baby," originally recorded by the underrated vocalist Maxine Brown. While B. B. King earned his own right to mainstream success, Franklin's cover of King's most successful singles "The Thrill is Gone" and "Why I Sing the Blues" helped solidify his career as a touring artist for the next forty-plus years. This was a period in which Franklin began to understand the power of her ability to introduce older R&B and blues artists to younger crossover audiences. Interestingly, Franklin's four originals on *Spirit in the Dark* especially the title song (which, admittedly, pales alongside her live Fillmore West version) and "Try Matty's," find Franklin achieving the full mastery of the very genres that she had previously gestured toward with covers.

With the covers that appear on *Young, Gifted, and Black* and *Let Me in Your Life* (1974), Franklin had achieved a quality of sublimity that coincided with a period that found her at the height of her creative power. There's not even a novice Franklin fan that wouldn't put the Franklin originals "Rock Steady" and "Day Dreaming" on their list of favorite Queen of Soul tracks. Yet Franklin's cover of the title track, "Young, Gifted, and Black," with her signature piano playing pushed to the front of the mix, transforms Nina Simone's stately anthem into something otherworldly and multigenerational; listeners only need to consider at least two of the hip-hop songs that sampled it—Heavy D's "Yes, Y'all," twenty years after Franklin's version, and Rapsody's "Laila's Wisdom," forty-five years after—as evidence of its reach and appeal. Elton John had not yet achieved his first number-one hit in the United States ("Crocodile Rock"), when Franklin recorded his "Border Song (Holy Moses)," which initially appeared on the British rocker's second album, *Elton John* (1970). Additionally, Franklin broadly reimagined the Delfonics' "Didn't I (Blow Your Mind)," with a Freddie Hubbard's *Red Clay*–styled intro, and updated Otis Redding's "I've Been Loving You Too Long" as a soulful slow drag. The standout was Franklin's rendition of the Jerry Butler classic "A Brand New Me," which she turns into a rollicking celebration of self-love, closing with a nearly minute-long piano solo that is among the best of her studio recordings.

At the time that Franklin recorded "Until You Come Back to Me" for *Let Me in Your Life*, few people knew it was a cover. Written and recorded by Stevie Wonder in 1967, Wonder's version was not made publicly available until the release of his anthology, *Looking Back* (1977). For Franklin, it would be the last top-five pop hit of her Atlantic career, and an example of her taking on her "soul man" peers. The album's title track was a cover of a sparse Bill Withers song, which, courtesy of Donny Hathaway, becomes a slice of electrified funk. In the spirit of "Day Dreaming," Franklin offers a whispering breeze of a version of Bobby Womack's "I'm in Love" (1968), which was first recorded by Wilson Pickett in 1967. Franklin had previously covered Womack on her 1973 studio album, *Hey Now Hey (The Other Side of the Sky)*, which includes a stellar, seven-minute version of "That's The Way I Feel about Cha," produced by Quincy Jones a year before he broke through with his prototypical jazz/pop with *Body Heat* (1974). Finally, Franklin offers a slow and sassy version of Marvin Gaye and Tammi Terrell's "Ain't Nothing Like the Real Thing" that takes the Motown track to a level of sensuality that Gaye himself had just begun to explore with *Let's Get It On*, released the previous year. *Let Me in Your Life* contains two of Franklin's most impressive studio performances on "Oh Baby" and "If You Don't Think"—both written by her, and potentially the best evidence of the singer at her vocal peak.

The only other match to these songs is the album's closer, Franklin's cover of Leon Russell's "A Song for You." After Donny Hathaway released a studio version of the song in 1971, "A Song for You" became a big session song for soul singers. Originally recorded on Russell's eponymous debut in 1970 as the opening track, the song was rescued from obscurity a year later by Andy Williams, who made a career of recording "middle-of-the-road" (MOR) fare, starting with his popular version of Henry Mancini's "Moon River" in 1960. Helen Reddy and the Carpenters also gave the song with the MOR treatment in the early 1970s, which could be said to betray Russell's vision of the song, as a White artist comfortable working in soul and blues idioms. Russell has some real street cred: he was instrumental in the early success of the Greenwood, Archer, and Pine Street Band, later known as the Gap Band, which featured vocalist Charlie Wilson, and he also co-wrote "Superstar" for the Carpenters, which later became a signature tune for Luther Vandross, who perhaps performed the song more closely to the way Russell may have originally imagined it.

That same year as Williams's version of "A Song for You," and one of the few times the song was released as a single, Merry Clayton recorded a version for her self-titled solo album. Perhaps best known for her duet with Mick Jagger on the Rolling Stones' "Gimme Shelter" (1969), Clayton also provided backing vocals on Russell's debut. Her version of the song is significant in light of the fact that her album featured contributions from bassist Wilton Felder and pianist Joe Sample, both of the Crusaders (who also contributed to Marvin Gaye's *Let's Get It On*), as well as session guitarist David T. Walker, who appears on many Motown recordings in the early 1970s, and the legendary Billy Preston, contributions that illuminate the song's resonance among soul and jazz performers. Jazz vocalists Carmen McRae and Billy Eckstine recorded versions of "A Song for You" in the early 1970s, as did Al Wilson ("Show and Tell"), Freda Payne ("Band of Gold"), and Lou Rawls, to name just a few. The Temptations also recorded their own, very fine version, featuring Dennis Edwards on lead vocals.

When Donny Hathaway covered A Song for You" on his second album *Donny Hathaway* (1971), which also included covers of songs by Mac Davis, Billy Preston, George Clinton and Van McCoy, Russell's composition provided much for him to work with. One could be forgiven for thinking that "A Song for You" was Hathaway's song; the late stylist gave it such personal touch that his catalog is unimaginable without it, though it would be nearly a decade after Hathaway's studio version—and a year after his death—that most listeners would hear his live version of song on *In Performance*. By then, Russell was a footnote to his own composition.

Hathaway was in the studio when Aretha Franklin recorded the sessions that became *Let Me in Your Life* (1974), which should be remembered as Franklin's last great studio recording, and among the top three of her best recordings. Though Hathaway played acoustic and electric piano on the Bobby Womack–penned single "I'm in Love" (which topped the R&B charts) and Franklin's cover of Stevie Wonder's "Until You Come Back to Me," which was her last major pop hit until "Freeway of Love" more than a decade later, he does not appear on Franklin's version of "A Song for You," which closes the album. Franklin could have decided to make a statement by taking the song to church, as Hathaway did, but instead she chose to swing it, accompanying herself on the electric piano, perhaps as a nod to the exquisite and underrated Quincy Jones–produced album that precedes *Let Me in Your Life*. Franklin's version, which opens with her playing a solo on a Fender Rhodes, her vocals lagging slyly just behind the beat, might be the definitive version, if only because no one could sing along with her. When Franklin's performances of songs from the American Songbook were more nuanced, they achieved an aura of originality.

Franklin continued to make covers, even later in her career, after she left Atlantic and recorded for Clive Davis's Arista Records, such as the Rolling Stones' "You Can't Turn Me Loose" and the Doobie Brothers' "What a Fool Believes" on her first Arista album in 1980. On her most commercially successful album, *Who's Zoomin' Who?* (1985), Franklin covers "Sweet Bitter Love," a song she first recorded during her legendary Clyde Otis sessions that had remained in the can for decades. Roberta Flack included a version of the song on her 1971 album *Quiet Fire*. On Franklin's 1985 version, you can hear an artist paying tribute not simply to the music and the artists that came before her, but to the long journey that had brought her to that moment.

Franklin's last studio album, *Aretha Franklin Sings the Great Diva Classics* (2014), found the artist covering songs by Etta James, Gladys Knight, Gloria Gaynor, Chaka Khan (via Whitney Houston), Diana Ross, and, most famously Adele, adding her own Aretha-ish spin on "Rolling in the Deep." Also included on that last studio is another rendition of "People," a song best known for launching the career of Franklin's contemporary Barbara Streisand in 1964 that Franklin had previously recorded in 1964 as part of the Otis sessions, but, like "Sweet, Bitter Love," it, too, was not released. Franklin's inclusion of the song on this last album served as a coy reminder of what could have been—film, stage, television, if we are to follow the arc of Streisand's career—and what had to be. Franklin might have been the greatest soul singer to ever live, but to crown her the "Queen of Soul" would be to limit the full range of her mastery of the American Songbook, and therefore to the very definition of what the American Songbook could be. Franklin, in effect invented a new American Songbook, or what could simply be called Aretha Franklin's American Songbook. Nowhere would this be more apparent than when Franklin walked into the New Temple Missionary Baptist Church in Los Angeles in 1972.

"I'll Be a Bridge": Redefining the American Songbook

Two months short of her thirtieth birthday, and less than two weeks before the release of her eighteenth studio album, *Young, Gifted, and Black*, Aretha Franklin entered the New Temple Missionary Baptist Church in Los Angeles to record a live gospel album. Backed by the Southern California Community Choir, under the direction of her longtime friend and mentor the Reverend James Cleveland, the subsequent recording eventually sold over two million copies and remained the best-selling gospel album of all time for more than twenty years. Firmly established as the Queen of Soul, Franklin was at the peak of her artistic powers when she recorded *Amazing Grace*, and the album stands as the best testament of Franklin's singular genius after its release in June 1972.

In a tellingly titled *New York Times* review of Aretha Franklin's *Young, Gifted, and Black*, published in March 1972, "Aretha's Blooming Thirties," critic Don Heckman describes the album as "an extraordinary, eclectic set of material."[35] To date, Franklin had earned six Grammy Awards, and nearly a dozen of her singles and several of her albums had gone gold; she was easily the most commercially successful Black woman vocalist of all time. Culled from sessions recorded in late 1970 and throughout 1971, *Young, Gifted, and Black* marks the beginning of what might be called Franklin's most sustained period of artistic genius. Franklin's choice to record tracks like Elton John's "Border Song," Jerry Butler's "Brand New Me," Lennon and McCartney's "The Long and Winding Road," and Nina Simone's "Young, Gifted, and Black," alongside originals like "Day Dreamin'," "All the King's Horses," and the infectious "Rock Steady" was as much the decision of an artist who had earned the right to record any-thing she wanted as it was the expression of a woman who felt she finally had control over her life and career.

Franklin made the album while living in New York City, after years of working in the shadow of her father, the legendary preacher Reverend C. L. Franklin, and under the professional guidance of her first husband, Ted White. In her autobiography, *From These Roots* (1999), Franklin writes of this period, "I see those days as a tremendous growth period and declaration of my independence. I was rediscovering myself."[36] Of *Young Gifted, and Black*, Franklin adds that with that album she felt "free and willing to take creative risks."[37] Part of that rediscovery, apparently, entailed Aretha going back to church, in which her lived experiences while recording *Young, Gifted, and Black* may have served as a portal.

Franklin is adamant in her memoirs that *Amazing Grace* didn't mark a return to church, in a spiritual sense, but "when I say 'took me back to church,' I mean recording in church. I never left church. And I never will."[38] Franklin's very first recording, "Never Grow Old," was recorded in her father's church in 1956. Her first album, *Songs of Faith*, released a year later, contained recordings collected from live performances of Franklin while on tour with her father. In the interim years between that release and *Amazing Grace*, Franklin had, with other artists, contributed to the mainstreaming of the Black gospel aesthetic in popular music and culture. Though Franklin had long wanted to make a full-fledged live gospel recording, the immediate impetus for *Amazing Grace* might have been one of Franklin's most triumphant performances: her three-night stand with King Curtis at Bill Graham's Fillmore West in March 1971, an engagement that resulted in the recording *Live at the Fillmore West* (later reissued in full as *Don't Fight the Feeling: Live at the Fillmore West*). In-troducing Franklin and her music to one of the iconic sites of late 1960s and early 1970s counterculture seemed like a risky endeavor at the time. As writer Mark Bego describes the venue in his book *Aretha Franklin: The Queen of Soul*, "There were no chairs and bleachers . . . the audience sat cross-legged on the floor, or stood up and grooved to the music being performed on stage. People in the audience freely passed around joints during the shows."[39]

It was Jerry Wexler, Franklin's longtime producer, who was largely behind the Fillmore West engagement, in an effort to counter the inclination to view Franklin simply as a soul singer. Wexler's ambitions were likely geared largely toward broadening her commercial appeal, whereas Franklin may have had greater aims regarding the American Songbook. Bego quotes Wexler as saying, "We want these longhairs to listen to this lady. After that there'll be no problems."[40] Franklin still had to deliver, and she did, tackling material like Stephen Stills's "Love the One You're With" and Bread's "Make It with You" for the first time. Stills had begun his career with Buffalo Springfield ("For What It's Worth"), moved on to a solo career (during which he recorded "Love the One You're With"), and spent time in a supergroup that included Buffalo Springfield bandmate Neil Young, Graham Nash of the Hollies, and David Crosby of the Byrds.[41] "Make It with You" was the most popular of the songs by Bread, who, with tracks like "If," "Baby I'm-a Want You," and "Aubrey," might be thought of as the founders of soft rock. Franklin had little trouble taking on the songs.

The same could be said of Franklin's version of Paul Simon's "Bridge over Troubled Water," which in retrospect might be the only song Franklin recorded over those three nights that might be considered part of the American Songbook, and indeed Simon himself might be the only composer that would be considered in that light. Released in 1970, "Bridge over Troubled Water" was the biggest hit of Simon & Garfunkel, the duo whose singles "The Sound of Silence" (1965), "Homeward Bound" (1966), and "Mrs. Robinson" (featured in the 1967 film *The Graduate*, starring Dustin Hoffman) epitomized the 1960s pop-folk sound. The song, which was the title track of the pair's final studio album, earned them a Grammy Award for Record of the Year, and, for Simon, a Grammy for Song of the Year in 1971. As a single, "Bridge over Troubled Water" was a bit of a departure for the group, as it featured Garfunkel on lead vocals, as opposed to the shared harmonies that marked most of their previous hits. The song also included a distinct reference to the Black gospel tradition. According to Simon, the song's title was inspired by an ad-lib performed by Claude Jeter, lead vocalist of the Swan Silvertones, on their 1958 version of "Mary Don't Weep," who sang at the song's close, "I'll be a bridge over deep water if you trust in my name."[42]

Simon's referencing of the Black gospel tradition resonated with Black artists, including the Supremes (with new lead Jean Terrell) and the Jackson 5 (with Jermaine Jackson on lead vocals), who recorded versions of the song in 1970, as well as Franklin's labelmate Roberta Flack, who included a version on her third studio album, *Quiet Fire* (1971). All of the various renditions hewed fairly close to the original in style, particularly Flack's. Franklin's version, of course, was another matter, beginning with a background vocal arrangement in which the trio of Brenda Bryant, Margaret Branch, and Pat Smith open with the refrain, "Don't trouble the waters, leave it alone, why don't you, why don't you, let it be / Still waters run deep, yes, it do," at once signaling the music of the Beatles and the Four Tops, whose Smokey Robinson composition "Still Water (Love)" was their last big hit before departing Motown for ABC-Dunhill in 1973. The Beatles' "Let It Be" was a more complex citation, and even a reminder, as Franklin's version of the Lennon and McCartney anthem had actually first been included on Franklin's *This Girl's in Love with You*, two months before it appeared as the title track and penultimate single on the Beatles' final studio album. Franklin had been sent a demo of the recording prior to the song's release, and, notably, Billy Preston plays keyboards on both the Beatles studio version and Franklin's Fillmore West performance. In citing and recording "Bridge over Troubled Water" and "Let It Be," Franklin had sung herself into the pantheon of contemporary White pop music; the two songs sat atop the pop charts for eight weeks in the period during and immediately following Franklin's appearances at the Fillmore West. As David Remnick would write some years later, "Just as Otis Redding quit singing 'Respect' after hearing Aretha's version ('From now on, it belongs to her'), Simon and Art Garfunkel forever had to compete with the memory of this performance."[43] As if to add a coda to her claim on the American Songbook, on the closing night of Franklin's Fillmore West stand, she closed with a rendition of Diana Ross's "Reach Out and Touch (Somebody's Hand)"—the lead single of Ross's debut solo album, which wouldn't be released for another month—essentially previewing the Ashford and Simpson composition for the Fillmore West audience. If Franklin had earned the right to essentially claim the "hippie" songbook (in the hippies' house, no less), she ultimately did so on her own terms, with her own music.

With the exception of the third night, where Franklin closed the show with "Reach Out and Touch (Somebody's Hand)," Franklin ended the first two nights with a suite of "Dr. Feelgood," "Spirit in the Dark" and an extended reprise of "Spirit in the Dark."[44] On all three nights Franklin's repertoire consisted of hits like "Respect," "Call Me," and "Don't Play That Song" that were written by others, in addition to the covers noted above; "Spirit in the Dark" and "Dr. Feelgood" are the only original compositions Franklin performed at the Fillmore West, making it notable that she essentially ended all three nights with those songs. I'd like to suggest that Franklin wasn't asserting her claim to interpreting and re-animating the American Songbook, but contributing to it with her own compositions. The third night of the suite was significant in particular, because Franklin was joined by Ray Charles on the reprise of "Spirit in the Dark." Charles's comments to David Ritz offer some perspective on the way Franklin wrote music that could serve as a common language across genres: "She sits me down at her electric piano and has me doing her 'Spirit in the Dark.' Never played the thing before. Didn't know the words. But Aretha's spirit was moving me and I got through it. She had me play a long solo on electric piano. . . . She's turned the thing into Church."[45]

In his book *Higher Ground: Stevie Wonder, Aretha Franklin, Curtis Mayfield, and the Rise and Fall of American Soul*, scholar and critic Craig Werner writes, "'Spirit in the Dark' evokes the sense of political community that seemed to be slipping away."[46] As Franklin writes about that night, "Soul oozed out of every pore of the Filmore. All the planets were aligned right that night, because when the music came down, it was as real and righteous as any recording I'd ever made."[47] Billy Preston, who accompanied Franklin on organ for the Fillmore dates was less refined in his response: "The hippies flipped the fuck out."[48] A year later, Franklin's father addressed the crowd on the second night of the *Amazing Grace* sessions, recalling a trip with his daughter to Italy, where the Italian audience knew very little English, but enough to say, as Reverend Franklin did, in a faux accent, "Aretha! 'Spirit in the Dark'!" Franklin had not only mastered the American songbook, but had become the very spirit of the thing.

One critic described *Amazing Grace* as "Aretha Franklin returns home," and indeed much of the preparation for the two nights of performances at the New Temple Missionary Baptist Church was intended to make Franklin feel comfortable. In the mix were members of Franklin's regular studio band, including bassist Chuck Rainey, guitarist Cornell Dupree, and drummer Bernard Purdie, the latter two veterans of the King Curtis band that backed Franklin at the Fillmore West. In addition to her father, Reverend Franklin, who provided remarks on the second night, gospel singer Clara Ward attended the recording. As Franklin admits in *From These Roots*, "Along with my dad, Miss Ward was my greatest influence. She was the ultimate gospel singer—dramatic, daring, exciting, courageous. . . . She took gospel where gospel had never gone before."[49] If *Amazing Grace* represented a homecoming, it was because the recording recalled Aretha's home life two decades earlier, when a young ambitious and talented musician and choir director James Cleveland was living in the Franklin household.

Of Cleveland, Franklin would later write, "James helped shape my basic musical personality in profound ways. . . . I was blessed to meet James so early in his career."[50] By the time Cleveland joined Franklin for the *Amazing Grace* sessions, he had long been established as one of the leading gospel stars of his generation, best known for his composition "Peace Be Still" and his stunning choir arrangements. Cleveland was himself at the peak of his powers in 1972. Franklin's longtime producer

Jerry Wexler realized as much and would recall that the "arrangements were between [Franklin] and James Cleveland. Those arrangements, some of them were traditional—and some of them were things that she and James Cleveland put together." Yet, as Antonia Randolph notes in her review of the *Amazing Grace* documentary, released forty-six years after the recording, listeners were not privy to the interpersonal dynamics of the performance. "Did Rev. James Cleveland, master of ceremonies at Los Angeles' New Temple Missionary Baptist Church, which was hosting Aretha Franklin's two-night concert in 1972, grip the back of her dress while she was singing 'Amazing Grace'?" Randolph asks, observing that "Cleveland's grasp was familiar, familial, and not exactly friendly. It was possessive in the way that men are of women and adults are of children. His re-centering of himself is part of a long tradition of Black men limiting the role of Black women in church."[51]

Franklin's involvement in the production of *Amazing Grace* was no small matter. As Franklin rather pointedly expresses in her memoir, "As much as I appreciated the soulful studio environment in which Atlantic placed me and the sensitive musicians who played by my side, one point was deceptive and unfair: I was not listed as a co-producer."[52] As recounted in *Nowhere to Run: The Story of Soul Music*, Franklin later told Gerri Hirshey that "I always worked on my sound, my arrangements, before I went into a studio with a producer." Hirshey confirms this point: "There's no better evidence than Aretha's own notes from those fabled sessions. They are written in a girlish, slanted hand on yellow legal pads. They actually look like homework, as Aretha claims they were."[53] Like her music itself, this ephemera presented by Hirshey serves as a reminder of just how studied Franklin was in the choice of her music. It was to Wexler's credit that he understood from the time he started working with Franklin in 1967 that she had the best idea about how she should sound. Franklin's piano playing on many of her Atlantic recordings testified to that understanding. Franklin's point in her comment to Hirshey was that she needed formal recognition for her coproducer status. *Amazing Grace* is the first Franklin recording on which she is listed as a coproducer, cementing her place in the pantheon of American music as founded upon her own authorship.

The song list from the first night of the live recording reveals the eclecticism that would become the hallmark on Franklin's recordings in this era. American Songbook fare like Rodgers and Hammerstein's "You'll Never Walk Alone" from the 1945 musical *Carousel* (the song was also an early hit for Patti Labelle and the Bluebelles) were chosen alongside traditional gospel standards like "What a Friend We Have in Jesus" and "Precious Memories" (popularized by Sister Rosetta Tharpe), as well as original tunes like Clara Ward's "How I Got Over" and even Marvin Gaye's "Wholy Holy," with which Franklin opens. As Ed Pavlic writes, "Franklin's 'Wholy Holy' swerves away from soul's sexuality and even from gospel's intensely personal address. Instead she returns Gaye's song to its roots as an Old Testament address to a collective in crisis."[54]

The variety in Franklin's selections was a product of the multiple worlds her success forced her to bridge. Nowhere was this more apparent than her medley of "Precious Lord, Take My Hand/You've Got a Friend," which combines the most popular compositions of the "Father of Gospel," Thomas A. Dorsey (in whose Chicago church Cleveland got his start) and singer-songwriter Carole King, whose "(You Make Me Feel Like) A Natural Woman" was one of Franklin's signature recordings. As choir director Alexander Hamilton told Aaron Cohen, "It was Aretha's idea. She was the one I heard present it. Again, it came naturally. Not about if, it's about how."[55] The brilliance of Franklin's seamless performance of the songs represents not merely an acknowledgement of the greatness of the songs she selected from the American Songbook, but the realization of Franklin's own cultural gravitas, which had the impact of elevating Dorsey—largely unknown to Franklin's mainstream fans—to the level of King, who at the time was considered the quintessential singer-songwriter of her generation. Franklin's efforts can be compared to what scholar and critic Walton M. Muyumba, borrowing from Tim Parrish, calls "democratic doing and undoing." Writing about the improvisational techniques of another African American musical genius, Charlie Parker, in his book *The Shadow and Act: Black Intellectual Practice Jazz Improvisation and Philosophical Pragmatism*, Muyumba writes, "Parker's music 'undoes' status quo American musical performance theories by offering new modes for 'doing' or improvising American music."[56] To Muyumba's point, Franklin's performance enacts an undoing of a logic that would separate mid-twentieth-century gospel music from 1970s singer/songwriter pop, while doing the work of placing an overlooked composer such as Dorsey on a more elevated plane.

Franklin's merging of Dorsey and King can additionally be read as an act of generosity that would be reinforced a year later when Franklin gave her Grammy Award for Best Rhythm Blues Performance (awarded for *Young, Gifted, and Black*) to former labelmate Esther Phillips, whose *From a Whisper to a Scream* was also nominated that year. Noted critic Leonard Feather describes Franklin's recognition of Phillips as "a rare noblesse oblige gesture": a term that translates into the "obligation of nobility." Phillips was only a few years older than Franklin and, like Franklin, began her career as a teen. On the road as a performer since the age of thirteen, in 1949, Phillips seemingly acquired a level of experience and trauma powerfully reflected in her music and her voice. "In fact, she scared me to death," Shirley Anne Williams writes, "that raw nervi-ness in her tone that was as much reminiscent of Billie Holiday as it was of Dinah [Washington], the one she was always compared to. Esther's voice seemed to me like an open wound, proclaiming that its owner had survived unspeakable things."[57]

When Phillips reemerged with a cover Ray Price country classic "Release Me" in the early 1960s, one of the many periods in which she struggled with addiction, she was poised, more so than Franklin, to fill the void left by Dinah Washington's death. Phillips's debut for Kudo Records, *From a Whisper to a Scream* (1971)—one of the great hybrid soul, jazz, and blues albums from that era—included a stellar cover of Gil Scott-Heron's "Home Is Where the Hatred Is," a song about addiction, and "Baby, I'm for Real," written by Marvin Gaye and originally recorded for Motown by the Originals. Franklin's generosity at the Grammys was not lost on the industry; Phillips had her biggest success two years later with a disco cover of Washington's "What a Diff'rence a Day Makes" before succumbing to liver disease in August 1984, ten days after the death of Franklin's father.

What ultimately makes *Amazing Grace* such a powerful reflection of Aretha Franklin's talent and stature is the response of the audience, composed of traditional churchgoers, fans, critics, gospel royalty, and Mick Jagger. Cleveland makes note of the atypical crowd in his opening comments, telling the audience, "I'd like for you to be mindful, though, that this is a church, and we're here for religious service. . . . We want you to give vent to the spirit. Those of you not hip to giving vent to the spirit, then you do the next best thing." By the time Aretha segues into "How I Got Over" after her stirring duet with Cleveland on "Precious Memories," it is clear that the crowd has caught the spirit; "How I Got Over" elicits a false start as Cleveland tells folk, "You know y'all threw us off just then. Don't clap till we get it open." The crowd was thus ripe when Franklin delivered what might be the definitive performance of her career.

"Amazing Grace" is the most traditional of all traditional hymns, and not a gospel singer (or country or blues singer, for that matter) worth their salt hasn't spent some time putting their unique spin on it. For all of those suspicious of Franklin's seemingly sudden desire to come "back home" to the church, this performance would put all concerns to rest. Clocking in at over sixteen minutes, including Cleveland's introduction, "Amazing Grace" features Franklin unadorned, with simply the accented backing of organist Ken Lupper and Cleveland on piano. The performance has the feel of a testimony or even a spiritual purging, the crowd audibly in step with Franklin through every turn of phrase and melismatic flourish. Hirshey recalls that Cleveland "stayed at the piano until he broke down in tears" during the performance. "Amazing Grace" would be Franklin's closing number on the opening night, and there was little reason to believe that on the second night she would match the emotional level of her performance on "Amazing Grace." What the documentary *Amazing Grace* reveals is the extent to which Franklin had usurped the privileged position of Black male clergy, represented by Reverend Cleveland, with her performance.

The second night opened with "What a Friend We Have in Jesus" and Gaye's "Wholy Holy," two of the four songs Franklin performed on both nights. Perhaps anticipating a letdown after the first night, Cleveland says to the crowd, regarding the opening hymn, "You only get out of it what you put in." Cleveland's warning, however, wasn't necessary. After a rather perfunctory performance of the opening tracks, Franklin launches into a sequence of five songs as impressive as any suite of songs recorded in the idiom of African American music. Beginning with a rousing rendition of the hymn "Climbing Higher Mountains," Cleveland slows the tempo with an improvised blues riff, doing call and response opposite Franklin, that serves as an introduction to the hymn "God Will Take Care of You." The significant action in the song occurs nearly two-thirds in, when Cleveland again takes the mic, urging the crowd to a higher level. "Over in the sanctified church, when they begin to feel like this," Cleveland exhorts, "all the saints get together and they join in a little praise. I wonder can I get you to help me say it one time," as the crowd yells, "Yeah," several times in unison, before the musicians unleash a torrent of sanctified rhythm. This section of the performance can best be described as the "pedagogy of Black Gospel," as Cleveland literally provides instruction for "catching the spirit," at the same time making transparent the more intimate details of African American community. The sheer brilliance of the moment lies in Cleveland's use of the segment as a musical transformation of the song from a spiritual ballad to a down-home stomper: you can hear him on the piano cueing the musicians and the choir for the cold start of "Old Landmark," highlighting the genius that is often born of utility.

When the pace shifts again for Franklin's stellar version of the Caravans' classic "Mary Don't You Weep," the crowd is nearly spent, and fittingly so, as Franklin undertakes her own version of gospel pedagogy. At the time of the performance, the Caravans were largely known as gospel's first supergroup, counting the legendary Albertina Walker, Dorothy Norwood, Inez Andrews, and Shirley Caesar among its ranks at one time or another; Cleveland himself had been an accompanist for the group in the mid-1950s. The Caravans were to gospel in the 1950s and 1960s what Art Blakey's Jazz Messengers were to jazz: a high-end finishing school for the genre's elite. Given this legacy, it was a propos that Franklin would perform one of the group's most important songs. The song, originally recorded by the Fisk Jubilee Singers in 1915, tells the story of Lazarus of Bethany: a figure that, in biblical lore, is brought back from death by Jesus. The Caravans recorded the song in 1959 a year before the Swan Silvertones, the latter's version of course cited as inspiration for Paul Simon's "Bridge over Troubled Water," and was later inducted into the Library of Congress's National Recording Registry in 2015, one hundred years after the Fisk Jubilee recording. Franklin's choice to claim the Caravans version—instead of crediting the song as "traditional," member Inez Andrews is given sole authorship in the liner notes—spoke volumes about how Franklin thought to reconstitute the American Songbook.

Ostensibly a song about the power of Jesus to deliver believers from adverse conditions, Franklin's performance of "Mary Don't You Weep" provides commentary on Black America in a historical moment that functioned, in part, as an extended period of collective grief and mourning, in the aftermath of a number of deaths: those of Martin Luther King Jr. (a close confidante of Franklin's father), Fred Hampton, Bunchy Carter, students at Jackson State, and countless others who sacrificed their lives in support of the civil rights and Black Power movements, in addition to her musical director, King Curtis, who was killed only months after the Fillmore West recording and her legendary stand at the Apollo in 1971. Franklin and Cleveland's arrangements transform "Mary Don't You Weep" into a dirge, but, in the spirit of much of the best of Black expressive culture, builds on cathartic possibilities. "As a nineteenth century spiritual it came loaded with metaphor: Israelites = black people and Pharaoh's Army = white pursuers" Cohen writes. "How these themes resonated among congregants at a Watts church in 1972 could fill another book."[58]

Midway through the song, Franklin begins to explicitly retell the story of Lazarus—her vocals vacillating between singing and preaching, not unlike the style for which her father was known, recreating Jesus's resurrection of Lazarus. As Franklin sings,

> Jesus said, "For the benefit of you who don't believe,
> Who don't believe in me this evening, I'm gonna call him three
>   times"
> He said, "Lazarus," hmmmm, "Lazarus, hear my, hear my voice,
>   Lazarus" . . .
> He got up walking like a natural man.

At face value, Franklin's "Mary Don't You Weep" offers a powerful example of gospel music's capacity to perform exegesis, but I'd also like to suggest that, in Franklin's hand, it resurrects the very idea of progressive community, a concept literally under siege at the time Franklin made her recording. Less an act of resurrecting a mythical savior, Franklin's performance was an attempt to recover "beloved" community: a community that, as constituted in the New Temple Missionary Baptist Church during those two nights in January 1972, embodied the kind of "imagined" community that would one day elect a Black president more than three decades later.

Franklin ended the suite with a fifteen-minute version of "Never Grow Old," seemingly putting an exclamation point on the inexhaustible idea of beloved community ("I have heard of a land on the faraway strand / 'Tis a beautiful home of the soul"). "Never Grow Old," also known as "Where We'll Never Grow Old," was written by James Cleveland Moore in the second decade of the twentieth Century and recorded by the legendary Carter Family in the 1930s, and later by country star Jim Reeves two years before his death on his 1962 album *We Thank Thee*. Franklin had recorded a version of "Never Grow Old" in 1956 at the age

of fourteen that at the time was released by a local label and later reissued on the 1965 album *Songs of Faith*; thus, this was not terrain that was
unfamiliar to Franklin. As Anthony Heilbut writes, "By applying her
ancestors' sensibility to some of the classic American songs, she virtually
colonized American music for the Gospel sound."[59]

By the time Franklin and Cleveland concluded the evening with a
second rendition of "Precious Memories," after impromptu comments
from Reverend Franklin, it was evident to many in the audience that
they had borne witness to something genuinely transcendent. Heilbut
said it best: "At fourteen, she imagined an afterlife where 'we'll never
grow old'; ten years later she sang of a bitter earth, where 'too soon we
grow old.' At fifteen she was singing of a fountain filled with blood; three
years later, she was singing 'it ain't necessarily so.'—From singing the
plaintive hymns of the eighteenth and nineteenth centuries she moved
to the greatest melodies of the twentieth."[60] On those two nights in Los
Angeles, folk may not only have witnessed the greatest singer of the
twentieth century at her peak, but the peak moment of a musical tradition that had, indeed, changed the world.

5

Decamping Wakanda

The Archive as Maroon

"This is why we can't have nice things." This admonishment has at times been directed toward those—a critical class of Black thinkers and writers, if you will—who are inclined to offer a less-than-affirmative critique of whatever is *this* moment's iteration of "nice things." As if such hypercritical observations ensure that Black cultural production will survive a White critical establishment accustomed to devouring, as in destroying, that which looks too different, these critics can drain the joy of consuming Blackness. This is a reminder that to actually have "nice things," to build on where you might be in the world, literally or figuratively, is to intend to stay put, a collective decision that has often been fraught with the reality of a culture given to fugitivity—or, to put it another way, a culture (always already) on the run.

The history of Black flight has animated many of the existentialist tensions in Black political thought and culture. Its prominence is evident in the myriad "runaway slave" narratives that have populated the Black imagination via the nineteenth-century reflections of Harriet Tubman, Fredrick Douglass, Solomon Northup, and Harriet Jacobs, among so many others, as well as more recent fare like Melina Matsoukas's film *Queen and Slim* (2019). As Lake Micah writes in a review of Ta-Nehisi Coates's *The Water Dancer* (2019), yet another example, "Slave narratives, perhaps the first true literary tradition attributable to blacks in the Americas" are "a fusion of the true and the incredible," "tales of psychosomatic deliverance, and a prototype for the Negro autobiography later to come."[1] That these narratives have at times been overdetermined in Black cultural expression speaks to the fact, as Alex Zamalin argues, that "culture has always played a crucial role in the black political imagina-tion because it was rarely given space in the US public sphere."[2] Yet what has also animated the Black imagination are images of the *there* that Black flight anticipates. Promised lands, freedom lands, Black utopias, and even the afterlife: all serve as metaphors for the *there* that partially inspires Black flight. Wakanda, the Black utopia found in the film *Black Panther* (2018), is one of the most recent and popular examples of this theme.

Wakanda, a world created by Stan Lee more than fifty years ago in the *Black Panther* comic and updated many times since, such as in Ryan Coogler's finely pitched Hollywood film and Reginald Hudlin's animated series, is a timeless extension of *there* as imagined by any number of gen-erations of Black folk who sought blueprints for flight and freedom in the imaginative realm. As N. D. B. Connolly writes, "Dreams of a place like Wakanda began sometime around 1512 in the Caribbean mountains and forested hills above the mines and fields of Spain's colony, Santo Domingo. Then and there, Africans in the Americas first broke away from slavery to form their own societies with indigenous island people."[3] Contemporary iterations of this theme of Black utopia include George Clinton's Mothership Connection, Julie Dash's Georgia Sea Islands, Lee "Scratch" Perry's Black Ark, or Harriet Jacobs's attic, to name just a few.

Many of these promised lands, including Wakanda, might be de-scribed as "hidden in plain sight"—cloaked in some way. One of the joys of the *Black Panther* series was in its previously *known* obscurity, re-called nostalgically by a generation of Black folk either as a Black comic book or a ten-episode animated series produced for BET by filmmaker Reginald Hudlin that no one ever expected would become a linchpin of the Marvel Universe: a maroon archive, in and of itself, which existed in a liminal space between official Black culture and mythical nostalgia. As such, this chapter contemplates the possibility that these so-called uto-pias might take physical or metaphorical form in ways that disrupt per-ceptions of what they actually are. What does it mean to think of Black ephemera—random, inconsequential Blackness—as fugitive archival matter, as marooned archives? And what of the question of aesthetics, particularly in the context of abstract expression, which, as Zamalin argues, was made political by Black utopia, "because it revised the normative horizon necessary for liberation"?[4] These themes can be found in the work of Ghanaian filmmaker John Akomfrah, whose film *The Last Angel in History* precedes the *Black Panther* film by more the twenty years, and in the extant archives of Black life.

Decamping Wakanda

Much has been made of the confrontation between the cautious T'Challa and the "woke" Killmonger in the film *Black Panther*—both characters as extensions of a substantive debate within Black thought about isolationism versus engagement that is historically rendered as nationalist verses integrationist debates within Black America. As Adam Serwer observes, "*Black Panther* is about a highly advanced African kingdom, yes, but its core theme is Pan-Africanism, a belief that no matter how seemingly distant black people's lives and struggles are from each other, we are in a sense "cousins" who bear a responsibility to help one another escape oppression."[5] Serwer also notes how the "woke" Killmonger's desires easily devolve into a demand for Black hegemony, which lies dormant in Wakanda itself and might explain the relationship of the Jabari Tribe to these strains of Black thought, who choose to remain in isolation, but within Wakanda's borders. Indeed it is the Jabari Tribe, as representing an alternative stream of Black thought within the *Black Panther* film, that animates my interest in Wakanda—specifically, the tribe's choice to *hide in plain sight*, if you will, as Maroons.

However they function in the world, Black people have done so with a critical understanding of the value of cultivating a world of Blackness beyond the gaze of Whiteness. This often compelled the old cultural guard of the 1960s and 1970s to romanticize, even memorialize, Black institutions that seemingly only served the logics of legal segregation, like the Negro Leagues and historically Black colleges and universities.

One of the more resonant examples of a Black utopia, or, more fittingly, "promised land" narratives of the late twentieth century, is Derrick Bell's short story "Afroatlantica Landing," from his collection of short fiction *Faces at the Bottom of the Well* (1992). In this collection, and others such as *And We Are Not Saved: The Elusive Quest for Racial Justice* (1987) and *Gospel Choirs: Psalms of Survival in an Alien Land Called Home* (1997), Bell utilizes short fiction and parables, to make more accessible insights derived from the field of critical race theory with regard to questions of racial and gender discrimination and debates about legal remedies to these issues.

In "Afroatlantica Landing," the mythical island of Atlantis emerges from the ocean, and despite the imperialist desires of the United States and others to colonize the land, no one can survive on the island; landing teams are literally unable to breathe there, with the exception of a lone African American, who is then followed by a party of African Americans who are also able to survive on the island. Bell writes, "The party felt exhilarated and euphoric . . . it was an invigorating experience of heightened self-esteem, of liberation, of waking up," and as such the discourse around the region—now referred to by the characters as "Afroatlantica"—shifts from that of American colonialism and imperialism to that of Black American emigration.[6] This discursive shift within the short story could be interpreted as Bell attempting to bring some closure to the ongoing debates about the so-called "Negro Problem."

Yet the possibilities rendered by the "reparations subsidy" offered by the US government to entice the mass emigration of Black Americans—to be paid back if said Black Americans chose to return within a decade—were fleeting.[7] When Black Americans mount ships with the intention of settling Afroatlantica, the memories of Marcus Garvey's Black Star Line in the collective memory, the island disappears as mysteriously as it appeared. Yet, as Bell writes, "They felt deep satisfaction—sober now, to be sure—in having gotten this far into their enterprise, in having accomplished it together . . . the miracle of Afrolantica was replaced by a greater miracle. Black discovered that they themselves actually possessed the qualities of liberation they had hoped *to* realize *in their new homeland.*"[8] A cautionary tale from the late Bell, who demystified legal theory for lay audiences in these series of short story collections, "Afroatlantica Landing" highlighted the fluidity of the promised land, if not freedom itself, and the relative power associated with movement and flight, notions that find resonance in examples of Black marronage.

The inclusion of a third stream of Wakanda thought, if you will, maps loosely onto the experience of American Maroons, as described by Sylvianne A. Diouf in her book *Slavery's Exile: The Story of American Maroons.* As Diouf writes, American Maroons "stood at the intersection of three worlds. One was their refuge, another the white controlled territories of the field, The Big House outbuildings, and sometimes the Big House itself."[9] Of the third more liminal site of marronage, Diouf writes, "the third was the physical and social terrain carved out by the enslaved community, from the quarters to the neighboring plantations and fields"—what we might think of as a site of Blackness as subterfuge and meaningful play. As Diouf notes, "To be successful maroons needed to build and maintain a symbiotic relation with these three geographical and social modes."[10] Of the physical terrain inhabited by American Maroons, "borderlands and hinterlands formed the 'maroon landscape,' a vast area whose several parts were connected by secret paths, discreet trails, and waterways navigated under cover of night and whose outer, intangible, limits reached, dangerously, into the plantations and cities."[11]

Diouf's description of American maroon life on the margins evokes notions of cultures of secrecy and interiority, of the need to develop social and cultural practices that are not meant to be accessible in the public sphere, that pivot on sustainability and survival, the consumption of which as commodities would be unfathomable. This is not to deny that American Maroons engaged in commercial practices; as Diouf notes, "Maroons traded goods in the underground market because they needed articles they had grown accustomed to and could not find in the woods or had trouble getting on plantations."[12] Yet in these commercial practices, and in the creation of domestic spaces in secluded places, where spirituality, kinship, and intimacy could be cultivated, American Maroons were creating culture that would also exist as an extension of marronage.

If we think of the *Black Panther* franchise, in all of its earlier iterations, as that which was formerly hidden in plain sight, and the Jabari Tribe as a particular example of a maroon society within the franchise, I'd like to consider both as elements of Black ephemera—specifically, as marooned and even fugitive ephemera. In his book *Freedom as Marronage*, Neil Roberts notes that "Maroonage conventionally refers to a group of persons isolating themselves from a surrounding society in order to create a fully autonomous community."[13] But Roberts adds nuance to this definition, suggesting that "contemporary political theory"—and contemporary mainstream cultural criticism—"lacks a sufficient vocabulary to describe the activity of flight and the dialectical mechanisms operating during the flight process."[14] He writes, "Marronage fills the discursive void. Marronage is a multidimensional, constant act of flight."[15] Taking some liberties with Roberts's observation that "freedom is not a place; it is a state of being," I'd like to offer the following remix: "The [archive] is not a place [or thing]; it is a state of being."[16]

The Last Angel and the Fugitive Archive

In light of my interest in embodying Black ephemera as maroon, among the various forms of marronage identified by Roberts I am particularly struck by what he describes as "sociogenic marronage," or "macropolitical flight whereby agents flee . . . through non-fleeting acts of naming, vèvè architectonics, liberation, reordering of the state of society, and constitutionalism."[17] As Roberts describes it, "[Sociogenic marronage] is a non-sovereign state of being whose conception of freedom is shaped by cognition, metaphysics, egalitarianism, hope for refuge, and the experiences of masses in a social and political order. *Condition, not place, is vital to its phenomenology*" (my emphasis).[18] Roberts's notion of sociogenic marronage finds cultural resonance in his reading of the influential Carribeanist Édouard Glissant, in whose *The Fourth Century* (*Le Quatrième siècle*), Roberts locates the blueprint for sociogenic marronage in four stages: "rearticulating a philosophy of history"; reconciling two theories of recognizing history and projecting forward in "Retour" ("the yearning to return to a single origin and fixed state of being") and "Détour" ("the desire to acquire freedom in a place or medium other than your transplanted homeland"); "resistance"; and "Antillanité," which, Roberts suggests, encompasses cultivating "collective experiences and convert[ing] them into conscious expressions".[19]

Whereas Glissant was concerned with recovering a lost history (that is, an archive) of his native Martinique, filmmaker John Akomfrah seems rather consumed with recovering something more ephemeral in *The Last Angel in History* (1996). In this film Akomfrah introduces the figure of the "data thief," whom narrator Edward George also describes as a "bad boy, scavenger, poet figure." The "data thief" is essentially a time traveler, going back to the past, and even to the future, to recover "techno fossils" and fragments of Black culture either lost to circumstance and memory or stolen. Cassandra L. Jones describes *The Last Angel in History* as an exploration of a "utopian view of the internet as a site of liberated information prevalent during the 1990s. This free flow of data allows the marginalized 'thief' to pilfer information, dislodged from time, joining the past and present in a fluid yet decidedly black, identity."[20]

Akromfrah and George were founding members of the Black Audio Film Collective (BAFC), which also included Reece Auguiste, Avril Johnson, Trevor Mathison, Claire Joseph, and Lina Gopaul, who, with Akomfrah and later member David Lawson, formed Smoking Dog Films in 1999. In many ways, BAFC was born out of a crisis of the archive: an effort to piece together narratives about Black identity in Britain via what these filmmakers referred to as "slide-tape-texts." As curator Zoé Whitley writes, "Imagery and ephemera for the slide tapes came from a variety of sources . . . unwanted books and back issues of National Geographic; pictures were reproduced from colonial textbooks, volumes checked out from a college library. . . . The artists would frequently buy titles, and then sell them back to the same booksellers after capturing desired images."[21]

Critical to their use of slide film—the material of choice, given the collective's lack of resources prior to the availability of digital film—was their approximation of the moving image. Of the materiality of slide film, Whitley notes that "layering is made possible by its transparent surface, and its very existence is dependent on a visible transition from formation to dissolution."[22] Thus, for the BAFC, the functional value of "slide-tape-texts" mirrored a theoretical one, as they were "a constant working of writing and writing," where the "slide-tape-texts were evolving variations of their theme," as Whitley observes.[23] The BAFC's ethics of repurposing in its early days represented one of the ways that the collective negotiated the crisis of the Black archive. In many regards, then, the "data thief" in *The Last Angel of History* might be considered a metaphor for the BAFC's work.

The themes of liminality (as evidenced in the use of slide-tape-texts) and loss run throughout many of Akomfrah's films. Culture remains in the realm of ephemera in *The Last Angel of History*; rarely can anything be concretely recovered, beyond an impression or a gesture. Culture exists in the film as more of an absence, a ghost-like presence, or what Richard Iton refers to as a "duppy state," which "marks the potent afterlife, mocking persistence, and resurgence—rather than the remission—of coloniality: the state that is 'there and not there' at the same time."[24] Laura U. Marks is even more specific: "*The Last Angel of History* is composed around ruins and palimpsests . . . a view that history is almost entirely lost to us, unless one can seize on the briefest of clues as they flash in the rubble."[25]

The Last Angel of History, and Akomfrah's work more generally, seem most concerned with the communal aspects embedded in the recovery of culture and the excavation of "ruins." Stoffel Debuysere makes a similar point in writing about Akomfrah's earlier film *Handsworth Songs* (1986), a meditation on the Handsworth riots of 1985, in which violence broke out in a largely Black and Asian section of Birmingham, England, in response to police brutality. The riots occurred four years after similar riots had taken place in Handsworth, which had one of the highest unemployment rates in Britain during the period. Some of the disaffected were progeny of the "Windrush": a generation of Caribbean migrants to Britain, so named because they first arrived in the late 1940s via the HMT *Empire Windrush*. The Windrush generation was also marked by the failure of the State to provide adequate opportunity after the specific labor needs that instigated their arrival dissipated, as well as by England's later attempts to renege on the promise of citizenship.[26] As the film captures and Debuysere writes, "The sense of loss that transpires is a loss of place and time, of history and identity, a loss that cannot be recovered but leaves behind its traces, in images of arrival and words of longing."[27]

Like *Handsworth Songs*, *The Last Angel of History* is obsessed with the traces, resonances, and residue of Black culture—to use the words of Christina Sharpe, what is left "in the wake"—as if chasing a fugitive culture. The question of why culture might be "on the run" speaks to the existential realities of the way culture might be lost, and the structural realities in which culture might also be stolen. Beyond macrodiscussions of Black cultural loss, where the transatlantic slave trade looms large, for the purposes of my discussion of Black ephemera I am more concerned with the microlevels on which this loss might manifest. In terms of Black marronage, as well as the attributes of fugitivity and hiding in plain sight, how does one carry culture? Or, more specific to this project, how does one travel with an archive, even an archive that, as I argue, exists more as ephemera than in boxes and bins? On a basic level this is a question of capacity, as in what literally can be used to carry archives forward. Krista Thompson observes accordingly in her book *Shine: The Visual Economy of Light in African Diasporic Aesthetic Practice*, "Blackness continues to connote fungibility." As such, the Black archive might itself be thought of as fungible.[28]

Marks alludes to this fungibility with regard to the lack of material culture in *The Last Angel of History*. Writing about Akomfrah's use of montages throughout the film, Marks identifies two kinds: one that exists stationary within the frame—what we might think of as the always already known within the archive, recognizable as visual hypertext—and another that is "decidedly noncognitive . . . in which worlds of images speed by our own eyes, too fast to comprehend" and viewers are left with shadowy impressions.[29] These images, along with Akonfrah's use of in-frame triptychs (which would become a regular feature of his films and installations), often of computer screens, places at the forefront his use of databases as digital ephemera. "The reason we cannot really see the images in *Last Angel*'s subliminal montages is that the film is not really showing us images: it is showing a database," Marks writes. "The Data Thief is collecting all possibly relevant fragments into a vast database, of which we perceive only a very few entries."[30] Indeed, as narrator George notes in the film, the data thief is armed with a "black box," a handheld device that seems to function as a data collector. In this way, *The Last Angel in History* anticipates the emergence of the Internet and smartphones as mainstream tools for communication, data collection, and sharing, as well as broadband and big data.

I reference big data here to suggest that the data thief is not simply recovering lost Black ephemera, but siphoning Black ephemera from more pronounced entities—the State, global corporations—who possess ownership in *this* moment; hence the term "data thief." Here musician George Clinton's observation in *The Last Angel of History* that "Black had become commercial" is of note in thinking of Black culture as not only a commodity, but also as an accompaniment, literally, to American empire. To address a question of capacity with regard to ownership of data, I'd like to think a bit beyond the obvious examples of corporations and those with individual wealth (like art collectors) as "culture vultures" or "culture bandits." Accepting the premise that Black culture, even as analog, was always already big data, and that it was always well-resourced entities—universities, museums, national archives, entertainment conglomerates—that possessed the greatest capacity to house, maintain, archive, and thus profit from Black culture (however ill-gottenly gained), what is to be said about the shift from analog to digital, where the archives themselves become more expansive and more ephemeral, and thus more expensive to maintain? Jones is clear on this question: "The data thief moves through archives, gaining access to locations previously denied him, slipping past the gate-keepers of sites of knowledge production. With his ability to move with impunity through artificially constructed barricades, he liberates knowledge for the consumption of all."[31] In a moment when Black archival matter functions as contraband, Akomfrah had little choice but to figure Black cultural workers, including critics—both represented in *The Last Angel of History*—as being engaged in illicit activity.

If the data thief is consumed with reclaiming what had been lost, there's the additional concern over what also gets lost in the transference of archives from analog to digital. Krista Thompson takes this up in her book *Shine: The Visual Economy of Light in African Diasporic Aesthetic Practice*, where she writes of street photographers in the Caribbean who, when creating digital representations, "habitually erase the files after printing them, in effect creating non reproducible images like Polaroids. These forms of picture-making are not solely bound to celluloid or built of pixels but appear both to invest in and to disavow, exceed, or eschew the material image."[32] While these photographers might simply be concerned with maximizing available digital space—reminiscent of how Motown would erase and reuse tape in the 1960s to maximize their utility—these actions suggest a commitment to producing a nonreproducible culture that exists beyond excessive commodification.

Thompson's discussion highlights the elusiveness of the Black archive, existing in an uncertain state, not unlike the physical aspects of Black marronage, in which enslaved Africans in the eighteenth and nineteenth centuries resisted the reach of a dehumanizing and exploitative market culture by embracing a condition of unsettledness. The photos by the Caribbean photographers, she writes, "linger in between representational states, appearing simultaneously like an analog and digital photographic form, like a still photograph or a moving image."[33] To personify archives as American Maroons is to think of Black archival matter as committed to "foolproof concealment, the exploitation of their natural environment," where, as Diouf writes, "secrecy and the particular ecology of their refuges forced them to devise specific ways to occupy the land and to hide within it."[34] Here I'd like to think of containers and the ability of marooned Black archival matter to adapt to the technologies of a given time. This is in part what the film's narrator George refers to when he describes blues artist Robert Johnson—the patron saint of *The Last Angel of History*—as selling his soul (as the popular mythology suggests) for a "Black technology."

I'd like to settle on the sound of Johnson's guitar, and sounds that more generally might have appeared as an abstraction even to Black audiences when Johnson's new technology first emerged in the 1930s. In his book *Abstractionist Aesthetics: Artistic Form and Social Critique in African American Culture*, Phillip Brian Harper observes the proclivity among social critics and audiences for Black art that connotes "modes of depiction that are properly race-proud and affirmative," which asserts an "empiricist demand that racialized representations perceptibly mirror real-world phenomena, however favorable—or not—any particular portrayal may seem."[35] Harper speaks here about the visual realm, which, in Black abstract art, is admittedly overdetermined, but he is also concerned with the "extent that this positivist ethic restricts the scope of artistic practice."[36] His concerns highlight the sense that Black realism—which, for the sake of argument, I'll term the Black "Really, Real"—is overdetermined, generally in Black art, and inherently more reproducible and thus commodifiable, to say nothing of the hypervisibility tethered to Black realism. Commercial and even Black communal desires for the Black "Really, Real" go against the need and desire for fugitive and maroon arts practices. Harper argues for the "displacement of realism as a primary stake in African American cultural engagement," citing the "critical utility of an alternative aesthetic mode" that he characterizes as abstractionism.[37]

Challenging the hegemony of visual art as the site of Black abstract art, Harper suggests that "we might on the contrary imagine that African American music offers an optimum site for abstractionism-driven critique. Music is, after all, held to constitute the quintessence of black culture while at the same time being generally conceived as the epitome of aesthetic abstraction."[38] Harper's suggestion resonates with the work of Akomfrah and the BAFC, whose collective genius lies in its reimagining of the contents of the Black archive as not quite historical documents, not quite photographs, and not quite film. Critical to this reimagining is the collective's utilization of music as archive material. As Whitley observes, "What is audible is never an afterthought meant solely to accompany an image, but rather an integral part of the audiovisual experience."[39] Gopaul adds, "Music creates an emotional landscape. . . . Creating an inner sound world has always been our biggest tool."[40]

In *The Last Angel of History*, Akomfrah locates Lee "Scratch" Perry, Sun Ra, and George Clinton as critical interlocutors—three artists working within the genres of reggae, jazz and funk whose work serves as archival material for much contemporary Black popular music, notably hip-hop, and could easily be read, per Harper, as abstractionist. Akomfrah's use of Perry, Clinton, and Sun Ra as artistic triptychs within the film was in part inspired by the work of music critic John Corbett, who argues that the trio "constructed worlds of their own, futuristic environs that subtly Signify on the marginalization of black culture."[41]

Of particular interest is Corbett's observation that the three musicians use containers—Clinton's "Mothership," Sun Ra's "Arkestra," and Perry's "Black Ark"—as unreasonable vessels for travel in discursive space, and by "unreasonable," I'd like to suggest that Corbett means disruptive.[42] In this sense, the fictive trio trouble concepts of space—the idea of space travel functioning as a more on-the-nose metaphor for all three artists—which in their collective worldview serves as a metaphor for "social marginalization," or of "being elsewhere, or perhaps of making this elsewhere your own."[43] That on-the-nose quality of space travel also places the three artists, along with *The Last Angel of History*, within the realm of science fiction, or what André M. Carrington adroitly refers to as the "speculative fiction of Blackness."[44]

Carrington describes this "speculative fiction" as a system of cultural production that coalesces around the concepts of "Afrofuturism, surrealism, Otherhood, and haunting," which in their own ways reconsider "how genre conventions and the distinctions between them have played a role in the struggle over interpretations of what it means to be Black."[45] All four concepts are relevant to thinking about *The Last Angel of History*, but the concepts of Afrofuturism and surrealism resonate in particular because they, as Carrington argues, "draw our attention to aspects of African American culture that would otherwise go overlooked."[46] As a counter to the realism that Harper scrutinizes, Black science fiction or Black speculative fiction might be thought of as one aspect of Black abstractionism. Writing about *The Last Angel of History*'s own relationship to "African diaspora science fiction," Marks suggests that the genre "unpacks fragmentary artifacts that indicate a buried past, modeling history on imaginations of the future. It mourns pasts that can never be recollected, and incorporates unknowns when facts do not serve."[47]

As musicians invested in broad and fantastic mythologies, George Clinton, Sun Ra and Lee "Scratch" Perry negotiate what Harper considers, the "delicate balance between subtle sophistication and incomprehensible obscurity."[48] What Harper terms a "delicate balance" represents important aspects of Black representation: to mirror the genius of Black musical innovation and interpretation in a form that is accessible and recognizable, and thus readily available for affirmation by a skeptical mainstream, while willingly pushing that genius to the margins of musical illegibility, so as not to be easily reproducible and commodifiable. This is the challenge of the Black archive writ large, the double move of reclamation and obscurity, claiming the value of the Black archive as meaningful, living, and knowable culture (to those who have long claimed the Black folk lacked culture), yet resisting desires to reduce the Black archive to its universality in the marketplace, in which its prominence might be misconstrued as evidence of cultural inclusion and equity.

With this tension decidedly unresolved, I'd like to briefly return to the *Black Panther* film franchise, if only as a false or at least unsatisfiable contrast to *The Last Angel of History*, despite their shared legacies to Black Science Fiction or Afrofuturism (to highlight an overdetermined term), and in light of questions of hypervisibility, marronage, fugitivity and abstraction. Unlike the promised land of marronage, *Black Panther* is not a promised land *hidden* in plain sight, but simply a promised land— and, really, what is promised here?—*in plain sight*. As a cultural product, *Black Panther* demands additional sets of principles of survival for Black cultural workers and artists that are not unlike what many previous generations responded to in light of the historic trading and trafficking in Black cultural production. American Black cultural production (or, at least, the means of its production) manages to be both obscure and overdetermined at the same time. Accordingly, the production of Blackness *in plain sight*—to be hidden would almost be an oxymoron within a consumer capitalist structure, hence the value of abstraction—has generated legitimate wealth for a small number of African Americans (and quite a few more folk of non-African descent) and inspired charges of both real and imagined cultural appropriation, exploitation, and theft of resources that were intended to be more than mass consumables—the very conditions that give rise to Akomfrah's "data thief."

The material question at hand is what comes after a *Black Panther*, or any hypervisual and hyperaccessible Black cultural production, given the issues of ownership and capacity that the *Last Angel of History* mediates (Michael Jackson's whole career post-*Thriller* and, increasingly, Beyoncé's, could be embedded in this inquiry). What should the reasonable expectations be, since the material stakes of production and consumption have seemingly changed due to the brand's success? Margo Natalie Crawford offers some insight in her examination of the Black Arts Movement in her book *Black Post Blackness: The Black Arts Movement and Twenty-First-Century Aesthetics*: "Blackness remains that elusive 'Flash of the spirit' that moves through the Black Arts Movement to twenty-first century black aesthetics."[49] The Black Arts Movement represented a then-unprecedented flowering of *national* Black cultural production (subtly distinct from the Harlem Renaissance), which manifested itself across multiple media platforms, including television, film, music, literature, drama, and visual art. It was a moment that was unsustainable for a number of reasons, including the lack of viable Black-owned infrastructures of production and the ambivalence experienced by Black cultural workers with regard to making Blackness accessible to a larger audience.

For Crawford, the sustainability of the movement can be referenced in those arts collectives, like AfriCOBRA and BLKARTSOUTH, that were committed to a politics of abstraction and an aesthetics of anticipation. As Crawford writes, "The Black radical imagination is profoundly anticipatory. Anticipation opens up a new way of thinking about the relationship between earlier and later cultural moments" as "the temporary dissonance between what has already settled into recognizable movement and what is emerging creates the ongoing flow of Black aesthetics."[50] Crawford argues that these productive tensions find resonance in notions of the "not yet finished"—"the unsettled nature of the [Black Arts Movement] as it moved through the different regions of the United States and transnational sites of pan-Africanism"[51]—and an aesthetics of "just left behind," where *Black Panther* might be viewed as a rearview iteration of Blackness that informs but does not define Black cultural production.[52] The sustainability of Black culture is deeply implicated in its portability, and perhaps aesthetic freedom is connected to our willingness to "just [leave] behind" Wakanda.

The existential crisis of what it means to carry culture—an archive—as opposed to leaving it behind, explains, in part, a move toward Black interiority by Black cultural producers or what Crawford describes as a "public interiority." Citing the antimuseum ethos of the Black Arts Movement ("What can blackness be when it is not treated like an object in a museum?"), Crawford notes that this "public interiority was created when inner space was mobilized, during the BAM, through outdoor murals," specifically highlighting the Wall of Respect mural in Chicago produced in 1967. Public murals like the Wall of Respect represent efforts to channel Black interiority to a distinct Black Public—in this instance, Chicago—while also conveying the expansiveness of Blackness in ways that resist institutional containment. Created by the Organization of Black American Culture (OBAC), a multiplatform arts collective that began to form around gatherings arranged in 1966 by literary critic Hoyt W. Fuller, poet Conrad Kent Rivers, and Gerald McWorter (the future Abdul Akalimat), the Wall of Respect was notable in the implicit ephemeral aspects of its creation and its ultimate destruction.

As Rebecca VanDiver writes, "The Wall functioned as a mirror of sorts and responded in medias res to the events of the day. Once in place, the mural was no longer the product of the OBAC artists, but a part of the surrounding community."[53] In this way, the Wall of Respect anticipates the kinds of crowd-sourced projects that would emerge in the digital era, often out of necessity, purposefully constructed to be ultimately ephemeral in response to shifting digital landscapes. As artist Jeff Donaldson told Crawford, the Wall of Respect was "never meant to be a permanent thing; it was meant to be something that changed with the movement," adding that "once the wall became a rallying point for a lot of things, the city's power brokers were nervous."[54] The Wall of Respect serves as a reminder of the possible dangers of what gets left behind for a fugitive culture. Such was the case with the Wall of Respect, which was destroyed along with the building it was painted on after a suspicious fire in 1971. Not surprisingly, the Wall of Respect survives in memory as a form of Black interiority—in the shape of the many who carry the wall with them.

Black Genius and the "Precarity" of the Archive

The ethic of "just left behind" that Crawford addresses in *Black Post-Blackness* and the cultivation of a public interiority speak directly to the idea of a fugitive archive: How does one index and project forward that which is left behind when a fugitive culture decamps? Whereas Crawford was most concerned with traditional visual arts, in light of the work of Akomfrar and the Black Audio Film Collective I'd like to consider the role of the moving image as a form of public interiority.

As much as *The Last Angel of History* narrates an ongoing struggle between Black cultural production and capital, Black bodies and commerce, in the midst of forced and intentional migrations, Akomfrah's later film *Precarity* offers a meditation on what gets lost, what disappears, with that decampment. Given the obsession of many with origin narratives—as much to claim some corporate ownership as to mark as illegitimate the Black genius that might have been at that origin's foundation—it becomes the labor of artists, critics, and theorists alike to animate the afterlives of fugitive archives long left in the wake. This is more than recovery work, or even the work of discovery (which it so often must be), but the work of imagination and creativity, as fictive realities that align with the very business of disappearing in plain sight: the slip of the hand is the slip of the archive. As Christina Sharpe offers in her book *In the Wake: On Blackness and Being*, "Rather than seeking a resolution to blackness's ongoing and irresolvable abjection, one might approach Black being in the wake as a form of consciousness."[55] Both Louis Armstrong and Akomfrah might have considered the early twentieth-century jazz musican Buddy Bolden as an example of that consciousness.

"Old Buddy Bolden blew so hard that I used to wonder if I would ever have enough lung power to fill one of those cornets" wrote Louis Armstrong, himself considered an authenticator of the origin story of jazz, of his experience as a five-year-old outside of Funky Butt Hall when he presumably first heard Charles "Buddy" Bolden play.[56] Armstrong adds a caveat to his observation: "Buddy Bolden was a great musician, but I think he blew too hard. I will even go so far to stay that he did not blow correctly. . . . Bolden had the biggest reputation, but even as a small kid I believed in finesse."[57] Dead men like Bolden, who "finally went crazy," as Armstrong describes, are in no position to dispute the assertions of jazz's arguably greatest innovator and ambassador, especially when no recorded archive of your genius exists. One could argue that by appearing in the second chapter of an autobiography whose aim is to establish Louis Armstrong as the alpha and omega of America's classical music, published in 1954 at a moment when be-bop and hard bop were rendering him a musical and racial relic, Armstrong doth protest too much.

Nearly two decades before *Precarity*, Akomfrah produced *The Wonderful World of Louis Armstrong (1999)* for the BBC—one of the first projects from Smoking Dog Films. "At the time, I was convinced that Armstrong was the foundational figure of jazz," says Akomfrah, but he was encouraged to take another run through the jazz archive after reading Michael Ondaatje's fictionalized account of Bolden in his 1976 novel *Coming through Slaughter*.[58] In his *New York Times* review of the book, Anatole Broyard writes, "The author gives us all the broken pieces and leaves it to us to infer the final form."[59] It was that unfinished aspect of Bolden's story that made him appealing to Akomfrah as an "emblematic diasporic figure" whose "historical traces are thin, the presence is fragile . . . but you know he's there because he's left this kind of ghost line of his presence in the music." Bolden, he added, was "symptomatic of the African Diaspora."[60]

In *Precarity*, Akomfrah's visual meditation on the life and art of Buddy Bolden, the filmmaker seeks not to recreate the moment that could be mythically referred to as a birth, nor does he seek to tell the facts of the story, but dares to provide glimpses into the literal precarity of Black genius and thus the precarity of the archive. Who is to care for and nurture the genius of those for whom citizenship—and, worse still, humanity—was thought to be at best a liminal existence? Yet any attempt to document the genius of Bolden, the one who blew so hard, will be rife with that which was not documented and thus can never be documented. As Michael Ondaatje writes in *Coming through Slaughter*, "There is only one photograph that exists today of Bolden and the band . . . as a photograph is not good or precise, partly because the print was found after the fire."[61] Bolden's peak years from 1899 to 1907 began at the dawn of the phonograph, only two years after Thomas Edison's invention was trademarked as the gramaphone, but who would waste such a cutting-edge technology on capturing a "genius" that Bolden's Blackness suggests, and some might have believed could not possibly exist in him?

Throughout *Precarity*, audiences bear witness to images of Blackness in the form of photographs rendered pristine under the cover of water's flow, all too familiar "deep river(s)" like the ones Jubilee Singers turned into a Negro standard in the late 1800s. In an interview Akonfrah acknowledges, "The key deities of West Africa are water-centered, and most of them are deities of memory."[62] Water, in this case, becomes yet another container for fugitive archives; as Akonfrah explains, "When you want to summon the gods, you pour libations, you pour water on the ground, and you start a series of incantations, and it's through the incantatory logic of your speech that they are supposed to come"—or, by extension, the "incantatory logic" of the fugitive archive.[63] In the film we hear Bolden, voiced by Christopher Udoh, "I am the only thing alive. I am one with the water." and the totality of water as a container is made apparent, yet water—flow—is also a metaphor for a nonextant archive, in that it can never be fully captured.

As Allyson Nadia Field's writes in her book *Uplift Cinema: The Emergence of African American Film and the Possibility of Black Modernity*, "Language surrounding non-extant film largely falls into three categories of terms, often invoked in combination: the historical artifact, the perishable organic, and the spiritual. . . . The last category answers the perceived lack evoked by the first two, and thereby establishes film restoration and preservation as a near-messianic solution, invoked with terms such as saving and resurrection."[64] Fields notes the responsibilities of scholars of Black film to "treat non-extant films as having the same concerns and import as their extant counterparts. If we do not look adjacently at these elements of film history . . . we risk missing the rich, albeit ephemeral, archive of the majority of films produced in this period."[65] While Fields is referring specifically to early Black cinema, her observations are also applicable to the nonextant archives of musical figures such as Buddy Bolden. The crisis of the nonextant archive is in part the crisis of Black genius—a genius that was obscured, ignored, and disregarded in its formative moments, as the documented silence and invisibility of Black Genius—the lack of evidence of things unseen and unheard to offer a Baldwinian mix—is reflected in the White gaze as indices of a genius that was always already lacking in the archive.

Hence, Bolden's "biographer" David Marquis could argue, echoing his source material, that "Bolden was not a genius: he attempted to follow through on the music and couldn't, which caused him great frustration and led to the public displays of rebellion against society that were his downfall and acted as a catalyst in his monumental battle with alcohol," as if Bolden simply lived in his head with the music and didn't live in a world. Marquis writes as if society was some innocuous force in Bolden's life, and that his life was not defined by the violence and trauma that accompanied the policing of the color line.[66]

Marquis further asserts of the music that would claim Bolden as its innovator, "Although their sound was alien to some, it had an appeal, especially to a liberated, post-Civil War generation of young blacks."[67] Here Marquis highlights the music and ethos of a generationally specific cohort, particularly those born after the Emancipation Proclamation like Bolden, who might fully understand the claim, via Udoh's Bolden, that "being a problem is a strange experience." Udoh is remixing Du Bois's well-known query "How does it feel to be a problem?"[68] It is with this query that Du Bois builds out his concept of double consciousness, which Akomfrah deploys in the film as six distinct properties—fluidity, plasticity, fugitivity, enjambment, waywardness, and immanence—with the film's triptych. This further complicates Du Bois's now flattened existentialist observations about Black life in ways that may only have been legible to the cohort of late nineteenth-century Black Americans to which Bolden belonged. Notably, those six properties of double consciousness might also represent dimensions of Black nonextant and fugitive archives as well.

Bolden's story presumably ends in the Louisiana State Insane Asylum, where he was committed in 1907 and remained until his death twenty-three years later. Marquis suggests that Bolden did, on occasion, pick up his instrument while institutionalized and "seemingly retained traces of his old touch and mannerisms."[69] Ondaatje offers some idea of how Bolden might have processed his new surroundings: "Here. Where I am anonymous and alone in a white room with no history and no parading. So I can make something unknown in the shape of this room. . . . I first began to play, back when I was unaware that reputation made the room narrower and narrower.[70] We might consider Bolden to be grappling with containment and containers here: a lack of which rendered genius illegible to a world both oblivious to and suspicious of Black genius and a sound forever lost to interiority, for even the ephemera that Bolden produced is no representation of what he might have heard in his head. Marquis notes that few "were aware of his former reputation. He was just another black patient who talked to himself, babbled incoherently and walked around ritualistically touching objects."[71] Bolden could be said to have struggled with a fugitive archive for which there was no technology for presentation, his babbling a form of afrofuturist signaling to Robert Johnson, Billie Holiday, Jimi Hendrix, Nina Simone, as well as a host of other Black futures.

Significantly, since there are no recordings of Bolden playing, the music of *Precarity*, represented in the film with moving images of Bolden's band, is rendered silent, wholly given to interiority. That we might think of fugitive archives as possessing qualities of interiority and silence, yet still "musical," in this instance, offers another layer to considering the project of a fugitive Blackness. Throughout *The Last Angel of History* and *Precarity*, Akomfrah makes a compelling case for the centrality of the musical and the sonic—culture that you can indeed carry with you—as the most critical conduit, portal, or container for Black fugitive archives. Though much has been said about the digital nature of Black fugitive archives, the relationship the of digital and the analog is a rich site to explore the fugitivity of the Black archive.

"Like half-eaten cake": Analog Interiorities and the Black Archive

Harper notes the paradoxical role of Black music as "at once the most abstract and the blackest of all the arts."[72] Even as Harper acknowledges Black music as the "most abstract" and the Blackest of arts, he offers this caveat: "However, the means by which music accedes to blackness—and, more to the point, racial blackness itself—consists not in specifically sonic modality but in a narrative discursivity that is not properly musical at all."[73] What Harper signals here is the relationship between music and narrative, beyond the obvious function of lyrics. What stories do the sounds of Blackness tell? What does the sound of Blackness tell us about its own fugitivity? Harper offers, "If African American blackness is itself a function of narrative, the disclosure of narrative's socially abstracted quality would seem to promise an equally unsettling and productive disturbance of received ideas about both that blackness and the sociopolitical contexts in which it derives its meaning."[74] We might also think of fugitive archives as serving such a function.

In a historical moment of Blackness perhaps most powerfully articulated in the hegemony of Black visuality, Black sound—music and other discourses of sound culture—seemingly no longer functions as the singular lingua franca of the Black American experience. The utility of Black music was most pronounced in its accessibility: as a live, community-based form as well as through recorded media and its analog distribution via the airwaves. With the emergence of relatively inexpensive handheld digital technology, which was revolutionized more than a generation ago with the personalization of the listening experience with the Walkman, the ease with which the visual can be placed in the service of Blackness, both as archive and live action, might be unprecedented.

This contemporary era has been defined by acts of Black self-documentation—the selfie as the new mode of communal and aspirational Blackness, as well as in the production of Black visual archives. As art historian Krista Thompson observes, "Technologies facilitate a shared visual literacy and spectacular visibility, which is manifest in the way diasporic subjects engage in shared performances of visibility—practices that involve staging the act of being seen and being seen in the act of being seen."[75] Perhaps these images also signal communal fugitivity, if we are to consider their function as visual travelogues of communities in transit, experiencing statelessness, or sheltering-in-place, for whatever reasons. Accordingly, we might also acknowledge the use of handheld digital technology as a means of countersurveillance of the State, particularly in the many instances of police malfeasance against Black and Brown bodies. This latter role mirrors that of photojournalists, Black and White, who captured many of the iconic as well as everyday moments of the Black liberation movement of the 1960s and 1970s.

As historian Mark Speltz notes in his book *North of Dixie: Civil Rights Photography Beyond the South*, however, "Photojournalists made hundreds of photographs during the civil rights era, but only a small percentage ever made it to print. Many of these beckon us to look past the most dramatic scenes."[76] Even as projects like Speltz's help to unearth aspects of the Black archive of the 1960s, they offer yet more examples of the corporate control of representations of Blackness—a fact often highlighted when digital dives reveal those archives not to be fugitive, but owned by, for example, Getty Images, as the company's stamp on many of these images and prominent warnings about reusing them remind us. In contrast to these corporate-owned photographic archives, we are witnessing both the crowdsourcing and sharing of visual content on social media platforms like Twitter and Instagram (albeit also corporately owned) that help transverse the political, editorial, and intellectual property constraints faced by photojournalists in the 1960s, for example, and some curators of the Black archive in the contemporary moment.

Additionally, with mainstream media platforms and cultural institutions in need of content, first as a response to the "Obama era" and then as a gesture to obscure the lack of real racial equity in the face of rebranded White supremacy, we have seen a proliferation of high- and middlebrow Black visual culture in the form of highly publicized exhibitions, such as Kara Walker's *A Subtlety, or the Marvelous Sugar Baby*,

Carrie Mae Weems's retrospective at the Guggenheim, and Kehinde Wiley's *A New Republic* and *Soul of a Nation: Art in the Age of Black Power, 1963–1983*, which was originally mounted at the Tate Modern before traveling to the United States. To this we might also add cinematic efforts such as Steve McQueen's *12 Years a Slave*, Ava Duvernay's *Selma*, and, of course, *Black Panther*.

I would argue that the sweet spot, if you will, of contemporary Black visual culture has been in the arena of music-based short film—a form beyond the record-label-produced promotional music videos that were popularized with the advent of MTV and Black Entertainment Television in the early 1980s. There has been a palpable relationship between Black visuality and Black sound: consider, for instance, the role of Black commercial music in framing and promoting the Blaxploitation film genre in the 1970s. These films often privileged Black music as product, with the soundtrack recording the most viable mode of promotion, at the expense of visual concerns, particularly given the dearth of Black visual artists in the production of Hollywood-based Blaxploitation films, save the examples of Michael Schultz (*Cooley High, Car Wash*), Gordon Parks Sr. (*Shaft*), and Gordon Parks Jr. (*Superfly*).

Fifty years after Melvin Van Peebles's independent *Sweet Sweet Sweetback's Baadasssss Song* (1971) birthed the Blaxploitation era, with a soundtrack by the relatively unknown Earth, Wind, & Fire (whose eponymous debut album came out just months before the soundtrack), a symbiotic relationship between music and visuals persists in Black cultural production. Beyoncé's visual album *Lemonade* (2016) was directed by experimental filmmaker Khalil Joseph, who has also lensed FKA Twig's "Video Girl," Flying Lotus's "Until the Quiet Comes," and Shabazz Palace's "Belhaven Meridian," which pays homage to L.A. Rebellion filmmaker Charles Burnett's *Killer of Sheep* (1977). In writing on contemporary music video, Alessandra Raengo and Lauren McLeod Cramer suggest that Joseph hails from a generation of Black filmmakers who are returning to a practice and tradition that "self-consciously uses visual and sonic citations from various realms of Black expressive culture including the visual and performing arts, fashion, design, and, obviously, the rich history of Black music and Black music production."[77] Raengo and McLeod specifically cite the work of Hype Williams in the mid-1990s and early 2000s, whose influence, they argue, "extends beyond his signature luminous visual style; Williams distinguished the Black music video as a creative laboratory for a new generation of artists such as Arthur Jafa, Kahlil Joseph, Bradford Young, and Jenn Nkiru."[78] Critical to this work in music video is a return to the archive that, I would argue, is premised in part on placing the analog in conversation with the digital.

Kahlil Joseph's visual shout-out to Charles Burnett's *Killer of Sheep* in "Belhaven Meridian" serves as one example of the recovery of a previous generation of artists and archivists working with maroon (and, dare I say, wayward) Black archives: archives that refuse to behave—or, to say it another way, with the help of Raengo and Cramer, are "unruly." Burnett's attempt to capture the ephemera of everyday Black working-class life in *Killer of Sheep* and the mercurial aspects of Black working-class lives are indicative of modes of interiority that are not of value in the marketplace, that in its mundaneness actively resist having any value beyond the lives that live through that experience. Burnett's *Killer of Sheep* was reflective of the ethos of the generation of Black filmmakers who emerged out of the UCLA film school in the 1970s, often referred to as the L.A. Rebellion, who were committed to capturing the insularity of Black life, as a direct contrast to the spectacle of Black life that was being produced in Hollywood via Blaxploitation films such as *Shaft* and *Superfly*, among dozens of others.

The L.A. Rebellion anticipate the formation of the Black Audio Visual Collective in Britain in the early 1980s, as well as provide direct inspiration for contemporary filmmakers, like those cited by Raengo and Cramer, as well as others including *Black Panther* director Ryan Coogler, Ava Duvernay, and the late John Singleton, who attended film school across town at the University of Southern California. L.A. Rebellion member Haile Gerima established a film pedagogy lab at Howard University, where he trained Young and Nkiru, as well as Ernest Dickerson, Malik Sayeed, and Arthur Jafa. Importantly for the L.A. Rebellion, Black music "constituted a model of actualization, of exploration, and of intergenerational relations—a living archive of the past and a laboratory for the imagination of the future."[79] The L.A. Rebellion's use of music was the most important link to these younger directors, who utilized the techniques of the earlier generation in the service of a genre—the music video—that didn't really exist for the L.A. Rebellion.

Charles Burnett's *Killer of Sheep* demonstrates some of the strategies that Black filmmakers have used to leverage Black music as a disruptive force in the context of long-form cinema. As Morgan Woolsey notes in her essay "Re/soundings: Music and the Political Goals of the L.A. Rebellion," filmmakers like Burnett, Julie Dash, and Larry Clark sought to "depathologize the wide range of musics of the African diaspora" and "expand understandings of what 'Black' music could sound like."[80] Specifically, Woolsey cites Burnet's oft-stated desire for *Killer of Sheep* to function as a "history lesson" in Black music. Burnett's investment in the popular music of earlier generations of Blacks counters claims that those genres of music are dead, and that the living artists who work within those genres have nothing to offer to contemporary listeners.

In a film that so brilliantly exploits the archive of Black music for the purposes of illuminating the exteriorities and interiorities of Black working-class life in Los Angeles in the 1970s, the most striking musical occasion occurs with the use of Dinah Washington's "This Bitter Earth" in a moment of intimacy between the protagonist Stan (Henry Gayle Sanders) and his wife (Kaycee Moore). Embodied in their slow drag, which abruptly ends when the music does as Stan leaves the frame, "This Bitter Earth" offers a *quiet* disruption to the drudgery of Stan's life and a glimpse of possibility for his wife. Indeed, Stan's wife reflects on that moment as "memories that just don't seem mine, like half-eaten cake." These comments highlight the fleeting aspect of their moment of intimacy, which acknowledges both the nature of their relationship and indicates how intimacy might function as a form of ephemera within maroon archives, if we might again consider Harper's notions about narrative.

This disruption—the use of an early 1960s classic in an era marked by the electronic pulsations of disco and funk—functions like a return, if not from the dead, but of a *stranger*, which, in the colloquialism of Black life, is not so much someone who is not known, but who has not been seen in some time. As Kevin Quashie writes, quiet is "often used interchangeably with silence or stillness . . . quiet, instead, is a metaphor for the full range of one's inner self—one's desires, ambitions, hungers, vulnerabilities, fears."[81] This moment of quiet in *Killer of Sheep*, as a decidedly analog disruption, mirrors the quiet in which actual Maroons would have moved in their efforts to travel from outposts to family and friends who might have been on plantations; indeed, the way in which Stan leaves the frame, after his dance, mirrors this ethos.

"Hello Stranger": Fugitive Analogs in the Black Digital Era

Burnett's use of the Black musical archive in *Killer of Sheep* serves as citation in Barry Jenkins's *Moonlight* (based on playwright Tarell Alvin McCraney's *In Moonlight Black Boys Look Blue?*). Like *Killer of Sheep*, the soundscape of *Moonlight* is filled with a gorgeous contemporary score by Nicholas Britell—enhanced by Britell's application of the "chopped and screwed" technique that emerged in the Houston hip-hop scene of the early 1990s. In *Moonlight*, Jenkins draws on the analog Black musical archive on two particular occasions, to enact moments of sonic and emotional disruption not unlike Barnett's use of "This Bitter Earth" in *Killer of Sheep*.

In the first instance, the main character, Chiron—known as "Little" when portrayed as a child and "Black" as a young adult—witnesses his mother Paula (Naomie Harris) engage in a seemingly stimulant-induced shimmy to Aretha Franklin's "One Step Ahead." Paula is, in fact, dancing for an unnamed suitor, who presumably provides her with drugs. In her review of the film, Stephane Dunn decries the fact that "the mother Jenkins creates in *Moonlight* is disappointingly typical since we primarily get one dimensional portrayals of black mothers or black women with addiction issues, especially poor and working class black women, "adding that "we do not get a glimpse of her story and worse because we don't, and she mostly traumatizes her son for his perceived lack of correct manliness, she personifies the imagery of dysfunctional black mothering in the hood."[82] In contrast to Dunn's point, the sonic disruption of "One Step Ahead" offers a brief glimpse into Paula's interiority; she becomes the embodiment of the "half-eaten cake" that Stan's wife memorializes in *Killer of Sheep*. That Franklin's song is likely best known to contemporary audiences as source material for Mos Def's "Ms. Fat Booty" ("ass so fat, you can see it from the front") only highlights Paula's own unspoken recollections of her former self: younger, clean, voluptuous, and without a child.

In its depiction of the main character Little/Chiron/Black, *Moonlight* imagines the concept of emotional marronage, as the character travels between the comforts of his hypermasculine exteriority and the unfreedom of his queer interiority. The film depicts Little/Chiron/Black—portrayed by Alex Hibbert, Ashton Sanders, and Trevante Rhodes—throughout his life, from his experiences of emotional abandonment in childhood; his struggles with colorism as a dark-skinned teen; moments of same-sex intimacy with childhood friend Kevin (portrayed by Emmy Award–winning actor Jharrel Jerome as a teen and André Holland as an adult); and his incarceration in juvenile hall. A late-night phone call from Kevin, when both are adults, sets the scene for the characters' reconnection at a diner in Florida, where Kevin is a cook.

Jenkins doubles down on the idea of archive here, using Caetano Veloso's version of "Cucurrucucú Paloma" as the soundtrack to Chiron's drive to Florida. As Jenkins explains, "It's the same song used in Wong Kar-wai's *Happy Together*. It's a direct homage. Even the way we framed the car driving down the highway is the same. . . . It was the first movie I would say that I saw that was outright a queer film."[83] The tension Chiron experiences between his exteriority and interiority is made manifest when "Cucurrucucú Paloma"—which he listens to in the car—quickly cuts to a chopped and screwed version of Jidenna's "Classic Man" as he gets out of the car at the diner where Kevin works. This tension is also rendered as a divide between analog and digital in that "Cucurrucucú Paloma" is a song about being lovesick, written and first recorded in 1954 by Tomás Méndez and covered in an acoustic style by Veloso in Kar- wai's film. The chopped and screwed version, Jidenna's "Classic Man," is by definition digitally manipulated and features lyrics (distorted as they may be) that celebrate traditional patriarchy, minus some of the toxic- ity. Echoing the observations above about Barnett's use of analog-era music, particularly with "Stan's Wife," Jenkins offers "I wanted the music to express the consciousness of the character and not necessarily . . . the propulsion of the plot."[84]

Signaling a shift back to the analog, and thus interiority and intimacy, Franklin's "One Step" returns upon Chiron's entrance into the diner. Upon Chiron and Kevin's "pound" and embrace—Chiron had been sit- ting at the counter for almost the entire length of "One Step" before being recognized—Kevin comments, "You still can't say more than three words at a time." This hearkens back to Jenkins's comments about how the music served as a site of interiority for the film's characters, and, for my purposes, as an emotional archive. After Kevin prepares the "chef's special" for Chiron, as he had promised in his phone call, the duo, now sitting in a booth, begin to reminisce while "Our Love" by the Edge of Daybreak plays in the background.

In accompanying a moment of Chiron reluctantly bearing his soul to Kevin, "Our Love" offers another example of "analog" soul in the film— the song is another instance of Jenkins doubling down on the sonic archive. The Edge of Daybreak was formed in the late 1970s at the Pow- hatan Correctional Center outside of Richmond. *Eye of Love*, the Edge of Daybreak's debut album, was recorded in September 1979, in one take, and had been long forgotten (there were only a thousand copies pressed) until it was reissued by Numero Uno Records in 2015, a year before the release of *Moonlight*. The use of the song and its attachment to the group is notable for its narrative value, making deep connections to the generational reality of mass incarceration for Black men and the value of nurturing their humanity, in this case via the musical and culinary arts, as Kevin learned to cook while he too was in prison. The group's mantra, as articulated in the liner notes—"Our bodies are in prison, but we want our hearts and minds to be with the free world. The Edge of Daybreak symbolizes the morning when each of the band members will be free"—suggests that their music was the very embodiment of a "fugitive archive," recorded in one take, as one might if on the run.[85]

Chiron and Kevin's reunion turns sideways when Chiron admits that he is living in Atlanta "trapping" (i.e., dealing drugs). Kevin's admonishment ("That ain't you") is met with an abrupt response from Chiron—"Nigger, you don't know me"—at which point "Our Love" fades. The conversation is briefly interrupted as the last paying customers exit the diner and Kevin begins to bus the tables. When he sits down again across from Chiron, Chiron asks, "Why'd you call me?" Kevin explains that a man came into the diner and played a song on the jukebox, which Kevin then plays: R&B and pop singer Barbara Lewis's "Hello Stranger." Along with "Baby I'm Yours" (1965), "Hello Stranger" is one of Lewis's best-known recordings. Written by Lewis, it topped the R&B charts and peaked at #3 on the Hot 100 Pop chart in 1963. The song would later be covered by several artists including British singer Elkie Brooks, the Capitols (as the B-side to their 1966 pop hit "Cool Jerk"), and Yvonne Elliman of *Saturday Night Fever* fame, whose version was a top-15 pop hit. Queen Latifah, recording by her given name, Dana Owens, included "Hello Stranger" on her first all-vocals album, in 2004.

I offer the list of covers of Lewis's "Hello Stranger" to make the point that Jenkins had a wide range of versions to use in the film. Ellison's cover was a legit pop hit, for instance, and Queen Latifah's version might have been more familiar to some film audiences. However, there is something about the analog sonic quality of Lewis's original that achieved the necessary affect within the narrative context of the film. From a narrative standpoint, Jenkins's use of Barbara Lewis's "Hello Stranger" marks *Moonlight*'s penultimate moment, as it brilliantly mines the collective interiority of Chiron and Kevin. This notion of a return (literally in the phrase "Hello Stranger") serves both as a signifier of Chiron and Kevin's reunion as well as a sonic return of a Black musical archive that animates memory and nostalgia not only for the film's characters, but also for audiences who might lament, "They don't make them like this anymore."

In his book *Film Blackness: American Cinema and the Idea of Black Film*, Michael Boyce Gillespie highlights what he describes as Jenkins's "quiet tonality" as it functions in his first full-length film *Medicine for Melancholy* (2008), set in San Francisco. As Gillespie writes, *Medicine for Melancholy* "organizes quiet as interiority force, an affective arrangement of the film's pulsing speculation on black capacities. . . . The film's quiet conjures the politics of black becoming, fantasy, and the cultural geography of San Francisco."[86] Jenkins explains that he included "Hello Stranger" in the film because "when I lived in San Francisco, there was this soul night that happens on Tuesdays where they would play only vinyl 45s. It was for grown folks. . . . Every time that song came on, I just got this feeling, you know? It was overwhelming. And I wanted to give this feeling to the audience."[87] Jenkins's comments highlight the limitations of formats in the digital era, where vinyl seven-inch 45 RPM records and their ten-inch 78 RPM predecessors are more obscure than long-playing twelve-inch 33 RPM records, which was the standard for album-length recordings throughout much of the twentieth century.

Vinyl 45s, or "singles," were notable for their short length, generally under three minutes, which often necessitated severe editing from the album-length versions of songs, or two-sided versions of the same song literally edited as part 1 and part 2. Yet, because of their accessibility, affordability (in comparison to album-length recordings), and disposability, 45s were the format of choice for the masses, particularly in the late 1950s and 1960s, when Black music became integrated into the mainstream of American consumption. In fact, Black music—I'm thinking in particular of Motown here—might have been thought of as more disposable in comparison to the album-oriented rock music that began to populate FM radio in the late 1960s. Indeed, save the example of Black jazz artists, one would be hard pressed to think of album-length recordings by Black soul or R&B artists that possessed the cultural gravitas of the Beach Boys' *Pet Sounds* (1966) or the Beatles' *Sergeant Pepper's Lonely Hearts Club Band* (1967), until perhaps Sly and the Family Stones' *Stand* (1969).

With the shift to digital recordings in the early 1980s and the emergence of the compact disc (CD) as a primary format, 45s largely disappeared from the landscape of popular music, except as collectables. One might experience happening upon a 45 or hearing the crackling and scratches that accompany its repeated plays as one might experience seeing a stranger; in fact, there is now at least a generation of Americans who have never seen an actual 45 to begin with. Yet 45s proved invaluable to Black archival practices, even if they were considered to possess little or no value for those who controlled the intellectual property of these recordings. In the transition from the sounds of actual old records, such as the crackling and scratching from repeated listening, to the "clean" digital versions of songs that have been made available via streaming in recent years, something important is lost sonically and culturally. That crackling and scratching is as much a part of the archive as the music itself, to double down again on Harper's earlier point about narrative.

In the film *Fences*, director Denzel Washington utilizes music differently: as part of a cinematic rendering of an August Wilson stage production that was devoid of music. Washington largely stays true to August Wilson's "single shot" depiction of mid-twentieth-century Black Pittsburgh, though he counters with cinematic recollections of that era in which music and dance were some of the prominent features. Washington's directorial strategy demonstrates both a commitment to the integrity of Wilson's artistic vision, where language functions as the musical default, and a concession to the predominance of the visual in contemporary Black culture, where his capturing of the city of Pittsburgh might constitute Washington's most pronounced contribution to Wilson's vision.

One of Washington's other contributions is the use of Jimmy Scott's "Day by Day" as a mode of narrative disruption that sonically captures the interiorities of many of the film's main characters in ways that language cannot. Originally recorded in 1969 and appearing on the album *The Source*, Scott's rendition of "Day by Day" is distinguished by his impeccable phrasing. Yet there is also the issue of the quality of Scott's vocals, which are emotive and "ungendered," given the gender confusion Scott's voice has historically generated. As Nina Sun Eidsheim writes, "I see Scott as a musician-activist who carries out the micropolitics of voice by bringing unexpected timbral content (non-falsetto) to a form (black masculinity), thereby challenging the form's very definition."[88]

Beyond its ungendering, Scott's vocals could only be read as disruptive in the context of a film that is devoid of what might be described as commercial Black music. Yet Scott himself could be said to represent the challenges of the archive and the commercial viability of Black cultural production, whether it be the economic feasibility of interpreting a Black stage classic as a narrative film or the economic exploitation that for long periods kept Scott's music—his voice—out of commercial circulation.

Scott was born with Kallmann syndrome, a genetic disorder that arrests the puberty process. In Scott's case, it left him with boyish features into adulthood and a uniquely high-pitched voice. Blues guitarist B. B. King, who was a deejay in Memphis, Tennessee, in 1950, recalled his response to hearing Scott's first (and ultimately only) big hit, "Everybody's Somebody's Fool": "First off, I thought it was a woman. But then, no, it's a man. Young man who sounds like an alto sax. Young man with a sound all his own."[89] Scott might have been a singer with a "sound all his own," but the record was not all his own. Scott was simply a singer in Lionel Hampton's band, and when "Everybody's Somebody's Fool" was released, the record identified the artist simply as "Lionel Hampton, Singer with Orchestra." It would not be the only time this would happen. When a live session from 1950 in which Scott sings "Embraceable You" with Charlie Parker was released as a double album in 1977, the vocals were mistakenly attributed to female vocalist Chubby Newsome.

In spite of this hiccup, Jimmy Scott launched an influential solo career in the 1950s. Standout recordings from this period like "I'm Afraid the Masquerade Is Over" and "When Did You Leave Heaven?" would influence a generation of singers. As Marvin Gaye told biographer David Ritz, "I heard Jimmy back in the fifties . . . My entire career I longed to sing ballads—like Frank Sinatra or Nat Cole or Perry Como—but with the depth of Jimmy Scott."[90] Vocalist Nancy Wilson was even more emphatic, noting that she was "eighteen years old when I first heard ["When Did You Leave Heaven"] . . . I was playing clubs around Ohio and, because Jimmy's version, fell in love with the song." Wilson adds, "I had fallen in love with Jimmy's sensitivity the moment I'd heard 'Everybody's Somebody's Fool.' From then on, I followed his career and based my style on his."[91]

Whereas the history of Black musical production—and the Black archive more broadly—are replete with examples of corporate malfeasance, theft, and exploitation best exemplified in the term "a deal with the devil," in the case of Jimmy Scott the devil was embodied in the figure of Herman Lubinsky, the owner of Savoy Records, the label to which Scott signed with in 1955. As David Ritz describes Savoy Records and its owner, the label "is famous in the annals of American music for producing a large number of important classic recording," particularly among Black artists; James Cleveland, for instance, recorded for Savoy during his ascent in the 1960s. But Lubinsky was "infamous for his underpayment and even nonpayment" of artists.[92] Scott's time with Savoy dealt him a double blow, denying him both respect for his talent and access to his full financial worth as an artist. Not so ironically, Scott referred to Savoy as the "slave barracks."[93]

Scott recorded three albums for Savoy between 1955 and 1960, and a fourth album in 1975, after Lubinsky's death. With the exception of *Very, Truly, Yours* (1955), which included "When Did You Leave Heaven" and "Sometimes I Feel Like a Motherless Child" from *The Fabulous Songs of*

Jimmy Scott (1960), the albums were commercial failures. According to Scott, in the era in which Sam Cooke and the Coasters were breaking through to the pop mainstream, "Lubinsky wanted me to make more rock-sounding records . . . I just wasn't willing . . . I couldn't be sincere."[94] Scott returned to his native Cleveland, where he stayed until a chance encounter with Mary Ann Fisher, a former vocalist for Ray Charles, led to another opportunity for success.

Scott relocated to Los Angeles with Fisher, and Ray Charles, who had long been a fan of Scott's, leapt at the chance to record Scott on his ABC Records–distributed label Tangerine. The resulting album, *Falling in Love Is Wonderful* (1963), featured arrangements from Gerald Wilson and Marty Paich, who both arranged Charles's groundbreaking *Modern Sounds in Country and Western Music* (1962). According to Wilson, *Falling in Love Is Wonderful* is "really a long and intimate conversation between Ray's sensitive piano playing and Jimmy's sensitive voice."[95] In his biography of Scott, Ritz describes *Falling in Love Is Wonderful* as comparable with some of the best albums of the genre, including Frank Sinatra's *In the Wee Small Hours of the Morning* and Billie Holiday's near-closing statement *Lady in Satin*. Scott's version of "I Wish I Didn't Love You So" was likely as much an inspiration as Sinatra's version in Marvin Gaye's decade-long fixation with the song during his *Vulnerable* sessions, raising the question as to whether Gaye might have been trying to record his own *Falling in Love Is Wonderful* as well as *In the Wee Small Hours of the Morning* with *Vulnerable*.

If Gaye was inspired by *Falling in Love Is Wonderful*, he would have been among a small group of folk who got to hear the record. Shortly after it was released, the album was recalled, after Lubinsky claimed that Scott was still under contract with Savoy, and Charles's Tangerine label capitulated. Scott had already experienced some erasure with the album due to the cover image, which featured male and female models, as if he was simply the invisible conjurer of these moments of collective romance. The erasure became even harsher when, several years later, Tangerine released the record's original instrumental tracks, with organist

Will Bill Davis replacing Scott's vocals, on the album *Wonderful World of Love* (1969). By the time the Davis album had been released, Scott was embroiled in yet another drama in which his productivity and ability to make a living from his art was again undermined by specious claims of contractual obligations to Savoy and Lubinsky.

Producer Joel Dorn was a radio deejay in Philadelphia in 1963 when *Falling in Love Is Wonderful* was released. Dorn was working as a producer at Atlantic Records in 1968 when, on the advice of Duke Wade, a one-time manager of Ruth Brown and Ray Charles, Scott came to visit. Soon after that, Scott was in the studio to record *The Source*, which featured eight tracks, including stellar interpretations of the Righteous Brothers' "Unchained Melody," "Our Day Will Come" (most famously recorded by Ruby & the Romantics), and "Day by Day." Dorn called the album *The Source* because "for modern jazz singing—especially modern female jazz singers—Jimmy really is the indisputable source."[96] Dorn attempted to capture the spirit of the Tangerine session, with Bill Fischer and Arif Mardin (who would later produce Chaka Khan's first three solo albums) providing string arrangements, and with the accompaniment of Charles's longtime sideman saxophonist David "Fathead" Newman. The result was the most accomplished recording of Scott's career to date, of which "Day by Day" was the clear standout.

As a song that was part of Sinatra's early repertoire, much of the genius of Scott's rendition of "Day by Day" comes in the pacing. As Ritz describes it, Scott "takes it a tempo half the pace of Sinatra, elongating notes and rewriting melodies in a manner that seems to defy musical reason."[97] Viewed from a contemporary standpoint in which US Representative Maxine Waters's famous claim that she was "reclaiming her time" became a popular digital meme, Scott indeed reclaims his time in his rendition of the song; his pacing almost seems to recover—in one song, no less—all the time that had already been lost in his career. As Maroons on the plantation stole moments with loved ones, Scott's performance steals time, the song's title a reminder of the "one day at a time" ethos that shaped Black political agency right into the era in which Scott recorded the song.

Scott's performance of "Day by Day" also resonates with themes in Wilson's *Fences* and its Washington-directed film adaptation. Produced on Broadway in 1987 and adapted for the screen in 2010 with a cast led by Washington and Viola Davis, who reprised their roles in the film, the drama revolves around a middle-aged Black man, Troy Maxon, who lives with his wife and son in Pittsburgh's Hill District. Part of an archival project, *Fences* is among the ten plays that comprise Wilson's "century cycle," with each play taking place in a particular decade of the twentieth century, nine of them set in Pittsburgh. Maxon, a formerly incarcerated garbage man, challenges the City of Pittsburgh to let him to move from the back of the truck collecting garbage to the driver's seat—something that he achieves during the course of the drama. Yet if this achievement might be seen as a racial uplift metaphor in the early years of the modern civil rights movement, for Maxon it serves as a reminder of opportunities lost a generation earlier.

Fences is set a decade after Jackie Robinson broke the so-called "color line" in Major League Baseball—Roberto Clemente is in the third year of what would become a Hall-of-Fame career for Maxon's hometown Pirates—and Troy considers himself a talent who deserved an opportunity to have competed in the majors. Though the major leagues had been integrated for a decade, Maxon, who honed his skills in prison, is already in his early forties and past his prime. When Maxon's best friend, Bono (Stephen McKinley Henderson), insists that he "just come along too early," Maxon responds emphatically, "There ought not never have been no time called too early!" Many themes in *Fences* revolve around timing: the birth of Maxon's out-of-wedlock daughter eighteen years into his marriage to Rose, and the intergenerational tensions he experiences with his son Corey (Jovan Adepo), right on the cusp of Black student activism in the 1960s. Indeed "Day by Day" provides the soundtrack to a montage of the changing seasons after the film's dramatic peak.

Scott's album *The Source*, which features "Day by Day," is one of the few available examples of Scott at his own peak. He would not record on a consistent basis until he was well into his sixties and "discovered" by a generation of hipsters in the 1990s. As such, Jimmy Scott embodies the disappointment felt by Troy Maxon, who, in bitter rants, can only gesture toward his potential greatness as an athlete that segregation robbed him of the opportunity to fully realize. Scott's performance of "Day by Day" allows Washington to add a layer to Troy Maxson's trauma, and that which he visits upon his wife and his sons Lyons (Russell Hornsby), and, in particular, Cory. In this regard Jimmy Scott's voice provides space for a disruptive interiority, for those characters who are largely reacting to Troy's self-inflicted malaise. And how interesting would have been for Washington to have used Scott's "The Folks Who Live on the Hill," given the historical significance of Pittsburgh's Hill district, and Scott's own view that he recorded the song when "I was still dreaming of making my marriage work. I related to the song and its hopeful sentiment."[98] Dorn recorded with Scott in 1972 for an album that both knew would never be released, but, as Dorn laments, "I couldn't stand the idea that Jimmy Scott, at his absolute prime, was still not being documented." Scott's versions of "The Folks Who Live on the Hill" and "Day by Day" wouldn't be available to the larger public until the CD/digital release of *Lost and Found* in 1993, which included five tracks from *The Source* and five tracks from the 1972 session that was never released.

Scott's genius, though stifled throughout much of his career, was able to be captured via analog archives and their curation by folk like Dorn and his biographer David Ritz in ways that were not possible for Troy Maxon. Yet, as previously mentioned, *Fences* is also an archival project in part; the character of Maxon was partly inspired by Wilson's stepfather, David Bedford, "a talented black football player who, after failing to receive a much-hoped-for college scholarship, killed a man during a robbery and spent over 20 years in prison."[99] Bedford's career, too, had been stifled by social realities. Troy Maxon's tales of his own greatness allows Wilson and, later, Washington to make manifest not only the greatness of David Bedford, but a generation of men like him and like Scott, who were denied opportunities and whose lives were buried in archives unnamed and unclaimed. In the context of contemporary Black filmmaking and visual culture, songs like "Hello Stranger" and "Day by Day" and the uses to which they are put cinematically, function as analog hauntings into the digital era: akin to nostalgia and remembrance not unlike the Maroons in the digital archive, that return fleetingly, with each new technological advancement.

Coda

Writing and Living with Black Ephemera

The opening passage of my first book, *What the Music Said* (1999), begins with a remembrance of listening to Junior Walker and the All-Stars' "What Does It Take (to Win Your Love)" while sitting with my dad in an uncle's car. I told that story then, and recall it now, to make a collateral claim: as I write about the Black musical archive, I have lived with that musical archive. But, in many ways, it's an empty boast; what Black American adult, of a certain age, has not grown up in a house or an apartment where the various traditions of Black music flowed like the wind through open windows during those requisite Saturday morning house-cleanings? This was the case for even those families for whom the blues, R&B, jazz, and especially soul, as corruptions of Black church music, were always the devil's music, as my long-time teaching collaborator Patrick Douthit (9th Wonder) often comically notes.

Instead, I'll make another claim, about two Black American parents—one born in Georgia, the other in North Carolina and raised in Baltimore—who unwittingly made their only child a student of that archive. My parents were not churchgoers, and to my mind not particularly religious, but our apartment during my childhood was filled with the music of Shirley Caesar, the Mighty Clouds of Joy, Inez Andrews, the Soul Stirrers, the Dixie Hummingbirds and Tessie Hill. I say this not to make a point about the kinds of music that my parents listen to; to be sure, Luther Ingram, Jimmy Smith, Al Green, Jimmy McGriff, Teddy Pendergrass and Mille Jackson got their share of spins on the turntable. Rather, I want to note that there was something sacred, even devout about their listening practices. The centrality of recorded music in their lives could be gleaned from my dad's Fisher amplifier, which he bought in 1972, when I was six, and which survived long enough to see me graduate from college, to the huge speakers that served as mantles in our living room, and to the smaller speakers, one placed above a kitchen cabinet and another placed above my parents' bedroom door. Our seven-hundred-square foot, two-bedroom, third-floor apartment overflowed with music, and it was not unusual on a Saturday afternoon to hear it coming from our third-floor apartment when entering our five-story tenement. I had no choice but to imbibe the music.

And yet. In a six-month period in 1971, at age five, I witnessed the Supremes at the Apollo (post–Ms. Ross), the Jackson 5 at Madison Square Garden, and Aretha Franklin during her legendary residency at the Apollo. I remember the Supremes concert in particular because they sang "Stoned Love," my favorite song at the time, and because I lost a ring that my mother had given me under the seats (which became an excuse not to buy me another piece of jewelry until I was an adult). I can only recall the Jackson 5 as tiny figures visible from the nosebleed seats my mother was able to afford, though the group's *Third Album*, released the year before, was the first record that I ever asked my mother to buy for me.

For years, though, the Aretha Franklin concert stayed with me, not so much for the performance, but because Franklin's bandleader King Curtis—a legend in his own right—was stabbed outside his New York apartment a few months later, on my mother's birthday. I vividly recall my parents speaking in hushed tones about how they had "just seen him, with Aretha." A few years later, when, not yet aged 10, I started bingeing on Sam Cooke records after hearing his vocals on a K-Tel television commercial and coming across in my father's record collection King Curtis's tribute album to Cooke, recorded in 1965, a year after Cooke's death. That album became the portal to my lifelong obsession with Cooke. Indeed, one of my biggest professional laments is that my father didn't live long enough to see me talk about the singer in Kelly Duane de la Vega's film *The Two Killings of Sam Cooke* (2019), because

Cooke was his dude, much the way prepubescent Michael Jackson was my mine in childhood.

Much of this book is about the culture—the ephemera—that I've lived with for much of my life. I've come to understand that the practices of Black ephemera must be taught, that the ability to help curate archives that are kinetic, if not living and breathing in their own right, is a learned skill. Some of that archive I took for granted: my mother blasting Isaac Hayes's *Black Moses* 8-track on Saturday mornings while my father was at work; watching the documentary *King: A Filmed Record . . . Montgomery to Memphis* (1970) in high school and again in college and realizing that what stayed with me from the film was Nina Simone's haunting performance of "Why? (The King of Love Is Dead)." Before I ever heard Aretha Franklin's *Live at the Fillmore West* (1972) or *Amazing Grace* (1973), arguably the defining examples of her musical genius and cultural significance, I had my own frame of reference for her, having seen and heard her with my own five-year-old eyes and ears. *Live at the Fillmore West*, recorded in March 1971, was part of the same national tour that brought Franklin and Curtis to the Apollo in June 1971. *Live at the Fillmore West* meant that, even as a child, I understood that all should come to a stop when Ray Charles shows up on that third night to join Ms. Franklin on stage.

Black Ephemera has reminded me that for every movement forward, there are necessary returns to the archive. When Public Enemy's "Fight the Power" emerged as an anthem of Black protests during the summer of 1989, which witnessed the premiere of Spike Lee's third film *Do the Right Thing* (the song the film's literal anthem) and the shooting death of Yusef Hawkins, who was for my generation what Trayvon Martin would become for another generation more than thirty years later, it did so with a powerful homage to the Isley Brothers. "Fight the Power" was initially a funky call to resistance recorded by veterans of the rock & roll era, in 1975. "And when I rolled with the punches I got knocked on the ground / By all this bullshit going down" was a far thematic cry from their early hits "Twist and Shout" (1962) and "Shout" (1959). Yet even

"Shout" was made most legible in its riffs on the sanctified Black church. As Ronald Isley recalls, so intense were their references to gospel music that church groups rose up to petition radio stations to take it off the air.[1]

I was not surprised at all when the Public Enemy version of "Fight the Power reemerged in the streets of American cities during the summer of 2020 in the midst of protests against the State-sanctioned killings of Breonna Taylor and George Floyd, among so many others. Indeed, even Public Enemy returned to the well, producing a 2020 version of the song that featured Nas, Black Thought, and Rapsody. Even against the backdrop of Black Lives Matter and protests in support of police abolition stood the reality of a global pandemic, where the archive proved bountiful for those sheltering-in-place around the world. The mixtapes that I might have made thirty years ago to mark my anger, fear, rage, and hope have given way to Spotify and Apple Music playlists, some curated by well-known music journalists, public radio outlets, and artists themselves. D-Nice, a one-time protégé of hip-hop icon KRS-One who had moderate success in the early 1990s with the singles "Call Me D-Nice" and "25 Ta Life," remade his career as the host of Club Quarantine, a deejay set that he curated on Instagram Live. On any given night, Club Quarantine welcomed a host of bonafide celebrities, most notably former First Lady Michelle Obama.

For a moment, Club Quarantine returned the figure of the deejay—as opposed to radio host—to prominence as public curator of the Black musical archive. For me, Club Quarantine and other shelter-in-place deejay sets like 9th Wonder's Fass Auntie's Lounge recalled earlier times when deejays like Black New York WBLS-FM radio legends Frankie Crocker, Hal Jackson, and Vaughn Harper used the airwaves to educate audiences, not only about the Black musical archives, but about how the music intersected with Black social and political realities. I distinctly remember as a young adult hearing Aretha Franklin's "Take a Look," the Clyde Otis—penned meditation on race relations in the 1960s, and Donald Byrd's "Cristo Redentor" during Crocker's afternoon drive-time programs in the weeks after Yusef Hawkins's death and the subsequent protests led by Reverend Al Sharpton. My own social media practice of sharing Black ephemera is largely inspired by listening to Crocker and his comrades thirty years ago. I understand it as a necessary intervention, grounded in a responsibility to the archive and to those who produced and curated it before me—an intervention likely to go unnoticed, except, as Conrad Kent Rivers wrote three generations ago, "Some black kid is bound to read you."

Black Ephemera is the first full-length book I conceived since the death of my parents, more than a decade ago. Throughout my career, I've written about my father's role as my first musical interlocutor; it's only been since my mother's death that I've come to understand her formative role in both my musical taste and my intellectual practice. It's been during the no less than twenty times a year listening sessions (usually on Sundays) of Aretha Franklin's full *Amazing Grace* sessions, in sequence, that I've communed with my mother. That Stax Records, and Isaac Hayes and Johnnie Taylor in particular, figure so prominently in *Black Ephemera* is a direct outcome of my mother wearing out her 33 1/3 copies of Hayes's *Hot Buttered Soul* and *The Isaac Hayes Movement* and her 8-track copies of his *Black Moses* and Johnnie Taylor's *Taylored in Silk*. And then there's Reverend James Cleveland's "I Stood on the Banks of Jordan" ("You took my Father, you came back and got my Mother"): hearing it now, there's little I can do but break down in tears, something I did often while working on this book. Yes, "some Black kid is bound to read," but *Black Ephemera* is a reminder that some Black kid is also bound to listen.

ACKNOWLEDGMENTS

First, I'd like to thank my editor and friend Eric Zinner (I didn't forget this time) and his team.

For the better part of fifteen years, the late Richard Iton was a thought partner and generous interlocutor, having read and offered commentary on four of my books, including *Looking for Leroy*, which was published weeks after his death in the spring of 2013. Though this is the first book I've written without Richard's sage critical council, there is no small irony in the fact that a celebration gathering for his life and work presented me with two interlocutors who were critical to me thinking through this project. I am thankful for the friendship and generosity of Shana Redmond and Margo Natalie Crawford, who both pushed my thinking.

Jessica Marie Johnson and have come to think of ourselves as mind-kin. Admittedly, I apprenticed with Jessica's mind on so many things digital, until I found my own voice in this conversation, and it is Jessica, who I specifically thank for this project's title—a gift to me that was for her, no doubt, just a passing thought. I came to know Jessica because of her relationship with Treva Blaine Lindsey, who almost twenty-years after she began her graduate career as my student, now teaches me often and powerfully; Treva's friendship has been another gift as we transitioned from teacher and student to colleagues and peers.

I'd also like to thank I. Augustus Durham, Nura Sedique, Gloria Y. Ayee, Tyler Bunzey, Chavis Jones, Shontea Smith, Kenya Harris, and Sasha Panaram, who, like Treva before them, afforded me the opportunity to work with them as they took their own journeys in graduate school. The after-class gatherings over food, especially with Karen Jean Hunt, were priceless; I am thankful that you all have been in my life, and my work.

Shoutouts to Camille Jackson, Tyra Dixon, Wilhelmina Green and StacyNicole Robinson, who worked with me in various administrative capacities over the past few years, whose care and professionalism helped make me successful. Shoutouts also to Catherine Angst, who for a decade served as director of photography, editor, and producer of *Left of Black*, the video podcast that I helped launch in 2010, and Eric Barstow, who picked up the role when Catherine moved on at Duke, and who helped us pivot in the early months of COVID-19.

Many thanks to the team at the Hutchins Center for African & African American Research and the HipHop Archive and Institute at Harvard University, including OGs Henry Louis Gates Jr. and Marcylina Morgan, as well as Abby Wolf (#DDMF) and Krishna Lewis, who, during a magical fall in 2013, allowed me the time and space to think initially about this project. These thanks should also extend to Shirley Taylor, who provided a regular platform as part of the Apollo Theater's Education Program.

I'd like to thank thank my colleagues, past and present at Duke, especially in the Department of African & African American Studies, including Michaeline Crichlow, Sam Daly, Thomas DeFrantz, Wahneema Lubiano, Charmaine Royal, Karen Shapiro, Stephen Smith, Jasmine Nicole Cobb, Sandy Darity, Anne-Maria Makhulu, Joe Winters, Lee Baker, Rick Powell, Adriane D. Lentz-Smith, Tsitsi Jaji, and in particular the "Bad News Negroes," Kerry Haynie, Eduardo Bonilla-Silva, Maurice Wallace, Trina Jones and the incomparable Karla FC Holloway, James B. Duke Distinguished Professor Emerita of English. It goes without saying that my path has been much easier because of the support of the Dean's staff of the Trinity School of Arts & Science at Duke, including the Dean Valerie Ashby, Social Science Dean Rachel Kranton, Associate Dean Kevin Moore (#LGM), as well as the John Hope Franklin Center, the Franklin Humanities Institute and its director Ranjanna Khanna, the Forum for Publics and Scholars and its former director and founder Laurent Dubois, Duke Performances, especially during the tenure of Aaron Greenwald, and the Nasher Museum of Art, under the leadership of Sarah Schroth and now Trevor Schoonmaker.

My work is the by-product of the places and spaces where I find comfort. Shoutout to Beans Traders, which provided such a great space and the best Americanos over the years; the "Woke" Starbucks on Roxboro, where I spent a hundred or so crack-of-dawn weekends finding my voice in this project; the homie Dorian Bolden and his spot, the Beyu Caffe; and finally Jennings Brody and the staff of Parker & Otis. The veranda at the old Parker & Otis was one of the loveliest spots in all of Durham, and it gave me the gift of Ms. Joan Minor's friendship; I lament that I will not write another book on that veranda.

Thankful for my cohort of OGs, especially Lisa "L-Boogie" Thompson; Brother G (Guthrie Ramsey Jr.); Bakari Kitwana; Patrick Douthit (a.k.a 9th Wonder); Joan Morgan, the first and forever homie; and Frank Paul Jr., the best brother this only child has ever had. Thankful for the brotherhood of Phi Beta Sigma, especially the Delta Zeta Sigma alumni chapter of Durham, Noth Carolina: "BLU-PHI!" Thank you to Tanya McKinnon, who sees something bigger for me, and Michael Eric Dyson, for both the introduction to Tanya and more than twenty years of counsel and mentorship. Many thanks to my therapist of seven years, Kira Royal, and my barber of seventeen years, Tone Boone.

In the time since the last time we did this, one of my daughters, Misha Gabrielle, graduated from high school, went off to college in Chicago, graduated in the early months of COVID, and began her own graduate career at the School of the Art Institute of Chicago. I miss our early morning drives to swim practice and her running commentary about my sartorial choices, but so much of what I "see" in this project is because of the way she, as an art history student, curator, and photographer, helped me to look differently. When Misha headed to Chicago, it was her sister, Camille Monet, who rode shotgun, and in the process changed how I listened—to her, no doubt—but also to the music that filled the car on every drive to and from school. As Camille prepares for college, I will miss her probing mind, her constant challenges to *everything*, her taking notes in the back row of so many of my classes. More than with any of my previous projects, my daughters were a tactile part of this process. I will miss them being so close by. As I write these words, I am preparing to celebrate thirty years of marriage to Gloria Taylor-Neal, who remembers those early days when a young scholar's ambitions were bigger than even he could imagine, but who always had faith that I would realize those goals and she sacrificed accordingly. Gloria remains my rock and my "pearl."

NOTES

INTRODUCTION

1 "Jay-Z's Samsung Deal Signals a Musical Future Where the Rich Get Richer," *Guardian*, July 3, 2014, www.theguardian.com.

2 Howard Rambsy II, *The Black Arts Enterprise and the Production of African American Poetry* (Ann Arbor: University of Michigan Press, 2011), 18.

3 Rambsy, *Black Arts Enterprise*, 29.

4 Randall's edited volume *The Black Poets* was published by Bantam Books in 1971; it was the first anthology of Black poetry that I owned, and I'm sure that I am not alone among my generation of African-American writers and critics.

5 Quoted in Rambsy, *Black Arts Enterprise*, 77.

6 Rambsy, 85.

7 A traditional five-volume version of the encyclopedia was published by Oxford University Press in 2005.

8 "Encarta Africana, the First Comprehensive Encyclopedia of Black History and Culture, Launches Today" (press release), Microsoft, January 8, 1999, news. microsoft.com.

9 Lisa Nakamura and Peter A. Chow, "Introduction—Race and Digital Technology: Code, the Color Line and the Information Society," in *Race after the Internet*, ed. Lisa Nakamura and Peter A. Chow (New York: Routledge, 2012), 3.

1. LOVE IN THE STAX

1 Aram Goudsouzian and Charles W. McKinney Jr., eds., "Introduction," in *An Unseen Light: Black Struggles for Freedom in Memphis, Tennessee* (Lexington: University Press of Kentucky, 2018), 4.

2 Zandria F. Robinson, "After Stax: Race, Sound, and Neighborhood Revitalization," in Goudsouzian and McKinney, *Unseen Light*, 356.

3 In his essay on the "soul grandfather" Rufus Thomas, Charles C. Hughes notes some tensions at Stax with regard to producer and the MGs' guitarist, Steve Cropper, who was White. Thomas is quoted as saying: "Steve Cropper was a guitar player and that's all Steve Cropper was . . . some of the songs that Steve Cropper's name appeared on as producer and all of that . . . had no business at all on there." Thomas also states, "Steve Cropper had that white thing that said because you're black, you're supposed to do exactly what this white man says." Quoted in Goudsouzian and McKinney, *Unseen Light*, 242.

4 "Negro Named Veep Of Big Record Firm," *Chicago Defender*, August 12, 1967, 17.

5 "'Dock of the Bay' at 50: Why Otis Redding's Biggest Hit Almost Went Unheard," NPR, January 8, 2018, www.npr.org.

6 Anthony C. Siracusa, "Nonviolence, Black Power, and the Surveillance State in Memphis's War on Poverty," in Goudsouzian and McKinney, *Unseen Light*, 280.

7 "Meet Al Bell, Big Man in Record Biz: Memphis-Based Exec Heading Upward," *Chicago Daily Defender*, March 30, 1968, 13.

8 Robinson, "After Stax," 356.

9 Richard Harrington, "A Soul Man Returns: Superstar Isaac Hayes Helped Shape Pop Music. Now He's Back for More," *Washington Post*, September 24, 1995, G1.

10 Rob Bowman, *Soulsville U.S.A.: The Story of Stax Records* (New York: Music Sales, 2006) 181.

11 Bowman, *Soulsville U.S.A.*, 181.

12 Bowman, 182.

13 R. J. Smith, *The Great Black Way: L.A. in the 1940s and the Lost African-American Renaissance* (New York: PublicAffairs Books, 2006).

14 Bowman, *Soulsville U.S.A.*, 182.

15 Many thanks to my Duke University colleague Professor Anthony Kelley for pointing to the Doris Day citation.

16 Bowman, *Soulsville U.S.A.*, 290.

17 Gayle Wald, "A Singer's Singer," *Los Angeles Review of Books*, December 23, 2011, lareviewofbooks.org.

18 Bowman, *Soulsville U.S.A.*, 160.

19 Bowman, 160.

20 Robert Gordon, *Respect Yourself: Stax Records and the Soul Explosion* (New York: Bloomsbury, 2015), 285.

21 Charles Hughes, *Country Soul: Making Music and Making Race in the American South* (Chapel Hill: University of North Carolina Press, 2015).

22 The "corporation" was a collective of Motown producers that included Freddie Perren, Deke Richards, Alphonse Mizell, and Berry Gordy.

23 "'Lord, Let Me Be an Instrument': The Artistry and Cultural Politics of Reverend James Cleveland and the Gospel Workshop of America," *Journal of Africana Religions* 5, no. 2 (2017): 165.

24 "An Analysis of Performance Practices in African American Gospel Music: Rhythm, Lyric Treatment, and Structures in Improvisation and Accompaniment," *Popular Music* 34, no. 2 (May 2015): 197–225.

25 *Conversations with Nikki Giovanni*, ed. Virginia Fowler (Jackson: University of Mississippi Press, 199), 4.

26 Alisha Lola Jones, "'You Are My Dwelling Place": Experiencing Black Male Vocalists' Worship as Aural Eroticism and Autoeroticism in Gospel Performance," *Women and Music: A Journal of Gender and Culture* 22 (2018): 3–21.

27 Jones, "You Are My Dwelling Place," 4.

28 Jones, 5–8.

29 Ben Sisario, "Complicated Legacy of a Gospel Singer," *New York Times*, April 28, 2014, C7.

30 Robinson, "After Stax," 356.

31 Robinson, 356–57.

32 Robinson, 357.

2. "I GOT THE BLUES OF A FALLEN TEARDROP"

1 Manohla Dargis, "Surviving Katrina with a Big Personality and a Video Camera," *New York Times*, August 21, 2008, www.nytimes.com.

2 Courtney R. Baker, *Humane Insight: Looking at Images of African American Suffering and Death* (Urbana: University of Illinois Press, 2015).

3 Dennis Lim, "The Angry Flood and the Stories in Its Wake," *New York Times*, August 15, 2008, www.nytimes.com.

4 Dargis, "Surviving Katrina."

5 Kathleen A. Bergin, "Witness: The Racialized Gender Implications of Katrina," in *Seeking Higher Ground: The Hurricane Katrina Crisis, Race, and Public Policy Reader*, ed. Manning Marable and Kristen Clarke (New York: Palgrave Macmillan, 2008), 185.

6 Williams Cole, "Rising above the Flood: Kimberly Roberts, Scott Roberts, and Carl Deal," Brooklyn Rail, September 2008, brooklynrail.org.

7 Henrick Karoliszyn, "Trouble the Water Star 10 Years Later: 'People Should Never Think Katrina Is Over,'" Splinter, September, 24, 2015, splinternews.com.

8 Baker, *Humane Insight*, 110.

9 "Slow Motion" was the first single from Cash Money Records to top the pop charts. In recent years the label has largely been defined by the crossover pop success of Lil' Wayne and Drake.

10 Amber N. Riley, "Integrating Architecture into Digital and Public Humanities: Sites and Sounds + MediaNOLA," *Journal of Digital Humanities* 2, no. 2 (Spring 2013) //AU: (Please include URL)//

11 Brentin Mock, "A History of New Orleans Public Housing, Through No Limit and Ca$h Money Music Videos," City Lab, August 28, 2015, www.bloomberg.com.

12 Mock, "History."

13 Matthew F. Delmont, *Making Roots: A Nation Captivated* (Berkeley: University of California Press, 2016), 171.

14 Delmont, *Making Roots*,173.

15 Delmont, 172.

16 David O'Grady, "Low and Behold: Using Fiction/Documentary Hybridity to See the Real Damage of Hurricane Katrina," *Mediascape: UCLA's Journal of Cinema and Media Studies* (Fall 2008) fliphtml5.com.

17 O'Grady, "Low and Behold."

18 Clyde Woods, "Do You Know What It Means to Miss New Orleans? Katrina, Trap Economics, and the Rebirth of the Blues,"*American Quarterly* 57, no. 4 (December 2005): 1008.

19 Woods, "Do You Know What It Means."

20 Woods.

21 "Five Days of Bleeding," *Kirkus Reviews*, July 15th, 1992, 129.

22 Saidiya Hartman, *Wayward Lives, Beautiful Experiments: Intimate Histories of Social Upheaval* (New York: Norton, 2018), xiii.

23 Marisa J. Fuentes, *Dispossessed Lives: Enslaved Women, Violence, and the Archive* (Philadelphia: University of Pennsylvania Press, 2016) 143.

24 Sarah Weinman, "Before, and After, the Jogger: Survivors of the Real 'Central Park Five' Attacker Speak for the First Time," The Cut, June 3, 2019, www.thecut.com.

25 Marian Meyers, "African American Women and Violence: Gender, Race, and Class in the News," *Critical Studies in Media Communication* 21, no. 2 (2004): 105.

26 Stephen J. Mexall, "The Roots of 'Wilding': Black Literary Naturalism, the Language of Wilderness, and Hip Hop in the Central Park Jogger Rape," *African American Review* 46, no. 1 (2013): 101.

27 Aimee Meredith Cox, *Shapeshifters: Black Girls and the Choreography of Citizenship* (Durham, NC: Duke University Press, 2015), 9.

28 Angela Davis's groundbreaking *Blues Legacies*, published in 1998, brought new critical attention to early Black women blues performers.

29 Carl Arrington and Maryanne George, "Sippie Wallace and Bonnie Raitt Prove That Blues Birds of a Feather Can Flock Together," *People Magazine*, April 12, 1982, http://www.people.com.

30 Arrington and George, "Sippie Wallace and Bonnie Raitt."

31 Stephen Holden, "Bonnie Raitt Captures the Heart of Her Generation," *New York Times*, March 25, 1990, 2:29.

32 Jessica H. Howard, "Hallelujah!: Transformation in Film," *African American Review* 30, no. 3 (Fall 1996): 441.

33 Eva Jesseye, "Girl Movie Star Attributes Her Success to Hard Work," *Baltimore Afro-American*, July 27, 1929, 8.

34 Victoria Spivey, "Blind Lemon and I Had a Ball," *Record Research* 76 (May 1966): 9.

35 Robert Springer, "Folklore, Commercialism, and Exploitation: Copyright in the Blues," in "On the Blues in Honor of Paul Oliver," special issue, *Popular Music* 26, no. 1 (January 2007): 33–45.

36 Springer, "Folklore, Commercialism, and Exploitation."

37 Springer.

38 Dave Hepburn, "Victoria Spivey: Last of the Hot Blues Mamas," *New York Amsterdam News*, December 28, 1963, 19.

39 Jakob Nielsen, "The Art of Navigating through Hypertext," *Communications of the ACM* 33, no. 3 (March 1990): 298.

40 Billy Mills, "*Finnegans Wake*—the Book the Web Was Invented For," *Guardian*, April 28, 2015, www.theguardian.com.

41 Mills, "Finnegans Wake."

42 Henry Louis Gates Jr., *Signifying Monkey: A Theory of African-American Literary Criticism* (New York: Oxford University Press, 1989) 186.

43 Gates, *Signifying Monkey*, 186.

44 *Surrender* (1971) was produced by Ashford & Simpson.

45 Beck recorded several Stevie Wonder songs in this period, including "Superstition" (Beck appears on Wonder's *Talking Book*) and "Cause We've Ended as Lovers," a song that Wonder wrote for Wright after their marriage ended.

46 Motown released a digital collection of Rita Wright's recordings in 2015, under the title *Syreeta: The Rita Wright Years—Rare Motown, 1967–1970*.

47 Robert J. Sye, "Kaleidoscope," *Sacramento Observer*, April 24, 1969, 16.

48 Vashti McKenzie, "The McKenzie Report: Syreeta's Got a Brand New Report," *Baltimore Afro-American*, September 28, 1974, 11.

49 Quoted in Pierre Perrone, "Syreeta: Motown Singer and Sometime Mrs. Stevie Wonder" (obituary), *Independent*, July 9 2004, 35.

50 Perrone, "Syreeta," 35.

51 Emily Lordi, *Black Resonance: Iconic Women Singers and African American Literature* (New Brunswick, NJ: Rutgers University Press, 2013), 104.

52 Lordi, *Black Resonance*, 104.

53 Fred Moten, *In the Break: The Aesthetics of the Black Radical Tradition* (Minneapolis: University of Minnesota Press, 2003), 109.

54 Moten, *In the Break*, 109.

55 "Linda Jones, R & B Vocalist, Dies Suddenly," *New York Amsterdam News*, March 25 1972, D1.

56 Russell Gersten, quoted in the liner notes of *Hypnotized: 20 Golden Classics* (Collectibles-COL-CD-5452, 1994). //AU: Could you please clarify/confirm the name of the record label for this album?//

57 "Linda Another Choir Alumnus," *Baltimore Afro-American*, Jun 29, 1968, B11.

58 Ray Allen, "Shouting the Church: Narrative and Vocal Improvisation in African-American Gospel Quartet Performance," *Journal of American Folklore* 104, no. 413 (Summer 1991): 295–317.

59 Elaine Scarry, *The Body in Pain: The Making and Unmaking of the World* (New York: Oxford University Press, 1985), 54.

60 Robert G. O'Meally, "Review: The Black Sermon: Tradition and Art," *Callaloo*, no. 34 (Winter 1988): 198–200.

61 Linda Jones, "Things I Been Through", For Your Precious Love (Turbo Records – TU 7008, 1972) //AU: I'm uncertain if this quote is from the liner notes of this album, and to whom it can be attributed; could you please clarify?//

62 Michael J. Agovino, "Artist Carrie Mae Weems Talks Race, Gender, and Finally Getting the Recognition She Deserves," *Elle*, November 20, 2013, www.elle.com.

63 Deborah Willis, "Photographing between the Lines: Beauty, Politics, and the Poetic Vision of Carrie Mae Weems," in *Carrie Mae Weems: Three Decades of Photography and Video*, ed. Katheryn Delmez (New Haven: Yale University Press, 2012), 36

64 Robert Storr, "Carrie Mae Weems: Anyway I Want It," in Delmez, *Carrie Mae Weems*, 31.

65 Maurice Berger, "Black Performers, Fading From Frame, and Memory," *New York Times*, January 22, 2014, https://www.lens.blogs.nytimes.com.

66 Berger, "Black Performers."

67 Berger.

68 Dawoud Bey, "Carrie Mae Weems," *BOMB Magazine*, July 1, 2009, https://bombmagazine.org.

69 "Jackie Wilson, Rock Singer; Records Included 'Teardrops,'" *New York Times*, January 23, 1984, B6.

70 Jacqueline Trescott, "Heartbreak and Soul," *Washington Post*, October 28, 1996, D1.

71 Quoted in Tony Douglas, *Jackie Wilson: Lonely Teardrops* (New York: Routledge, 2005), 25.

72 Douglas, *Jackie Wilson*, 25–26.

73 Shana Redmond, *Anthem: Soul Movements and the Sound of Solidarity in the African Diaspora* (New York: NYU Press, 2013), 100.

74 Redmond, *Anthem*, 142.

3. "PROMISE THAT YOU WILL [TWEET] ABOUT ME"

1 James Baldwin, *The Evidence of Things Not Seen* (New York: Owl, 1985), 6.

2 Baldwin, *Evidence*, xiv.

3 Baldwin, 37.

4 Joe Vogel, *James Baldwin and the 1980s: Witnessing the Reagan Era* (Urbana: University of Illinois Press, 2008), 121.

5 Vogel, *James Baldwin and the 1980s*, 117.

6 Vogel, 118.

7 Vogel, 117.

8 Brenda Stevenson, *The Contested Murder of Latasha Harlins: Justice, Gender, and the Origins of the LA Riots* (New York: Oxford University Press, 2013), 155–56.

9 Andrea Ford, "Videotape Shows Teen Being Shot after Argument," *Los Angeles Times* October 1, 1991, B1.

10 It is not until the film's final scene that audiences realize that Caine's narration of the film takes place from the afterlife, leading critic Sharon Patricia Holland to suggest "when [Caine] dies at the end of the film, we feel cheated, almost lied to—the directors have displayed the ultimate "bad faith." In *Raising the Dead: Readings of Death and (Black) Subjectivity* (Durham, NC: Duke University Press, 2000), 21.

11 Felicia Lee, "Brooklyn Blacks and Koreans Forge Pact," *New York Times*, December 21, 1988, B1; John J. Goldman and Karen Tumulty, "Dinkins Tries to Break Black Boycott of Korean Stores, *Los Angeles Times*, September 22, 1990, A2.

12 Stevenson, *Contested Murder of Latasha Harlins*, 287.

13 Stevenson, 279.

14 Mike Davis, *City of Quartz: Excavating the Future in Los Angeles* (New York: Vintage, 1992), 251.

15 Davis, *City of Quartz*, 252.

16 S. Craig Watkins, *Representing: Hip Hop Culture and the Production of Black Cinema* (Chicago: University of Chicago Press, 1998), 198.

17 Stevenson notes that Ice Cube seems to indirectly reference Harlin's shooting death in the lyrics to "Black Korea," released in late 1991 and featured on *Death Certificate* (Lench Mob/Priority Records). Stevenson, *Contested Murder of Latasha Harlins*, 264.

18 Henry Jenkins, Sam Ford, and Joshua Green, *Spreadable Media: Creating Value and Meaning in a Networked Culture* (New York: New York University Press, 2013), 2.

19 See Tom Standage's *Writing on the Wall: Social Media, the First 2000 Years* (New York: Bloomsbury, 2013) for an overview of the history of Social Media.

20 For backstory on George Holliday, see Michael Goldstein, "The Other Beating," *Los Angeles Times*, February 19, 2006, I28.

21 *Glik v. Cunniffe*, 655 F.3d 78 (1st Cir. 2011).

22 Rose Hackman, "'She was only a baby': Last Charge Dropped in Police Raid that Killed Sleeping Detroit Child," *Guardian*, January 31, 2015, www.theguardian.com.

23 Stephane Dunn, "Fruitvale: Swansong for Oscar Grant, Trayvon Martin, and the Bruhs," NewBlackMan (in Exile), July 29, 2013, www.newblackmaninexile.net.

24 Usame Tunagur, "No Final Redemption? Fruitvale Station and the Academy's Ambivalence with Black Death," NewBlackMan (in Exile), March 3, 2014, www.newblackmaninexile.net.

25 Tunagar, "No Final Redemption?"

26 Shana Redmond, "'Sing about Me': Social Media Memorial and Inventory Form," *Current Musicology*, nos. 99–100 (Spring 2017): 37.

27 Matthew Linder, "'Am I Worth It?': The Forgiveness, Death, and Resurrection of Kendrick Lamar," *Toronto Journal of Theology* 33, no. 1 (2017): 107.

28 Rachel Kaadzi Ghansah, "When the Lights Shut Off: Kendrick Lamar and the Decline of the Black Blues Narrative," *Los Angeles Review of Books*, January 31, 2013, https://lareviewofbooks.org.

29 Karla F. C. Holloway, *Passed On: African American Mourning Stories, A Memorial* (Durham, NC: Duke University Press, 2002), 151–52.

30 Michael D. Shear, "Obama Starts Initiative for Young Black Men, Noting His Own Experience," *New York Times*, February 27, 2014, A11.

31 Holloway, *Passed On*, 147.

32 Holloway, 7.

33 Soyica Diggs Corbett, "Black Movements: Flying Africans in Spaceships," in *Black Performance Theory*, ed. Thomas F. DeFrantz and Anita Gonzalez (Durham, NC: Duke University Press, 2014), 129.

34 Diggs Corbett, "Black Movements," 130.

35 Diggs Corbett, 133.

36 Hashim Khalil Pipkin, "Gripping Mo(u)rning: Black Indignation, Artistic Rescue, and Fooling Death," NewBlackMan (in Exile), October 14, 2014, www.newblack-maninexile.net.

37 Redmond, "Sing about Me," 39.

38 "'Why?': Remembering Nina Simone's Tribute to the Rev. Martin Luther King Jr.," NPR, April 6, 2008, www.npr.org.

39 Fernando Gonzalez, "Freedom Drummer: Max Roach Keeps His Own Beat," *Boston Globe*, May 8, 1992, 47.

40 The song would be covered by fellow drummers Jack DeJohnette and Roy Haynes a year and four years later, respectively, and then recovered by vocalist Dwight Trible almost two generations later on an album by the collective Build an Ark in 2004, and in 2005 with a distinctive hip-hop interpolation that seemed to resonate after the reelection of George Bush in 2004.

41 Gregory Porter, "Nat 'King' Cole & Me," YouTube, September 26, 2017, www.youtube.com.

42 Porter, "Nat 'King' Cole & Me."

43 Michael Awkward, *Soul Covers: Rhythm and Blues Remakes and the Struggle for Artistic Identity* (Durham, NC: Duke University Press), 17.

44 Awkward, *Soul Covers*, 28.

45 Peter Guralnick, *Dream Boogie: The Triumph of Sam Cooke* (New York: Little, Brown, 2005), 271.

4. 'I'LL BE A BRIDGE'

1 Tom Kenny, "Marvin's Room," Mix, November 1, 2006, www.mixonline.com.

2 David Ritz, *Divided Soul: The Life of Marvin Gaye* (New York: De Capo, 2010), 214.

3 Kenny, "Marvin's Room."

4 Ritz, *Divided Soul*, 233.

5 Harry Weinger, quoted in Michael Eric Dyson, *Mercy, Mercy Me: The Art, Loves, and Demons of Marvin Gaye* (New York: Basic Books, 2004), 179.

6 Matt Micucci, "Year by Year: Five Essential Jazz Albums of 1955," JazzIz, March 21, 2019, www.jazziz.com.

7 Sinatra is quoted as saying in 1958, "It is Billie Holiday . . . who was, and still remains, the greatest single musical influence on me." Quoted in Jody Rosen, "Frank Sinatra and Billie Holiday: They Did It Their Way," *New York Times T Magazine*, October 19, 2015, 132.

8 Stephen Holden, "Frank Sinatra: A Hundred Years On, the Voice Resonates Still," *New York Times*, December 11, 2015, C1.

9 Micucci, "Year by Year."

10 Ritz, *Divided Soul*, 29–30.

11 Ritz, 30.

12 Ritz, 107–8.

13 In the spirit of Motown's assembly-line production style, both songs were also recorded, though not released until years later, by the Four Tops. The rich harmonies employed by the Four Tops on these tracks might have had an impact on Gaye when he returned to pop ballads and torch songs in the 1970s.

14 Junior Parker was immortalized in the intro to Al Green's "Take Me to the River" (1974).

15 Hughes, *Country Soul*, 153.

16 Hughes, 159.

17 Andrew Flory, "The Ballads of Marvin Gaye," *Journal of the American Musicological Society* 72, no. 2 (2019): 325.

18 Flory, "Ballads of Marvin Gaye," 326.

19 Lisa Barg, Tammy Kernodle, Dianthe Spencer, and Sherrie Tucker, "Introduction," in "Special Issue on Melba Liston," *Black Music Research Journal* 34, no. 1 (2019): 1.

20 Ritz, *Divided Soul*, 135.

21 In his research on Gaye, Flory reproduces transcriptions of Gaye's sessions from January and February 1967 ("Ballads of Marvin Gaye," 338–42).

22 Flory, 339.

23 Ritz, *Divided Soul*, 135.

24 Ritz, 240.

25 Flory, "Ballads of Marvin Gaye," 349.

26 Dyson, *Mercy, Mercy Me*, 181.

27 Dyson, 181.

28 Flory, "Ballads of Marvin Gaye," 350.

29 Ritz, *Divided Soul*, 240.

30 Sinatra left Columbia in 1960 to start his own label, Reprise, and *Lady in Satin* was the last album released in Holiday's lifetime and the only released by Columbia before her death.

31 Daphne Brooks, "Bold Soul Ingénue," *Take a Look: The Complete Aretha Franklin on Columbia*, 2011 (88697792792).//AU: Can you please clarify if this is from the liner notes of the album?//

32 Quoted in Michael Dwyer, "Solving the Mystery of Amazing Grace," *Sydney Morning Herald*, August 29, 2019, www.smh.com.au.

33 Richard Leppert and George Lipsitz, "'Everybody's Lonesome for Somebody': Age, the Body, and Experience in the Music of Hank Williams," *Popular Music* 9, no. 3 (October 1990): 268.

34 No small irony that when Columbia released a Franklin compilation in 2011 titled *The Great American Songbook*, both "Cold, Cold Heart" and "This Bitter Earth" were included.

35 Don Heckman, "Aretha's Blooming Thirties," *New York Times*, March 5, 1972, D28.

36 Aretha Franklin with David Ritz, *Aretha: From These Roots* (New York: Villard, 1999), 146.

37 Franklin and Ritz, *Aretha*, 141.

38 Franklin and Rita, 150.

39 Mark Bego, *Aretha Franklin: The Queen of Soul* (London: Robert Hale, 1990). 137.

40 Bego, *Aretha Franklin*, 137.

41 "Love the One You're With" was likely brought to Franklin's attention via organist Billy Preston, who partially inspired the song. The Isley Brothers covered the song in 1971, and Luther Vandross would cover it on his 1994 cover album, *Songs.*

42 Ben Sisario, "Claude Jeter, Gospel Singer with Wide Influence, Dies at 94," *New York Times*, January 10, 2009, www.nytimes.com.

43 David Remnick, "Soul Survivor: The Revival and Hidden Treasure of Aretha Franklin," *New Yorker*, April 4, 2016, 74.

44 The suite immediately precedes "Reach Out and Touch (Somebody's Hand)" on the last night.

45 Quoted in Ritz, *Respect*, 236.//AU: Please include a full citation (The Ritz sources Aretha and Divided Soul have appeared to now, but this is the first mention of Respect)//

46 Craig Werner, *Higher Ground: Stevie Wonder, Aretha Franklin, Curtis Mayfield, and the Rise and Fall of American Soul* (New York: Crown, 2004), 184.

47 Ritz and Franklin, *Aretha*, 139.

48 Billy Preston quoted in Ritz, 235.//AU: ("Ritz and Franklin" here?)//

49 Ritz and Franklin, 153.

50 Ritz and Franklin, 41.

51 Antonia Randolph, "In the Living Room with Aretha and James and C.L.: Review of *Amazing Grace*," *Scalawag*, September, 9, 2019, www.scalawagmagazine.org.

52 Ritz and Franklin, *Aretha*, 111.

53 Gerri Hirshey, *Nowhere to Run: The Story of Soul Music* (New York: Crown, 1984), 243.

54 Ed Pavlic, "Aretha Franklin's Soul," *Boston Review*, April 19, 2019, bostonreview. net.

55 Aaron Cohen, *Amazing Grace* (New York: Continuum, 2001), 95.

56 Walton M. Muyumba, *The Shadow and Act: Black Intellectual Practice Jazz Improvisation and Philosophical Pragmatism* (Chicago: University of Chicago Press, 2009), 31.

57 Sherley Anne Williams, "Returning to the Blues: Esther Phillips and Contemporary Blues Culture," *Callaloo* 14, no. 4 (Autumn 1991): 816–28.

58 Cohen, *Amazing Grace*, 90.

59 Anthony Heilbut, *The Fan Who Knew Too Much: Aretha Franklin, the Rise of the Soap Opera, Children of the Gospel Church, and Other Meditations* (New York: Knopf, 2012), 24.

60 Heilbut, *Fan Who Knew Too Much*, 24.

5. DECAMPING WAKANDA

1 Lake Micah, "Inhuman Bondage: Ta-Nehisi Coates's Turn to Fiction," *Bookforum*, December–January 2020, www.bookforum.com.

2 Alex Zamalin, *Black Utopia: The History of an Idea from Black Nationalism to Afrofuturism* (New York: Columbia University Press, 2019). 16.

3 N. D. B Connolly, "How *Black Panther* Taps into 500 Years of History," *Hollywood Reporter*, February 16, 2018, www.hollywoodreporter.com.

4 Zamalin, *Black Utopia*, 17.

5 Adam Serwer, The Tragedy of Erik Killmonger," *Atlantic*, February 21, 2018, www.theatlantic.com.

6 Derrick Bell, *Faces at the Bottom of the Well: The Permanence of Racism* (New York: Basic Books, 1992), 35

7 Bell, *Faces*, 36.

8 Bell, 45–46.

9 Sylvianne A. Diouf, *Slavery's Exile: The Story of American Maroons* (New York: NYU Press, 2014), 9.

10 Diouf, *Slavery's Exile*, 9.

11 Diouf, 10.

12 Diouf, 121.

13 Neil Roberts, *Freedom as Marronage* (Chicago: University of Chicago Press, 2015), 4.

14 Roberts, *Freedom as Marronage*, 8–9.

15 Roberts, 11.

16 Roberts, 11

17 Roberts, 116–17.

18 Roberts, 117.

19 Roberts, 152–67.

20 Cassandra L. Jones, "The Data Thief, the Cyberflaneur, and Rhythm Science: Challenging Anti-Technological Blackness with the Metaphors of Afrofuturism," *CLA Journal* 61, no. 4 (September 2018): 203.

21 Zoé Whitley, "Geography Lessons: Mapping the Slide-Tape Texts of Black Audio Film Collective, 1982–1984," in *John Akomfrah: Signs of Empire* (New York: New Museum, 2018), 10.

22 Whitley, "Geography Lessons," 12.

23 Whitley, 12.

24 Richard Iton, *In Search of the Black Fantastic: Politics and Popular Culture in the Post–Civil Rights Era* (New York: Oxford University Press, 2008) 136.

25 Laura U. Marks, "Monad, Database, Remix: Manners of Unfolding in *The Last Angel of History*," *Black Camera* 6, no. 2 (Spring 2015): 114.

26 "Windrush Generation: Who Are They and Why Are They Facing Problems?," BBC News, April 18, 2018, www.bbc.com.

27 Stoffel Debuysere, "Signs of Struggle, Songs of Sorrow: Notes on the Politics of Uncertainty in the Films of John Akomfrah," *Black Camera* 6, no. 2 (Spring 2015): 71.

28 Krista Thompson, *Shine: The Visual Economy of Light in African Diasporic Aesthetic Practice* (Durham, NC: Duke University Press, 2015), 33.

29 Marks, "Monad, Database, Remix," 116.

30 Marks, 122.

31 Jones, "Data Thief," 206–7.

32 Thompson, *Shine*, 16.

33 Thompson, 16.

34 Diouf, *Slavery's Exile*, 2.

35 Phillip Brian Harper, *Abstractionist Aesthetics: Artistic Form and Social Critique in African American Culture* (New York: NYU Press, 2015), 2.

36 Harper, *Abstractionist Aesthetics*, 2.

37 Harper, 2.

38 Harper, 10.

39 Whitley, "Geography Lessons," 12.

40 Quoted in Whitley, 12.

41 John Corbett, "Brother from Another Planet: The Space Madness of Lee 'Scratch' Perry, Sun Ra, and George Clinton," in *Extended Play: Sounding Off from John Cage to Dr. Funkenstein* (Durham, NC: Duke University Press, 1994), 7.

42 Corbett, "Brother from Another Planet," 18.

43 Corbett, 18.

44 André M. Carrington, *Speculative Blackness: The Future of Race in Science Fiction* (Minneapolis: University of Minnesota Press, 2016)

45 Carrington, *Speculative Blackness*, 22–23.

46 Carrington, 26.

47 Marks, "Monad, Database, Remix," 113.

48 Harper, *Abstractionist Aesthetics*, 72.

49 Margo Natalie Crawford, *Black Post Blackness: Te Black Arts Movement and Twenty-First-Century Aesthetics* (Urbana: University of Illinois Press, 2017), 17.

50 Crawford, *Black Post Blackness*, 40.

51 Crawford, 111.

52 Crawford, 115.

53 Rebecca VanDiver, "Before the Wall Came Tumbling Down: Ephemerality and Chicago's Wall of Respect, 1967–1971," *Space and Culture* 18, no. 4 (2015): 418.

54 Quoted in Margo Natalie Crawford, "Black Light on the Wall of Respect: The Chicago Black Arts Movement," in *New Thoughts on the Black Arts Movement*, ed. Lisa Gail Collins and Margo Natalie Crawford (New Brunswick, NJ: Rutgers University Press, 2006), 38–42.

55 Christina Sharpe, *In the Wake: On Blackness and Being* (Durham, NC: Duke University Press, 2016), 14.

56 Louis Armstrong, *Satchmo: My Life in New Orleans* (New York: Prentice-Hall, 1954), 23.

57 Armstrong, *Satchmo*, 23–24.

58 Interview of John Akomfrah with the author, Left of Black, May 14, 2018, www.youtube.com.

59 Anatole Broyard, "New Woman, Old Jazz, Hemingway," *New York Times*, April 24, 1977, BR4.

60 Interview of John Akomfrah with the author, Left of Black, May 14, 2018.

61 Michael Ondaatje, *Coming through Slaughter* (Toronto: House of Anansi, 1976), 3.

62 Laura Jaramillo, "John Akomfrah Blends Historical Witness and Imagination to Resurrect a New Orleans Jazz Legend at the Nasher," *Indy Weekly*, May 9, 2018, indyweek.com.

63 Jaramillo, "John Akomfrah."

64 Allyson Nadia Field, *Uplift Cinema: The Emergence of African American Film and the Possibility of Black Modernity* (Durham, NC: Duke University Press, 2015), 24.

65 Field, *Uplift Cinema*, 24.

66 David Marquis, *In Search of Buddy Bolden: The First Man of Jazz* (Baton Rouge: Louisiana State University Press, 1978), xvii.

67 Marquis, *In Search of Buddy Bolden*, 43.

68 W. E. B. Du Bois, "Strivings of Negro People," *Atlantic Monthly*, August 1897, 194–97.

69 Marquis, *In Search of Buddy Bolden*, 128.

70 Ondaatje, *Coming through Slaughter*, 82.

71 Marquis, *In Search of Buddy Bolden*, 128.

72 Harper, *Abstractionist Aesthetics*, 114.

73 Harper, 114.

74 Harper, 115.

75 Thompson, *Shine*, 10.

76 Mark Speltz, *North of Dixie: Civil Rights Photography Beyond the South*, (Los Angeles: J. Paul Getty Museum, 2016), 25.

77 Alessandra Raengo and Lauren McLeod Cramer, "The Unruly Archives of Black Music Videos," *JCMS: Journal of Cinema and Media Studies* 59, no. 2 (2020): 138.

78 Raengo and Cramer, "Unruly Archives of Black Music," 138–39.

79 Raengo and Cramer, 139.

80 Morgan Woolsey, "Re/soundings: Music and the Political Goals of the L.A. Rebellion," in *L.A. Rebellion: Creating a New Black Cinema*, ed. Allyson Nadia Field, Jan-Christopher Horak, and Jacqueline Najuma Stewart (Berkeley: University of California Press, 2015), 176.

81 Kevin Quashie, *The Sovereignty of Quiet: Beyond Resistance in Black Culture* (New Brunswick, NJ: Rutgers University Press, 2012), 6.

82 Stephane Dunn, "Queering the Cool: A *Moonlight* Review," NewBlackMan (in Exile), November 1, 2016, www.newblackmaninexile.net.

83 Matthew Schnipper, "Director Barry Jenkins on the Music That Made *Moonlight*," Pitchfork, November 29, 2016, pitchfork.com.

84 Michael Boyce Gillespie, "One Step Ahead: A Conversation with Barry Jenkins," *Film Quarterly* 70, no. 3 (Spring 2017): 60.

85 J. Bennett, "Prison Soul: The Edge of Daybreak Recorded Their 1979 Album Behind Bars in One Take," *Vice*, November 23, 2015, www.vice.com.

86 Michael Boyce Gillespie, *Film Blackness: American Cinema and the Idea of Black Film* (Durham, NC: Duke University Press, 2016), 120.

87 Kristen Yoonsoo Kim, "*Moonlight* Director Barry Jenkins on His Kendrick Lamar Moment and Making the Movie of the Year," Complex, October 24, 2016, www. complex.com.

88 Nina Sun Eidsheim, *The Race of Sound: Listening, Timbre, and Vocality in African American Music* (Durham, NC: Duke University Press, 2019), 92.

89 David Ritz, *Faith in Time: The Life of Jimmy Scott* (New York: Da Capo, 2003), 65.

90 Ritz, *Faith in Time*, 108.

91 Ritz, 95.

92 Ritz, 91.

93 Ritz, 92.

94 Ritz, 118.

95 Ritz, 129.

96 Ritz, 156.

97 Ritz, 155.

98 Ritz, 165.

99 Susan Koprince, "Baseball as History and Myth in August Wilson's *Fences*," *African American Review* 40, no. 2 (Summer 2006): 351.

CODA

1 Marc Myers, *Anatomy of a Song: The Oral History of 45 Iconic Hits That Changed Rock, R&B, and Pop* (New York: Grove, 2016), 23–27.

INDEX

ABOUT THE AUTHOR

Born and raised in the Bronx, New York, MARK ANTHONY NEAL is the James B. Duke Distinguished Professor of African & African American Studies at Duke University. He resides in Durham, North Carolina, with his wife and two daughters.